Talk Tech To Me

The Non-Technical Guide to Technology Recruiting

To Hope!
Be prepared
to build
better,
more resilient
organizations!

BRIAN FINK

Best,
Bri

Brian Fink

TALK TECH TO ME
The Non-Technical Guide to Technology Recruiting

ISBN-13:
ASIN:

Copyright 2023
All rights reserved.

For Ally and Maddie —
Who gave up their time with me to make this all happen for you.

Special thanks to Barbara Marks, Jason Singer, Rodney Walden, Cristina Moceri, Liz Whitehead, Chris Stanzione, Justin Hill, Anthony Cedeno, Michael Goldberg, Lauren Laughlin, Jenna Aronow, and Dan Lockhart — Each of them gave their time freely to critique and conjure the best out of me on this journey. Thank them for taking an early glance at these pages. They each understand the importance of community and the core strengths of recruiters and sourcers.

Contents

Introduction 1

How To Use This Book 5
    A Little Reminder About How Awesome You Are 8

A Boolean Primer 11
    AND 12
    OR (or the | symbol) 14
    NOT (or the - symbol) 15
    Parentheses ( ) 17
    Quotes " " 19
    Quick Review 20
    Some Advanced Commands That I Use with
    The Boolean Operators 21
    Why Did I Include a Boolean Primer? 26

What is the SDLC? 27
    Why Does the SDLC matter? 28
    Agile vs. Waterfall 29
    How Does the SDLC relate to the Internet 32

What Makes Up The Internet? 35
    Web 36

What Is An Application? 41
    Front-End Technologies 42
    Back-End Technologies 72

What Data Matters? 171
    Databases 172

What Infrastructure Does?...233
   What Makes Up The Infrastructure of a Web App?....234
   Common Job Titles: Who Does What and When Do
   They Do It?..291

Strategy Sessions..331
   What You Need To Get From a Kickoff Meeting........333
   High Volume Tech Hiring Strategies............................348
   Post Mortem..351

Next Level..357
   Front-end Developer..359
   Back-end Developer..374
   Full-stack Developer...380
   DevOps Engineer...390
   Quality Assurance (QA) Engineer...............................399
   Test Automation Engineer...408
   Mobile Developer..416
   Data Engineer..424
   Cloud Engineer..432
   Technical Architect..441
   Project Manager..450
   Scrum Master...459
   Technical Writer..467
   UX/UI Designer...475
   Security Engineer..485
   Machine Learning Engineer..493
   Data Scientist..502
   Infrastructure Engineer..510
   Site Reliability Engineer (SRE)...................................518

Final Thoughts..527

Chapter One

Introduction

I love recruiting, and moreso, I love helping others hone their recruiting skill set. And that's why I am writing this book. Just getting off the stage at Talent Acquisition Week 2023 in San Diego, I had a few moments with 10 different talent acquisition practitioners. Some of them were agency owners, a few corporate recruiters, and two sourcers. Everyone asked different questions; they ranged from how do you find developers, what types of Boolean strings do you use, to how do you know what you are looking for. One recruiter asked how I learned it all.

At first, I didn't do it on my own. I was proverbially baptized by fire. I went from sales recruiter to tech recruiter overnight. I messed up a lot. But, I learned to be curious and ask a lot of questions of clients and engineering talent. I learned from some of the best tech recruiters and sourcers like Shally Steckerl, Steve Rath, Ronnie Bratcher, and Shannon (Van Curen) Pritchett. One stands out, Steve Levy – who pushed me to go beyond the surface and get personal. Steve really challenged the way I think about recruiting and working with technologists. Steve has the advantage of being a software engineer who came to the recruiting field. Coming from sales, I was really transactional. Steve changed that.

Loosely, that's how I came up with my goals here. I want for you to be able to understand the technologies you are looking for, build the company where the best software developers in the world would want to work, find engineers who have the skills necessary to solve deep challenges, and radiate confidence while you are doing it. I want that confidence to be something rooted in your curiosity, empathy, and tenacity.

Realistically, you have all three of these core elements or you would not have decided to be a recruiter, sourcer, account manager, or burgeoning talent acquisition pro. You would not have picked up this book. You would not be looking (for me) to (help you) simplify the process – and that is exactly what I intend to do. I want you to be a great technical recruiter, and I hope you'll use this book as a cheat sheet to talk tech to clients, customers, hiring managers, team members, and most importantly, candidates!

We're going to get into a lot (in here) and also a lot out there. While we might take a look at Boolean search and different online hangouts, I want to encourage you to think and grow as a technical recruiter. As you go from novice to experienced wizard or sorceress, I want you to expand your net while contracting it. While that seems like an oxymoron, it made you think.

I want to encourage you to:

- Think about where the people you want to hire are hanging out?
- What conferences do they go to?
- Where do they live?
- What organizations do they belong to?
- What websites do they read?

Instead of casting a wide net with a job search on a paid online job board, use Github, Overflow, or Quora to limit your search to the smart people that contribute to opensource software. Go to the really interesting tech conferences. Great iOS developers will be at Apple's WWDC. Python engineers will be at PyCon. There are a bunch of open source conferences where you can slink around in the hallways, talk to everyone you meet, go to the technical sessions and invite the speakers out for a beer, and when you find someone smart, BANG!—you launch into full-fledged flattery mode.

But how will you understand and appreciate the conversations to be had with these potential candidates?

Listen up, buddy! I'm all about helping you grasp the tech you're after, creating a company that's so cool even the top software developers will beg to work there, snagging engineers with mad skills to tackle the tough stuff, and exuding confidence like a boss while you're at it. And that's the tech we will talk about.

Chapter Two

How To Use This Book

All right, there is a method to the madness of how this book is organized. You do not have to read it cover-to-cover, and can jump in here and there and everywhere. Web technologies can be a real headache to grasp. It's like trying to understand a foreign language, except instead of Spanish or French, you're trying to decipher tech jargon - and trust me, that's a whole different level of difficulty. But do not be alarmed, scared, or anxious, because this book divides web technologies into four sections and at each section I'll do a quick recap:

- **Internet**: sometimes called simply "the Net," is a worldwide system of computer networks – a network of networks in which users at any one computer can, if they have permission, get information from any other computer (and sometimes talk directly to users at other computers). In this section, we will discuss a few foundational internet technologies used to connect the world's computers together. **RECAP: the connection between you and the website.**

- **Application**: also referred to as an application program or application software, is a computer software package that performs a specific function directly for an end user or, in some cases, for another application. We'll get into the programming languages that are used to create the modern web. This section is going to be divided into two equally important parts – the front-end (the code your computer runs) vs. back-end (the code that the server runs). **RECAP: the brains of the website.**

- **Data**: refers to all the files, images, and cookies downloaded to a device when someone visits a website. This data provides information about a site user's location, behavior, and interests. How does this get organized? Being amble and able to store a user's data for a web application can make visiting the site a unique experience tailored to the needs and interests of each user. We'll jump into databases, cache, and search systems that customize each experience. **RECAP: how a website stores all the information.**

- **Infrastructure**: includes the hardware, software and services to maintain corporate Web sites, intranets, and extranets, including Web hosting services and Web software application development tools. Let's face it: web applications require a great deal of configuration and management besides the data and web application itself. To finish the cycle, we will delve into how web servers are used and what powers them. **RECAP: how the website is configured and managed on computers.**

In each of the four sections, I'll teach you about foundational underpinnings that comprise each technology, make it as simple as possible, offer some potential job titles that might be associated with each of the technologies, share some Boolean strings to aid in your search and potential interview questions (and answers) you might want to ask your candidates and see if your hiring managers feel that they are relevant to the conversations you'll have.

Mind you – this guide is meant to be an introduction. I will not teach you how to engineer a website or build the next Instagram. That is to say: I will not dive into the details that would be covered by an engineering book. This is not to be a substitute for having a real actual conversation with the hiring manager to see what they are looking for in their ideal technical candidate and hire!

Remember our goal: competency with confidence.

After reading this, you should have a clearer understanding of web technologies and their use. Many of the concepts here are simplified – and there's power in that simplification. It's my hope that simplification leads to curious confidence. Simplicity comes out from the synthesis of experience and wisdom. Simple is natural, easy, nice, and unpretentious. It often happens that great lessons of life, which are full of wisdom, spring from simple concepts which are also and paradoxically, even more, difficult to reach with full understanding.

Each section can also be read independently. For instance, if you're over learning about the internet, skip to the programming languages in the application section. If you want to learn more about AWS and Azure, skip ahead to learn all about web servers and infrastructure. If you want a refresher on Boolean Search, start there. Or maybe you're just here for the strings?

This is your adventure. Choose it.

A Little Reminder About How Awesome You Are

Ladies and gentlemen, let's dive deep into the world of recruitment for engineering jobs, and let me tell you why it's absolutely essential for recruiters to know the technologies associated with specific engineering roles. You see, in the fast-paced, ever-evolving world of technology, staying on top of the latest trends and innovations is not just a cool thing to do, it's a matter of survival in the modern business ecosystem.

Now, picture this. You're a recruiter looking for the perfect candidate to fill an engineering position at a prestigious firm. You're not just looking for a mere mortal with a shiny degree, no. You're seeking a rockstar, a one-of-a-kind genius who can leverage their technical expertise to catapult your company to new heights of success. But how are you supposed to find this unicorn without understanding the specific technologies that define their realm?

The technologies associated with a particular engineering job aren't just buzzwords; they're the lifeblood of the role. They are the tools that engineers use to sculpt the digital landscape, and they're constantly evolving. To find the right candidate, you need to understand these technologies as intimately as possible. This isn't just about separating the wheat from the chaff, it's about identifying the very best stalk of wheat in the entire field.

When you grasp the ins and outs of the technologies associated with specific engineering roles, you're able to ask the right questions and assess candidates' skills more effectively. This means you'll be more likely to identify the talent that can truly drive innovation and growth at your organization. It's not enough to merely dabble in the world of technology – recruiters must immerse themselves in it, or risk being left behind.

In the end, knowing the technologies associated with specific engineering jobs isn't just important for recruiters, it's downright crucial. The future of your company depends on it. So, my friends, let's strap in and embrace the wild ride that is technology. Only then can we hope to find those elusive unicorns and secure the brightest future for our organizations.

You've got this.

Chapter Three

A Boolean Primer

So what's Boolean search and why does it have anything to do with finding and understanding technical talent in a confident way?

I know, I know. Oh joy! Another mathematical theory to make our lives easier. Thanks George Boole. So, let's cut to the chase - Boolean search is a fancy way of saying you can use Google, Bing, DuckDuckGo, Exalead or some other search engines to look for candidate profiles. You know, instead of just aimlessly scrolling through pages of irrelevant junk. Just use a few magic words like "AND" and "OR" and "NOT" voila!

Relevant results at your fingertips. Thank goodness for Boolean search, because who wants to actually read through a whole page of information anymore?

But really, Boolean search is a type of search that uses Boolean logic to retrieve relevant information from a database. Boolean logic is a system of mathematical logic that uses binary variables to represent truth values of expressions. In Boolean search, the search query uses operators such as AND, OR, and NOT to combine keywords and phrases in a way that narrows or expands the search results. Boolean search enables users to specify conditions for retrieving information, making the search more precise and relevant to our needs.

Let's break this down: Boolean search is supposed to be this amazing tool that helps us find things faster and more precisely. Yeah, sure, if you use the right words and have the right logic. But let's be real, if you don't pick the right keywords, you're gonna end up with either a million irrelevant results or zero results at all. Who wants to waste time sorting through that?

What we intend to learn is what those right technical terms are and how we can use Boolean search to bring back relevant candidates. But, not every single candidate you find will have the skills and experience you're looking for. Adding Boolean keyword searches and expanding the complexity of your searches will help you find profiles that suit your needs.

Let's tackle the logic herein before jumping ahead to "using the right words."

AND

When you want to include two (or more) criteria in your search, the operator AND narrows down or constricts your search. For example, a Boolean search string for recruiting AWS Architects should include (aws AND architect). This will produce results that include both keywords.

Another way to think about it: you use AND as a boolean operator when you want to combine two or more conditions and all of them need to be true for the overall expression to be true. The AND operator returns true only if all of the operands are true. If any of the operands is false, the AND operator returns false.

When using Google, LinkedIn, Bing, DuckDuckGo, the AND operator is implied by the space between two or more words. For instance, if we were looking for Senior Database Engineer, we do not have to enter (senior AND database AND engineer) as the AND is implied. This will produce results that include all three keywords.

RECAP: Placing the AND operator between two conditions means that both conditions must be met in order for the result to be "true".

OR (or the | symbol)

The OR operator, on the other hand, allows us to expand our Boolean search results. Think of it like this: OR is used in situations where we want to determine if at least one of two conditions is true. It returns true if either of the conditions being compared is true, and returns false if both conditions are false. For example, if we have two conditions "A" and "B", the expression (A OR B) would be true if either "A" is true or "B" is true, or if both "A" and "B" are true.

Another way to think about it is that you use OR as a boolean operator when you want to combine two or more conditions and only one of them needs to be true for the overall expression to be true. The OR operator returns true if at least one of the operands is true

People might use different words to say the same thing. OR is particularly useful for synonyms, like (java OR "java 10" OR j2ee).

As alternative to using OR, you can also us the | symbol that appears about your enter/return key on your PC/Mac keyboard. The pipe as it is often referred to comes from the syntax of several programming languages.

RECAP: With the OR operator, only one condition has to be met for the result to be "true".

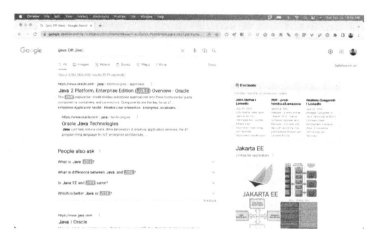

NOT (or the - symbol)

The NOT operator excludes unwanted terms from your sourcing search. You use NOT as a boolean operator when you want to reverse the value of a condition. The NOT operator returns the opposite value of the operand it operates on. If the operand is true, the NOT operator returns false. If the operand is false, the NOT operator returns true. The NOT operator is often used to reverse the value of a condition in an expression and make it easier to understand or to match the desired outcome.

The NOT boolean operator is like having a magic wand that can make things turn from "yes" to "no" and "no" to "yes". Let's say you have a toy box and you have toys inside it. The NOT operator can help you find out if the toy box is empty or if there are toys inside. If the toy box is full of toys, the answer is "yes, there are toys". But if we use the NOT operator, it turns the answer to "no, there are no toys". It's like a magic wand that can change the answer from "yes" to "no" and vice versa.

Instead of NOT, you could also use the minus symbol followed by your unwanted term without leaving a space like (NOT data) and -data.

RECAP: When NOT is used, all the conditions except the excluded ones must be true.

Parentheses ( )

You can use parentheses to group multiple search strings and set your priorities.

Priorities? What priorities?

You can enclose search terms and their operators in parentheses to specify the order in which they are interpreted. Information within parentheses is read first, then information outside parentheses is read next.

Think about your Boolean expression being a code that specifically looks for what you want and eliminates what you are NOT looking for in your search.

This will come in handy for complex candidate searches where you must combine different keywords. For example, ((developer OR designer) AND Java) indicates that Java knowledge is a must-have both for developers and designers. But, in a (designer OR (developer AND Java)) search, Java knowledge is important only for the developers you're looking for – not the designers.

Alternatively, you could think about it like this: use parentheses to nest query terms within other query terms.

You can enclose search terms and their operators in parentheses to specify the order in which they are interpreted. Information within parentheses is read first, then information outside parentheses is read next. For example,when you enter (java OR kotlin) AND app, the search engine retrieves results containing the word java or the word kotlin together with the word app in the fields searched by default.

If there are nested parentheses, the search engine processes the innermost parenthetical expression first, then the next, and so on until the entire query has been interpreted. For example,

((java OR kotlin) app) OR android

If the Boolean queries do not include parentheses, java OR kotlin AND app NOT android, the search engine will follow an order of operations like in math where AND and NOT are considered multiplication and are processed first, followed by the OR clause which is addition. Effectively, the search engine processes java

OR kotlin AND app NOT android as though the query has parentheses in the following places: java OR ((kotlin AND app) NOT android)

RECAP: Boolean operators (AND, OR, NOT) allow you to form compound searches by combining two or more terms together. Parentheses also allow you to group terms together.

Quotes " "

If you want Google to consider the exact phrase you're searching for as a complete phrase, you should put it in quotes. For example, leaving a blank space between "cloud" and "engineer" will provide pages that contain both of the words "cloud" and "engineer", but not necessarily together. You should type "cloud engineer" to get more relevant results when sourcing passive candidates on Google, Bing, LinkedIn, or DuckDuckGo. When Boolean operators are contained within a phrase that is enclosed in quotation marks, the operator is treated as a stop word. When this is the case, any single word will be searched for in its place.

Another way to think about it: if you want to make Google your loyal sidekick in your search for the perfect cloud engineer, you better put those keywords in quotes, otherwise you'll be sifting through pages of irrelevant information.

RECAP: when you are looking for an exact phrase, use quotes " ".

Quick Review

Search engines like Google use these Boolean operators as follows:

- AND: A space between two terms is interpreted as "AND".
- OR: Both the word "OR" and the pipe symbol (|) act as the OR operator.
- NOT: Putting a minus sign before a word (with no space) excludes the word from the search.
- ( ): Parentheses also allow you to group terms together.
- " ": Looking for an exact phrase or keywords.

Some Advanced Commands That I Use All The Time with The Boolean Operators

Party people, have you met the king of search engines? Yes, I'm talking about the one and only Google, with a whopping 75% of the market share. It's like having a personal librarian who can find any information you need in a snap - all neatly organized and sorted by relevance. But let's be real, sometimes you gotta dig a little deeper to find the real gems.

That's why you gotta get savvy with your search terms, and make Google work for you. And let me tell you, Google has some tricks up its sleeve - specific search commands to refine your search and get you to your goal faster. Think of it as speaking the language of the search engine. Just remember, always put that colon in front of your search term, and don't leave any room for errors - Google is a stickler for details. And the best part? You can even combine these advanced commands to make your search even more precise. So, get ready to level up your search game, folks!

To get started we are going to delve into two special commands that I use all the time with the Boolean operators we've already reviewed.

Those are the site: command and filetype: command. Let's delve into the magic these two commands release, or produce, or whatever magical things happen.

site:

Let's talk about the magic of Google search commands. Have you ever heard of the site: command? It's like having a VIP pass to all the pages of a domain, and trust me, it's a game-changer.

But wait, it gets even better.

When you combine the site: command with a juicy search term, Google will serve up all the subpages containing that keyword. It's like having a personal tour guide in the world of the internet - the possibilities are endless.

Let's say you want to find the best "cloud engineer" on the planet.

How do you do it?

Easy, just type in the magic query and let Google do the heavy lifting.

The example query will have Google searching through the sub-pages of cnet.com for your desired phrase, and voila! The results are right at your fingertips. But wait, there's more! You can even use basic operators to

TALK TECH TO ME

exclude certain domains during the search. It's like having a personal filter, making your search experience smoother and more efficient. So, go ahead and try it out, and watch the magic unfold!

site:cnet.com "cloud engineer"

Hmm.... let's get a little more specific than "cloud engineer." Let's look for study materials for cloud engineers who are going to take an Amazon Web Services (AWS) certification.

site:cnet.com "cloud engineer" (aws OR "amazon web services") (test OR certification)

23

RECAP: *The Google search command site: is your ticket to unlocking the secrets of a domain's index. With just a few keystrokes, you'll be able to see every single page that the search giant has deemed important enough to include in its index. Get ready to take control of your search results and uncover the hidden gems of the web!*

filetype:

Who likes free resumes?

Want to take your Google search game to the next level? Introducing the filetype: command! This tool will help you fine-tune your search results and only show you what you're looking for. For example, if you want to find PDF documents related to your keyword, simply add filetype:pdf resume to your search query and voila! Google will compile a list of all the freely accessible PDFs that match your criteria.

Let's try this search string to find resumes of developers who went to the Georgia Institute of Technology who knows Java.

filetype:pdf resume developer java "georgia institute of technology"

And that's not all, folks! Google supports other file types too, like "doc" and "jpg". So, whether you're looking for a specific document or image, the filetype: command has got you covered. Get ready to streamline your search results and find exactly what you need, lightning fast!

RECAP: looking for documents or files on the web is a cinch when you use the filetype: command to point Google towards those documents.

Why Did I Include a Boolean Primer?

Boolean operators are your ticket to unlocking the full potential of search engines. They're like the secret sauce of online searches, giving you the power to expand or narrow down your results with ease. Think of them as mathematical wizards, using a special syntax to work their magic and help you find exactly what you're looking for.

The idea is to use Boolean search to bring back relevant candidates, but not every candidate you find will have the skills and experience you're looking for. So, you need to use the right technical terms and expand the complexity of your searches to find the profiles that suit your needs.

Boolean search is versatile, valuable, and essential for anyone looking to get the most out of their online searches. So, if you want to take your search game to the next level, learn the basics of Boolean operators and start using them as we go through the example search strings as we work through the book together.

Chapter Four

What is the SDLC?

Let me tell you about the software development lifecycle, or SDLC. It's a process that software developers use to create, test, and deploy software applications. Think of it as a roadmap for building software.

It typically starts with requirements gathering, where the developers work with stakeholders to understand what the software needs to do and what features it needs to have. Then they move on to design, where they create a plan for how the software will be built and what tools and technologies will be used.

Next comes the development phase, where the actual coding happens. This is where the developers write the code that makes the software work. They also perform testing to make sure that the code works as intended and meets the requirements.

Once the code is developed and tested, it moves on to deployment, where it is installed on the end user's system. This is where the software is made available to users and is put into use.

But the lifecycle doesn't end there. Software requires ongoing maintenance and updates to stay secure and up-to-date. This is known as the maintenance phase.

Overall, the software development lifecycle is a critical process that ensures that software is built in a structured and systematic way. By following this process, developers can create high-quality, reliable software that meets the needs of users and stakeholders.

Why Does the SDLC matter?

The software development lifecycle (SDLC) is important for a number of reasons.

First, it provides a structured and systematic approach to building software, which helps to ensure that the software is developed in a predictable and consistent manner. This helps to reduce the risk of errors and bugs, and can improve the overall quality of the software.

Second, the SDLC helps to ensure that the software being developed meets the needs of its users and stakeholders. By following a rigorous requirements gathering and design process, developers can ensure that the software is built to meet specific needs and requirements.

Third, the SDLC helps to manage risk and control costs. By following a well-defined process, developers can identify potential problems early in the development process and take steps to mitigate them. This can help to prevent costly rework or delays in the project timeline.

Finally, the SDLC helps to ensure that the software being developed is secure and stable. By including testing and quality assurance processes in the development lifecycle, developers can identify and fix security vulnerabilities and stability issues before the software is deployed.

RECAP: Overall, the SDLC is important because it provides a structured and systematic approach to software development that helps to ensure the software being developed is of high quality, meets the needs of its users, and is secure and stable.

Agile vs. Waterfall

Well, hello there! Let's talk about two different ways of managing software development projects: Agile and Waterfall.

Waterfall is a more traditional approach that involves a linear, sequential process in which each phase of the project must be completed before moving on to the next. This approach is often used in large, complex projects with well-defined requirements, and it's known for its predictability and structure.

Agile, on the other hand, is a more flexible and iterative approach that involves continuous feedback and adaptation throughout the development process. With Agile, teams work in short sprints to deliver working software and get feedback from users, allowing them to make changes and adjustments as they go.

Agile is known for its flexibility and ability to quickly adapt to changing requirements or priorities, while Waterfall is more structured and predictable. Which approach is best depends on the specific needs of the project and the preferences of the development team.

Overall, Agile and Waterfall are two different project management methodologies that each have their strengths and weaknesses.

RECAP: Agile and Waterfall are two distinct software development project management methodologies. Waterfall follows a linear, sequential process, completing each phase before moving on, making it suitable for large, complex projects with well-defined requirements. Agile, on the other hand, is a flexible, iterative approach that emphasizes continuous feedback and adaptation, working in short sprints to deliver software and incorporate user input. Agile offers adaptability, while Waterfall provides structure, making the choice between the two dependent on project needs and team preferences. Ultimately, both methodologies have their own strengths and weaknesses in managing software development projects.

One More Comment: Understanding User Stories

Alright, buckle up folks, because I'm about to drop some knowledge on you. A user story is a tool used in agile software development to describe a feature or function from the perspective of the end user. It's a concise, plain-English description of what a user needs to be able to do, and why they need to do it.

In other words, a user story is like a little narrative that captures the user's motivation, the task they need to complete, and the benefit they'll receive from completing that task. It's a way of keeping the focus on the user and their needs, rather than getting bogged down in technical details or abstract concepts.

Now, some people might say that user stories are just a fancy way of writing requirements, but I'd argue that they're much more than that. A well-written user story can inspire empathy, creativity, and collaboration among team members. It can help everyone stay aligned around the user's goals, and it can serve as a powerful reminder of why we're building this thing in the first place.

So if you're a product manager, a designer, or a developer, and you're not using user stories in your agile process, then I'd say you're missing out on a valuable tool for building better products. And if you're not building better products, then what the hell are you doing with your life? Get with the program, people!

How Does the SDLC relate to the Internet, Applications, Data, and Infrastructure?

The software development lifecycle is closely related to the internet, applications, data, and infrastructure, as these are all key components of software systems.

When developing software that will be used on the internet, the SDLC can help ensure that the application is designed to meet the needs of users, while also taking into account the requirements of the internet environment, such as scalability, security, and connectivity.

Similarly, when developing applications, the SDLC can help ensure that the application is designed to meet the needs of users, while also taking into account the requirements of the platform it will run on, such as the operating system, hardware, and software environment.

In the context of data, the SDLC can help ensure that the software is designed to manage and process data in a secure and efficient manner, while also complying with relevant data protection and privacy regulations.

Finally, when developing software infrastructure, the SDLC can help ensure that the infrastructure is designed to meet the needs of the software system being built, while also taking into account the requirements of the underlying hardware and network infrastructure.

Overall, the SDLC provides a framework for designing, building, and deploying software systems that takes into account the complex and interrelated nature of the internet, applications, data, and infrastructure. By following a structured and systematic approach, developers can create software systems that are reliable, secure, and effective in meeting the needs of their users and stakeholders.

RECAP: The SDLC is important because it provides a structured and systematic approach to software development that helps to ensure the software being developed is of high quality, meets the needs of its users, and is secure and stable.

Chapter Five

What Makes Up The Internet?

At the risk of being known as Captain Obvious, our journey into tech recruiting starts with the Internet, the big kahuna of the digital world. The Internet, in its simplest form, is a vast network of interconnected computers and servers that allow us to access and share information from anywhere in the world. It's like a digital superhighway, connecting people, businesses, and organizations across the globe.

The Internet has revolutionized the way we communicate, work, and play. Thanks to the internet, we can now send emails, make video calls, shop online, stream movies and music, and so much more. It's a game-changer, folks! The Internet has transformed the world into a global village, breaking down barriers and opening up endless possibilities.

As a network of connections used to allow computer users to send and receive information, these connections are located all over the world and there are no central controllers where all the connections must pass. These connections are able to communicate effectively because of a standard set of protocols. A protocol is just a collection of rules; the internet runs on protocols, and these protocols are like a roadmap for computer communication. They tell the computers when to start sending information, when to stop, and how that information should be formatted. Think of it like a dance. The protocols are the steps, and the computers are the dancers. With these protocols in place, the computers know exactly what to do and when to do it, ensuring that the information is transmitted smoothly and efficiently. So, next time you're online, take a moment to appreciate the magic of internet protocols and the seamless communication they enable.

Web

The Web is a powerhouse of technologies that make the internet, well, the internet. It's a collection of tools that define how web pages are created (HTML), how they're linked together (URL), where they live (DNS), and how you can access them (HTTP). That's right, the Web is what makes the internet accessible, intuitive, and user-friendly. It's the glue that holds everything together and makes the digital world a reality.

But what are these concepts like HTML, URL, DNS, and HTTP?

HTML

HTML, or Hypertext Markup Language, is the backbone of the web. It's the language that web developers use to create and structure the pages you see on your screen. Think of HTML like the blueprint for a building, it gives shape and structure to the web pages and determines how the content is displayed.

HTML tags are like building blocks, they define the different elements on a web page, such as headings, paragraphs, images, links, and more. By using these tags, developers can create web pages that are both functional and aesthetically pleasing. It's a crucial tool in the web development toolbox, and without it, the web would be a lot less interactive and a lot less exciting.

But HTML is more than just a pretty face. It's also accessible and user-friendly, making it easier for people with disabilities to access information online. With HTML, developers can add alternative text to images, create captions for videos, and provide audio descriptions for multimedia content. That's right, HTML is making the web a more inclusive place, one tag at a time.

RECAP: HTML, or Hypertext Markup Language, is the fundamental language used by web developers to create and structure web pages.

URL

Let's talk about URL, or Uniform Resource Locator. URL is the address that takes you to a specific page on the internet. Think of it like the street address for a building. Just like you need a street address to find a building, you need a URL to access a web page.

URLs are the keys to the internet kingdom, they allow you to navigate from one page to another, find information, and connect with people and organizations from all over the world. They're simple, intuitive, and easy to use, making the internet accessible and user-friendly.

But don't let their simplicity fool you:. URLs are also powerful tools for SEO and marketing. By optimizing your URL structure, you can improve your search engine ranking, making it easier for people to find your content and engage with your brand.

RECAP: URL, or Uniform Resource Locator, is the address that leads to a specific web page on the internet, serving as a key to the internet for easy navigation, information finding, and connection with others.

DNS

DNS, or Domain Name System, is the system that translates human-readable domain names into machine-readable IP addresses. Think of it like a phone book for the internet. Just like you need a phone book to find someone's phone number, you need DNS to find a website's IP address.

DNS is the backbone of the internet, it's what makes it possible for you to type in a simple and memorable domain name, like "www.google.com", and be directed to the correct website. Without DNS, you would have to remember a string of numbers to access a website, and let's be real, who wants to do that?

But DNS is more than just a convenience, folks. It's also a critical component of internet security. By using DNS, you can protect your website from cyber attacks, prevent phishing scams, and ensure that your users have a safe and secure browsing experience.

So, there you have it, folks. DNS, the system that translates domain names into IP addresses, making the internet accessible, user-friendly, and secure. Get ready to dive into the world of internet infrastructure and see what DNS can do!

RECAP: DNS, or Domain Name System, is the system that translates human-readable domain names into machine-readable IP addresses, allowing for easy access to websites by simply typing a memorable domain name.

HTTP

Let's riff on this final component, HTTP, or Hypertext Transfer Protocol. HTTP is the protocol that defines how information is transmitted over the internet. Think of it like the language that web pages and servers use to communicate with each other.

HTTP is what makes the web possible, it's what allows you to request and receive information from a web server, whether it's to view a website, download a file, or access a web-based service. Without HTTP, the web would be a lot less accessible and a lot less useful.

HTTP is more than just a communication tool. It's also a key component of the web architecture, and it's critical to the performance and security of your website. By understanding HTTP, you can optimize your website's load time, improve its security, and ensure that your users have a fast and seamless browsing experience.

So, there you have it, folks. HTTP, the protocol that powers the web and makes it possible for you to access information from anywhere in the world. Get ready to dive into the world of web architecture and see what HTTP can do!

RECAP: HTTP, or Hypertext Transfer Protocol, is the protocol that defines how information is transmitted over the internet, serving as the language between web pages and servers and making the web accessible and useful.

Chapter Six

What Is An Application?

Applications are the lifeblood of the digital age. These computer software packages, also known as application programs or application software, are the tools that allow us to interact with technology and perform specific functions. And as we delve into the intricacies of web development, it's crucial that we understand the role of applications.

So, let's break it down.

Applications can either run directly for an end user or, in some cases, for another application. As we delve into the world of programming languages, it's essential that we distinguish between the two fundamental components that make up an application: the front-end and the back-end. The front-end, you see, is the code that your computer runs, while the back-end is the code that runs on the server. Both are equally important, and together they form the backbone of the web.

Front-End Technologies

Maybe you have heard of HTML, CSS, and Javascript? Front-end technologies refer to the tools and technologies used in the client-side of web development, which is responsible for the presentation and interaction of a website or web application. These technologies are used to create the user interface, handle user interaction, and control the behavior of a web page. Some of the most common front-end technologies include:

- HTML (Hypertext Markup Language) - used to structure the content of a web page
- CSS (Cascading Style Sheets) - used to style and design a web page
  - Bootstrap and Foundation - popular CSS frameworks for creating responsive and mobile-friendly designs
- JSON - used primarily to transmit data between a server and a web application
- WYSIWYG - used to see and manipulate the formatting of a document or web page in real-time,
- JavaScript - used to add interactivity and dynamic behavior to a web page
  - React, Angular, and Vue.js - popular JavaScript libraries and frameworks used for building dynamic user interfaces

These technologies work together to create the user experience and interactivity of a website, and are crucial for the success of any web-based project.

For mobile applications, you can also think of apps in the App Store (iOS) or Google Play Store (Android) as the "front-end" part of a mobile application. Typically, the front-end part of the web applications and the mobile application will talk to the same back-end application.

HTML

Consider this a double dip if you've previously read about HTML in the previous chapter, or an alternative explanation. Either way, let's answer the question: what is HTML?

If you visit your favorite website, maybe ebay.com or amazon.com, you can right click anywhere on the page and click *view page source*. The code you'll see is HTML.

The "unintelligible" code you see is actually the foundation of the web. The code you see is written in a language that computers can understand, and it's what allows the web pages to function and be displayed as intended.

Without this code, web pages would not be able to have the structure, design, and interactivity that we're used to seeing. HTML provides the structure for the content, CSS styles and designs the page, and JavaScript adds interactivity and dynamic behavior.

While it may look like nonsense to the average person, this code is the key to making the web work and providing a seamless user experience. Without it, the web would be much less functional and visually appealing.

Think of HTML like the frame of a house, it's what gives the website its form and holds everything together. The HTML tags, or building blocks, define the different elements on a web page, such as headings, paragraphs, images, links, and more. By using these tags, developers can create web pages that are both functional and aesthetically pleasing.

But HTML is more than just a pretty face. It's also accessible and user-friendly, making it easier for people with disabilities to access information online. With HTML, developers can add alternative text to images, create captions for videos, and provide audio descriptions for multimedia content. HTML is making the web a more inclusive place, one tag at a time.

Also important to mention is the Document Object Model (DOM); the DOM is a programming interface for HTML. It represents the structure of a document as a tree-like structure, where each node in the tree represents an element, attribute, or text content in the document. The DOM provides a way for programs to dynamically access and manipulate the content and structure of a document. This allows for dynamic and interactive web pages, as well as the ability to programmatically interact with a page using JavaScript. The DOM is considered the standard for representing and manipulating HTML in modern web development.

RECAP: HTML, or Hypertext Markup Language, is the fundamental language used by web developers to create and structure web pages.

JSON

Ever been on Google and as you are typing a query, the results magically appear in the search bar and on the page?

Maybe "magically" is a bit of a stretch.

When we discussed how HTML works and defines the content of the web page, we suggested loading the full page. But what if the whole page doesn't need to be updated?

What if you only need to update a portion of the page?

BAM!

Google's instant search feature sends only the search result information to your computer and not the other spurious formatting descriptions and instructions. To make this magic happen, they use JSON.

JSON, or JavaScript Object Notation, is a lightweight data-interchange format that is used to exchange data between the server and a web application. It's a text-based format that's easy for humans to read and write, and it's also easy for computers to parse and generate.

Now, imagine you have a bunch of data, like information about a person, and you want to send that data to another person or use it in a different program. You could write it down on paper, but that's not very efficient, especially if you have a lot of data. Instead, you could use JSON to structure that data in a way that makes it easy to transmit and easy to understand.

Think of JSON as a way of organizing information in a way that's both compact and readable. It's like a recipe for a cake - the recipe has all the ingredients and instructions needed to make the cake, and it's organized in a way that makes sense to both the baker and the person who's following the recipe. Similarly, JSON organizes data in a way that makes it easy for both computers and humans to use and understand.

And the beauty of JSON is its simplicity. It's based on JavaScript, so if you know JavaScript, you already know how to work with JSON. And because it's so lightweight, it's fast and efficient, making it a popular choice for exchanging data between different systems and applications.

RECAP: JSON is a simple and effective way to structure and exchange data between systems, making it a crucial tool in the world of technology.

XML

XML (eXtensible Markup Language) is a markup language that is used to store and transport data. Unlike HTML, which is used to display data and create web pages, XML is used to describe and store structured data in a way that is independent of the software or hardware that will be using the data. XML documents contain elements that describe the data and its structure, allowing software applications to easily access and manipulate the data.

One of the main differences between XML and HTML is that XML allows you to create your own custom tags, making it a more flexible and adaptable way to store and transport data. HTML, on the other hand, has a fixed set of tags that describe how web page elements should be displayed. Another difference is that XML is case-sensitive, while HTML is not. Additionally, XML requires that all elements be properly nested and closed, while HTML is more forgiving in this regard.

Overall, XML provides a more flexible and structured way to store and transport data than HTML, making it a popular choice for data exchange between different software applications and platforms.

RECAP: XML (eXtensible Markup Language) is a markup language used to store and exchange structured data in a human-readable format, allowing for more complex data structures than HTML.

WYSIWYG

But what if you are using an application like Microsoft Excel?

In this instance, you'll only see the output format and never the underlying code.

The world of digital documents and presentations is a complex one, and navigating it requires a certain level of know-how and technical expertise. Microsoft Word and its Office Suite are examples of WYSIWYG editors, which allow users to create and edit documents with ease, as the output document will look exactly like what is seen in the editor. WYSIWYG means "what you see is what you get."

However, the world of web pages operates differently. HTML is the language of the web, but it's not as simple to work with as Microsoft Word. Web pages are viewed through various browsers, such as Chrome, Firefox, and Safari, and each browser may interpret the document format differently. This requires a level of precision and care from the programmer when writing code to ensure the web page looks and functions as intended.

Although there are WYSIWYG editors available for HTML, they are limited in their functionality and are only suitable for very basic web pages. For more complex web pages, it's necessary to have a deeper understanding of HTML and the web development process.

RECAP: WYSIWYG (pronounced wiz-ee-wig) is a type of editing software that allows users to see and edit content in a form that appears as it would when displayed on an interface, webpage, slide presentation or printed document.

CSS

CSS is what gives web pages their style and design, making them visually appealing and easy to navigate.

Think of CSS as the interior design of a house, it's what determines the color scheme, font, and layout of a website. CSS allows developers to separate the content of a web page from its presentation, making it easier to maintain and update a website over time.

CSS is a powerful tool that allows developers to create unique and engaging user experiences. With CSS, they can change the background color of a page, adjust the spacing between elements, and add animations and transitions to make a website more interactive.

But CSS is more than just a way to make a website look good. It's also critical for accessibility and responsiveness. By using CSS, developers can ensure that a website is accessible to users with disabilities, and that it works well on different devices, from desktop computers to smartphones.

RECAP: CSS (Cascading Style Sheets) is used to style and layout web pages — for example, to alter the font, color, size, and spacing of your content, split it into multiple columns, or add animations and other decorative features

Bootstrap

Bootstrap is used when a quick and easy solution for creating a responsive, well-designed website is needed. It provides a pre-designed library of HTML, CSS, and JavaScript components, making it easier and faster to create a website compared to writing CSS from scratch.

It was originally developed by Twitter and is now one of the most popular front-end development tools for building websites and web applications. Bootstrap makes it easy for developers to create beautiful and functional websites, regardless of their experience level, by providing a set of pre-designed and tested components that can be easily combined and customized to fit specific needs.

RECAP: Bootstrap simplifies the process of creating consistent, user-friendly interfaces.

Foundation

Foundation is a responsive front-end framework that provides a set of CSS, JavaScript, and design patterns for building responsive websites and web applications. One might choose to use Foundation over CSS because it offers a pre-designed and tested set of UI components, along with a grid system and other features, which can make it faster and easier to develop and maintain a responsive, mobile-friendly website. Additionally, Foundation provides a consistent look and feel across different devices and screen sizes, which can be beneficial for user experience and brand consistency.

RECAP: Foundation is a responsive front-end framework used for developing responsive and mobile-first websites, providing a set of CSS and JavaScript tools for creating consistent, responsive designs with ease.

AJAX

AJAX, or Asynchronous JavaScript and XML, is a technique used for creating fast and dynamic web pages. It allows for the exchange of data with a server, updating parts of a web page without having to reload the entire page. AJAX has revolutionized the way we interact with websites, making web pages faster, more responsive, and more user-friendly.

With AJAX, web developers can create dynamic, seamless user experiences that were once impossible.

It's a powerful tool for creating the dynamic and interactive web pages that we all enjoy today.

AJAX uses the XMLHttpRequest object to communicate with the server, and can be used with other data formats such as JSON or plain text. The request and response are processed in the background, so the user can continue to interact with the page while the data is being updated.

This enables web developers to create more interactive and dynamic web pages, providing a better user experience. For example, instead of reloading a page to retrieve new data, an AJAX call can be made to retrieve the data and update the page dynamically.

RECAP: AJAX is widely used in modern web development, as it provides a way to update web pages asynchronously, without having to reload the entire page, resulting in a faster and more responsive user experience.

COOKIES

All right, students – we aren't talking about the ones that go with milk. No, no, no!

Cookies are small data files that are stored on your computer or device when you visit a website. They were created as a way for websites to remember information about you and your preferences, so that you don't have to keep entering the same information every time you visit the site. For example, if you log into a website, a cookie can be used to remember your username so that you don't have to enter it every time you return to the site.

Cookies are a crucial component of the modern web, they make it possible for websites to offer personalized experiences, store shopping carts, and track user behavior. They're also the backbone of many online advertising models, allowing advertisers to target specific audiences and measure the effectiveness of their campaigns.

However, cookies have also been a source of controversy due to privacy concerns. Some users are uncomfortable with the idea of websites tracking their behavior and collecting information about them, and there have been instances of cookies being used for malicious purposes, such as tracking users without their consent.

In the end, cookies are a double-edged sword. They make the web more convenient and personalized, but they also raise important privacy and security concerns. As with many things in the tech world, it's up to each individual to weigh the pros and cons and make a decision about how they want to use cookies.

RECAP: Cookies are small text files that are stored on a user's device when they visit a website. They are used to remember user preferences, browsing history, and other information about the user's interaction with the website.

Javascript

As we delve deeper into the world of web development, we come across a language that has revolutionized the way we interact with web pages - Javascript. JavaScript is so popular that it's the most used programming language in the world, used as a client-side programming language by 97% of all websites!

You see, before Javascript came along, web pages were pretty much just static documents. They were like brochures, presenting information but not much else. But with the advent of Javascript, web pages have become dynamic and interactive.

Javascript is a programming language that runs on the client side, that is, on the user's web browser. It allows developers to add behavior to web pages, making them more interactive and engaging.

Want to create a drop-down menu or an image slider? Javascript can do that.

Want to validate a form or add an auto-complete feature to a search box? Javascript can do that, too.

The beauty of Javascript is that it can interact with HTML and CSS, which are the other two fundamental building blocks of the web. HTML provides the structure and content of a web page, while CSS provides the styling. Javascript then adds the behavior and interactivity, making the web page come alive.

In short, Javascript is the glue that holds together the web and makes it dynamic and engaging.

Not to create confusion, there are several varieties, frameworks and libraries of Javascript, each with it's own pluses and minuses. There are several types of JavaScript, including:

- **Vanilla JavaScript**: This is the purest form of JavaScript, without any additional frameworks or libraries.

- **Library JavaScript**: This is pre-written JavaScript code that can be easily incorporated into a website to perform a specific task, such as jQuery or React.

- **Framework JavaScript**: This is a more comprehensive set of pre-written code that provides a structure for building a web application, such as Angular or Vue.

- **Server-side JavaScript**: This type of JavaScript runs on a server and is used to build server-side applications, such as Node.js.

- **Hybrid JavaScript**: This is a combination of library and framework JavaScript that provides both pre-written code and a structure for building a web application.

- **ECMAScript**: This is the standardized version of JavaScript, which is updated regularly to add new features and improve performance.

Each type of JavaScript has its own strengths and weaknesses, and the choice of which one to use depends on the specific requirements of a project.

RECAP: JavaScript is a scripting language that enables you to dynamically update content, control multimedia, animate images, and pretty much everything else.

Javascript Libraries and Frameworks

A JavaScript library is a pre-written collection of functions and methods that can be easily incorporated into a larger project to perform specific tasks, such as manipulating the Document Object Model (DOM) or making AJAX requests.

Frameworks provide a more structured and opinionated approach to building web applications, dictating the overall architecture and guidelines for building applications. This means that if you're using a framework, you're going to have to stick to its conventions and prescribed methods. On the other hand, a library provides a more flexible and customizable way to build an application, offering a set of tools that can be used as needed. So, when it comes to frameworks versus libraries, it's really a question of structure versus flexibility.

There are many popular JavaScript libraries and frameworks, and some of the most common ones include:

- **jQuery**: makes HTML document traversal and manipulation, event handling, and animation much simpler.

- **ReactJS**: render and update the view of web applications with a focus on declarative code and reusable components.

- **Angular**: framework for building dynamic, single-page applications (SPAs).

- **Vue.js**: for building user interfaces and single-page applications with a reactive and composable architecture.

- **Lodash**: provides a variety of functions for working with arrays, numbers, objects, and strings, making it easier to manipulate and analyze data

- **D3.js**: Data-Driven Documents is used for creating dynamic, interactive visualizations and charts using data from various sources

- **Chart.js**: allows developers to create beautiful and interactive charts for web applications.

- **EmberJS**: building scalable and complex web applications that provides developers with a productive and organized development environment by following the Model-View-Controller (MVC) pattern.

- **BackboneJS**: provides structure to web applications by providing models with key-value binding and custom events, collections with a rich API of enumerable functions, and views with declarative event handling

- **MeteorJS**: used for building web and mobile applications that allow for real-time updates and live data synchronization between the client and server.

- **SvelteJS**: eliminates the need for a virtual DOM and reduces the amount of code necessary for updates, resulting in faster and more efficient web applications.

- **PolymerJS**: uses reusable and composable custom elements that can interact with other elements on the page, enabling you to build large and complex web applications in a modular and performant manner.

Really quick side note: don't try committing all of this to memory. You've got this book as a reference guide. Be patient and persistent in your efforts. Technology and concepts are constantly evolving, so it's important to stay informed of the latest developments. Read industry blogs, attend events, and participate in online forums like Reddit, Quora, and Medium to stay current; let this just be a starting point on your Javascript journey.

jQuery

jQuery is a fast, small, and feature-rich JavaScript library that makes HTML document traversal and manipulation, event handling, and animation much simpler with an easy-to-use API[1] that works across a multitude of browsers. jQuery takes a lot of common

[1] Hey there - what's an API? API is the acronym for application programming interface — a software intermediary that allows two applications to talk to each other. APIs are an accessible way to extract and share data within and across organizations.

APIs are mechanisms that enable two software components to communicate with each other using a set of definitions and protocols. For example, the weather bureau's software system contains daily weather data. The weather app on your phone "talks" to this system via APIs and shows you daily weather updates on your phone.

tasks that require many lines of JavaScript code to accomplish, and wraps them into methods that you can call with a single line of code. jQuery was found on more than 80 million websites in 2022; jQuery has changed the way that millions of people write JavaScript.

jQuery makes it easy to select elements on a web page, handle events such as mouse clicks, and animate elements to create dynamic user interfaces. The library also has a huge community of developers who have created plugins to extend its functionality even further.

RECAP: jQuery is a JavaScript library that makes HTML document traversal and manipulation, event handling, and animation much simpler with an easy-to-use API that works across browsers.

ReactJS

React is a JavaScript library for building user interfaces that is highly efficient and flexible, allowing developers to create complex applications with ease. React is a JavaScript library developed by Facebook which, among other things, was used to build Instagram.com. Its aim is to allow developers to easily create fast user interfaces for websites and applications alike. React is primarily used for developing single-page applications and mobile applications, and it's known for its high performance and ability to handle large amounts of data.

React also uses a component-based architecture, where developers build UI components as individual, reusable elements; it lets you compose complex UIs from components[2].

React works by using a virtual DOM (Document Object Model)[3] which is a lightweight in-memory

---

[2] What is a component? Components are independent and reusable bits of code. They serve the same purpose as JavaScript functions, but work in isolation and return HTML. Components come in two types, Class components and Function components.

A class component in ReactJS is a type of component that is defined as a class, rather than a function. Class components allow you to use additional features such as lifecycle methods and state, which are not available in function components. The syntax for creating a class component is a bit different from that of a function component, as it requires the use of a JavaScript class and the render method. The render method returns the HTML-like code, known as JSX, that will be displayed on the page. Class components are generally used for more complex components that need to manage internal state or perform more advanced logic, such as making API calls, whereas function components are used for simpler components that only render UI based on their props.

A function component in ReactJS is a type of component that is defined as a JavaScript function. It is an alternative to class components and is used to create presentational components in ReactJS. Function components are simple, easy to write, and have a small footprint. They accept props as arguments and return a React element, which is then rendered to the screen. Function components are also referred to as stateless components because they do not have access to state, unlike class components.

[3] React uses a virtual DOM to update and render components efficiently. The virtual DOM is a simulated representation of the actual DOM, which is the tree-like structure that represents the

representation of the actual DOM. This allows React to make changes to the UI quickly and efficiently, without having to re-render the entire page.

When the state of your application changes, React updates only the components that need to change, making the process much faster than other traditional front-end frameworks.

RECAP: React is primarily used for developing single-page applications and mobile applications, and it's known for its high performance and ability to handle large amounts of data.

Angular

Angular is a JavaScript-based open-source front-end web application framework primarily maintained by Google and a community of individual developers. It allows developers to build dynamic, single-page applications that can run in a web browser. AngularJS uses two-way data binding, which means that changes made to the model are automatically reflected in the view and vice versa. This makes it easier for developers to manage the flow of data in their application.

HTML elements on a web page. When changes are made to the components, React updates the virtual DOM instead of directly updating the actual DOM. This allows React to determine the most efficient way to update the actual DOM, reducing the amount of time and resources needed to update the page. The virtual DOM also provides a fast and smooth experience for the user, as they are able to interact with the page without any delay.

In Angular, the application is built using components, which are modular pieces of code that can be reused throughout the application. This makes it easier for developers to manage the complexity of their application and keep the code organized.

Another key feature of AngularJS is its ability to handle dependencies automatically, making it easier for developers to manage the components and modules in their application. AngularJS also provides a set of built-in directives, which are special attributes that allow developers to extend the HTML language and add dynamic behavior to their application.

RECAP: Angular is a powerful and flexible front-end framework that makes it easier for developers to build dynamic and complex web applications.

Vue.js

Vue.js is a progressive JavaScript framework for building user interfaces, with a focus on simplicity, performance, and scalability. is a progressive JavaScript framework for building user interfaces. It is known for its simplicity, reactivity, and modularity. Vue.js follows a component-based architecture, where the user interface is composed of reusable components. The framework uses a template-based syntax, which makes it easy to write and understand the code. Vue.js also offers two-way data binding, which means that changes in the model are automatically reflected in the view, and vice versa. Additionally, Vue.js has a small size and good performance, making it a popular choice for building dynamic, responsive web applications.

RECAP: Vue.js is known for its simplicity, versatility, and performance, making it a popular choice for building dynamic user interfaces and single-page applications.

Lodash

Lodash is a JavaScript library that provides utility functions for common programming tasks, such as working with arrays, numbers, objects, and strings. It is designed to make it easier to write clean and maintainable code, and to reduce the amount of repetitive and tedious code that developers often have to write. Lodash provides a large collection of functions that perform tasks such as finding elements in arrays, merging objects, and formatting strings. It is widely used by developers due to its speed, consistency, and ease of use, and it is often considered one of the most essential libraries for JavaScript development.

RECAP: Lodash has a modular design, which allows developers to only include the functions they need, making it fast and lightweight.

D3.js

D3.js (Data-Driven Documents) is a JavaScript library used to create dynamic and interactive visualizations in web browsers. It allows developers to bind arbitrary data to a Document Object Model (DOM), and then apply data-driven transformations to the document. D3.js uses a declarative approach, making it easier for developers to create complex visualizations, animations, and charts. It also has a large and active community that provides a wealth of resources and plugins for developers to use. D3.js is used by a wide range of organizations, from news outlets to financial institutions, to create compelling data visualizations and to tell stories with data.

RECAP: D3.js is a JavaScript library for producing dynamic, interactive data visualizations in web browsers.

Chart.js

Chart.js is a simple and flexible JavaScript charting library for designers and developers. It provides an easy-to-use and flexible API for creating various types of charts, including bar charts, line charts, pie charts, and more. Chart.js is also highly customizable, allowing developers to change the appearance and behavior of charts to fit their needs. Additionally, it's open-source and has a large community of developers who contribute to its development and maintenance. Chart.js is a popular choice for data visualization on the web because of its ease of use, versatility, and strong performance.

RECAP: Chart.js is a JavaScript library that allows developers to create interactive charts and graphs on websites and web applications.

EmberJS

EmberJS is designed to make it easier for developers to create complex, scalable, and high-performing web applications by providing a set of conventions and tools that streamline the development process. Ember.js uses the Model-View-Controller (MVC)[4] pattern to structure the application code and provides features such as two-way data binding, computed properties, and a powerful router. It also has a large and active community, which provides a wealth of resources, add-ons, and plugins for developers to use.

---

[4] What's the MVC? The Model-View-Controller (MVC) is a design pattern used in software engineering to separate the code that defines the application's data structure (the "model"), the code that defines the application's behavior (the "controller"), and the code that defines the application's user interface (the "view"). The purpose of this separation is to make it easier to change or update one aspect of the application without affecting the others.

By separating the model, view, and controller, the MVC pattern helps to create a more organized and maintainable codebase. It also allows for a clear separation of concerns, making it easier for multiple developers to work on the same codebase at the same time

RECAP: With EmberJS, developers can create single-page applications that can handle large amounts of data and provide a smooth user experience.

BackboneJS

BackboneJS is designed to be minimalistic, making it a great choice for small to medium-sized projects. It provides a Model-View-Controller (MVC) architecture that helps organize your code into a more manageable structure. With Backbone.js, you can create dynamic and interactive web applications by defining models that represent your data, views that display that data, and routers that control the flow of your application. BackboneJS is known for its simplicity and elegance, making it a popular choice for developers who want to build web applications quickly and efficiently.

RECAP: BackboneJS is a JavaScript framework that provides structure to web applications by providing models with key-value binding and custom events, collections with a rich API of enumerable functions, and views with declarative event handling.

MeteorJS

MeteorJS is a full-stack JavaScript framework for building web applications. It provides a platform for building web applications using only JavaScript, from the client side to the server side. MeteorJS is designed to be fast, simple, and scalable, making it a popular choice for developers looking to build modern web applications quickly and efficiently. The framework provides a collection of libraries and packages that handle common tasks, such as data management, user authentication, and real-time updates, so developers can focus on building their application's unique features. MeteorJS integrates with popular front-end technologies like React, Angular, and Vue, as well as back-end databases like MongoDB[5].

RECAP: MeteorJS is a free, open-source JavaScript framework for building web and mobile applications. It provides a full-stack solution for building real-time web applications with a reactive programming model that makes it easy to build complex, scalable applications.

---

[5] What is MongoDB? MongoDB is a popular NoSQL database that is used to store and retrieve large amounts of data in a flexible and scalable way. Unlike traditional relational databases, MongoDB stores data in a JSON-like format called BSON (Binary JSON), which makes it easy to store, index, and query complex data structures.

MongoDB works by using a distributed architecture, which means that data is stored across multiple servers. This allows it to scale horizontally and support large amounts of data and high levels of traffic. It also provides high availability, as data is automatically replicated to multiple servers for backup and recovery purposes.

MongoDB uses a document-oriented data model, which means that each record in the database is stored as a document. This makes it easy to store and retrieve data, and it also allows for complex relationships between data to be stored within a single document, rather than across multiple tables.

SvelteJS

SvelteJS is a front-end JavaScript framework that uses a reactive and efficient approach to building web applications. It operates at the component level, transforming components into highly optimized JavaScript code during the build process, resulting in smaller bundle sizes and faster runtime performance compared to traditional frameworks like React or Angular. SvelteJS does not use a virtual DOM, making it a unique solution for building web apps that offers a simple and straightforward learning curve for developers.

It works by compiling code at build time rather than runtime, resulting in smaller and faster applications with a minimal footprint. SvelteJS focuses on a simple and reactive programming model, making it easier to build complex and dynamic UIs. The framework also provides a set of tools and features for building and testing applications, making it a popular choice for front-end developers.

RECAP: SvelteJS works by compiling components at build time, rather than interpreting them at runtime like other frameworks, resulting in fast and efficient performance.

PolymerJS

PolymerJS allows developers to create reusable and customizable web components. It uses declarative syntax to define the components, making it easy to build complex user interfaces with reusable, modular components that can be easily shared and integrated into other projects. It works by leveraging the latest web technologies such as web components and shadow DOM[6] to create scalable and performant web applications.

The elements created using PolymerJS are encapsulated and self-contained, allowing developers to easily build and manage complex user interfaces without affecting the rest of the application. PolymerJS also includes a powerful data binding system, allowing developers to easily bind data from one part of an application to another, making it easier to keep the UI in sync with the underlying data.

RECAP: PolymerJS allows developers to create reusable and customizable custom elements for building web applications.

[6] Wait... more DOMs? What is a Shadow DOM?

A shadow DOM is a feature of modern web browsers that allows developers to create isolated and encapsulated parts of a web page, called "shadow trees", that can have their own DOM tree, styles, and behavior, but are still connected to the main document and can affect or be affected by it. Shadow DOM provides a way to create reusable and modular components in web development, making it easier to manage and maintain complex applications.

JavaScript Summary

The popularity of JavaScript as the most used programming language in the world can be attributed to its ability to add behavior and interactivity to web pages, making them dynamic and engaging. JavaScript is a client-side programming language that interacts with HTML and CSS, enabling developers to create drop-down menus, image sliders, form validation, and search box auto-complete features. HTML provides the structure and content of a web page, CSS provides styling, and JavaScript adds the behavior and interactivity, making the web come alive. Simply put, JavaScript is the foundation of web development that brings all the pieces together to create an engaging user experience.

Back-End Technologies

Back-end technologies, like servers[7], databases[8], and APIs, are the unseen engines that drive the web and

---

[7] What is a server?

While this is covered in more detail in the Infrastructure section, I want to give you a quick, simple flavor for what a server is or could be. Simply put, a server is a computer system that provides data, resources, or services to other devices connected to it over a network, serving as the central source for the requests made by clients.

[8] What's a database?

make it possible to store and access vast amounts of information and data. Unlike front-end technologies, which are focused on creating visually appealing and interactive user experiences, back-end technologies are all about functionality and reliability. They're responsible for securely storing and retrieving data, processing requests, and serving up content to users. In other words, while front-end technologies are the showstoppers that grab our attention, back-end technologies are the unsung heroes that make it all possible.

Just like the engine of the car, electric or combustion, the back-end gets really complex really fast. But do not worry: this is going to get broken down in simple terms and concepts.

Understanding Back-End Programming Languages

Programming languages on the back-end are used to create the logic and structure for web applications and services. They allow developers to write code that runs on the server, rather than in a user's web browser, and are used to interact with databases, perform

---

While this is covered at length in the Data section, a quick primer is that a database stores and serves data. A database is a structured collection of data stored and organized in a specific manner, typically stored on a server, to allow for efficient querying, retrieval and manipulation of data.

computations, and generate HTML, CSS, and JavaScript for the front-end. Popular back-end programming languages include Python, Ruby, PHP, and Java, and they work by receiving HTTP requests, processing the data, and returning a response to the client. The code runs on the server and the output is sent to the user's browser, where it is then displayed as a web page.

You might be wondering why there are so many different programming languages on the back-end?

If we learned anything from all the varieties of Javascript, we learned the concept of efficiency and effectiveness.

There are many back-end programming languages because different languages are optimized for different tasks and work better for certain types of applications. Some programming languages are better suited for handling heavy loads of data and are more efficient at processing large amounts of information, while others are better suited for building complex web applications and provide more advanced features. Additionally, different organizations have different preferences and requirements, so they may choose to use a specific language that meets their specific needs. The widespread availability of a variety of programming languages allows developers to choose the best language for their particular project, which leads to a more efficient and effective outcome.

You'll find that many technology companies like Facebook started using only a few programming languages, and then, over time adopted more. For instance, Facebook was originally written in PHP, a language I will explore more. With the growth and complexity of Facebook, the company has also started using other technologies and programming languages, such as Hack (a dialect of PHP), React (JavaScript library), and GraphQL (query language) to tackle various challenges and improve performance.

What's Specification and Runtime?

In programming languages, specification and runtime refer to different stages of software development. The specification defines the structure and behavior of a programming language and includes its syntax, grammar, and semantics. The runtime, on the other hand, is the environment in which the language is executed and the code is executed.

We might explain the similarity between specification and runtime by saying that they are both crucial components of software development, working together to create a seamless experience for developers and end-users. The specification sets the standard for how a language should be used, while the runtime provides the environment in which it is executed.

However, they are also different in that the specification is a theoretical construct, while the runtime is the actual implementation of the language. The specification lays out the rules and guidelines for a language, but it is the runtime that brings those rules to life and makes them actionable. Therefore, understanding both the specification and the runtime is key to understanding and effectively using a programming language.

Think of it like this: the difference between specification and runtime can be explained as being similar to the difference between a set of blueprints and a construction site. The blueprints (specification) provide the guidelines and rules for building the house, while the construction site (runtime) is where the house is actually built and brought to life. In the same way, a programming language specification provides the guidelines and rules for writing code, while the runtime environment is where the code is executed and run.

Each programming language has one or more available runtime environments:

- **Ruby: The runtime environment for Ruby is the Ruby interpreter.**
- **Python: The runtime environment for Python is the Python interpreter.**
- **Java: The runtime environment for Java is the Java Virtual Machine (JVM).**
- **C#: The runtime environment for C# is the Common Language Runtime (CLR).**

In each of these examples, the programming language is used to write the code, and the runtime environment is responsible for executing the code. The runtime environment provides the necessary resources and environment for the code to run, such as memory management, security, and access to system resources.

What's a Compiler?

A compiler is a special type of program that takes in source code written in a high-level programming language and outputs an executable machine code. Think of a compiler like a translator who takes your written words in one language and converts it into another language that is readable by a different group of people. Similarly, the compiler takes your high-level code written in a language like Python or Java and converts it into low-level code that can be executed by the computer's processor. This process ensures that your code can run efficiently and effectively on a wide range of devices and operating systems.

Why So Many Languages?

As suggested, the widespread availability of a variety of programming languages allows developers to choose the best language for their particular project, which leads to a more efficient and effective outcome. There are a lot of languages, and there are features that make them special, nimble, and unique. These characteristics not only illuminate the trade-offs, but also explain why one language is a better choice for a particular use case.

Programming languages can be categorized based on their features as:

- **Low-level vs. High-level**
- **Object Oriented vs. Functional**
- **Dynamically Typed vs. Statically Typed**
- **Interpreted vs. Compiled**
- **Concurrency**

Low-level vs. High-level Languages

Low-level programming languages are computer languages that provide little or no abstraction from a computer's instruction set architecture. They are often closer to machine code and provide the programmer with direct access to the hardware. Some examples include Assembly language and C.

High-level programming languages, on the other hand, provide higher levels of abstraction and are more user-friendly. They have a more natural syntax, are easier to learn, and are generally more efficient for solving complex problems. Some examples include Python, JavaScript, and Ruby - all languages we will delve into.

The main difference between low-level and high-level programming languages is the level of abstraction they provide, which affects how close they are to machine code and how easy they are to use.

RECAP: Low-level programming languages operate closer to the machine language and hardware, while high-level programming languages are more abstract and user-friendly.

Object Oriented vs. Functional Languages

Object-oriented and functional languages are two different approaches to solving problems. Object-oriented languages focus on the idea of objects and the interactions between those objects to solve problems, while functional languages rely on functions and mathematical concepts to solve problems.

These two approaches have their own strengths and weaknesses, and the choice of which one to use depends on the specific requirements of the problem you're trying to solve.

Object Oriented programming focuses on creating objects that represent real-world entities and their interactions, and is often favored for its ability to model complex systems and encourage code reuse. On the other hand, Functional programming emphasizes immutability, pure functions, and avoiding side effects, making it well suited for tasks such as data processing and concurrency. However, it can sometimes result in more verbose code and a steeper learning curve for some developers.

Some popular object-oriented programming (OOP) languages are Java, Python, Ruby, C#, Swift, PHP, and Objective-C. These programming languages use OOP concepts such as classes, objects, inheritance, and encapsulation to structure and organize code.

Some popular functional programming languages include Haskell, Lisp, Scheme, Erlang, Elixir, and Scala.

RECAP: Object-oriented programming uses classes and objects to represent real-world concepts and their attributes and behaviors, while functional programming emphasizes immutability and treating functions as first-class entities that can be composed and passed as arguments.

Dynamically Typed vs. Statically Typed

Dynamically typed languages, such as Python and JavaScript, allow variables to change type during runtime and do not require the programmer to declare the type of the variable beforehand. Statically typed languages, such as Java and C++, require the programmer to declare the type of a variable before it can be used and do not allow for type changes during runtime.

Another way to think about it would be dynamically typed and statically typed programming languages refer to how they handle data types. In a dynamically typed language, the data type of a variable is determined at runtime, while in a statically typed language, the data type of a variable must be declared when it is created.

In other words, it's all about the data types!

RECAP: Dynamically typed languages determine the data type of a variable at runtime, while statically typed languages declare the data type of a variable when it is written in the code.

Interpreted vs. Compiled Languages

Interpreted and Compiled languages are two distinct approaches to programming, where Interpreted languages are executed line by line at runtime, whereas Compiled languages are translated into machine code before execution, leading to faster performance but also a longer development time.

These two approaches offer trade-offs in terms of speed, flexibility, and efficiency, and each has its strengths and weaknesses depending on the specific needs of a project.

Interpreted languages are known for their flexibility, as they do not need to be compiled before being executed. This allows for faster iteration and development, as changes made to the code can be immediately tested without the need to recompile the code. Additionally, interpreted languages often have more dynamic features, such as dynamic typing, which allows for greater flexibility in how the language can be used. They also often have more convenient error handling, as errors can be detected and reported on-the-fly, making it easier to debug code.

Compiled languages have the strength of faster execution times, as the code is compiled into machine code before it is run, allowing for optimized performance. Additionally, compiled code is often more secure as it is not easily readable in its compiled form, making it more difficult for malicious actors to exploit vulnerabilities in the code. Compiled languages also tend to have better error checking and debugging tools, making it easier to identify and fix issues in the code.

RECAP: Interpreted languages are executed line by line by an interpreter, while compiled languages are translated into machine code and executed as a standalone program.

Concurrency

Concurrency in computer programming refers to the ability of a system to handle multiple tasks or operations simultaneously. It allows multiple processes to run independently, at the same time, without affecting each other's execution. Concurrency enables programs to run efficiently and effectively by dividing a large task into smaller, manageable parts that can be executed in parallel, making it an important concept in modern programming.

Concurrency in computer programming can be explained using the metaphor of making hamburgers. Imagine a fast food restaurant where multiple customers place their orders at the same time and each order requires different ingredients to be assembled. The kitchen staff can handle these orders concurrently by working on multiple orders simultaneously, much like how threads in computer programming can handle multiple tasks concurrently. Just like in the kitchen, proper coordination and management is required to ensure that the orders are completed efficiently and without any errors, similarly in computer programming proper coordination and synchronization is required to handle concurrency.

Lastly, concurrency is important in computer programming because it allows multiple tasks to be executed simultaneously, improving the efficiency and performance of the program. In a concurrent system, multiple tasks can be executed in parallel, making better use of the available resources such as processing power, memory, and network bandwidth. This results in faster completion times and a more responsive user experience. Additionally, concurrency enables programs to handle multiple inputs and outputs at the same time, making them more scalable and able to handle increasing workloads.

RECAP: Concurrency in computer programming refers to the ability of a system to run multiple tasks simultaneously.

What's a Scripting Language?

A scripting language is a type of programming language that is designed for writing scripts, which are programs that are typically used to automate tasks or processes.

Scripting languages are often interpreted rather than compiled, which means that the code is executed directly by the computer's processor rather than being translated into machine language beforehand. This makes them well-suited for writing small to medium-sized programs, such as scripts for automating file transfers, processing data, or performing system administration tasks.

Scripting languages are also often used in web development for tasks such as form validation and handling user input. Some popular scripting languages include Python, Perl, Ruby, and JavaScript.

RECAP: Scripting languages are a type of programming language that are designed for writing small to medium-sized programs and automating tasks, and are often interpreted rather than compiled.

Exploring Algorithms

How do computers know what the hell we want them to do?

Enter algorithms.

An algorithm in computer programming is a set of instructions that tells a computer how to perform a specific task or solve a particular problem. It is a sequence of steps that can be followed to achieve a desired outcome, such as sorting a list of numbers, searching for a specific item in a database, or generating a new image or video.

Algorithms are fundamental to computer programming, and they can be used to solve a wide range of problems in many different fields, from scientific computing and data analysis to machine learning and artificial intelligence.

An algorithm typically takes some input data as its starting point, processes that data using a series of steps or operations, and produces an output or result. The quality and efficiency of an algorithm can have a significant impact on the performance of a program or system, and optimizing algorithms is an important part of computer programming.

Programmers use a variety of techniques and tools to design, implement, and optimize algorithms, including flowcharts, pseudocode, and formal mathematical notation. Overall, algorithms are a fundamental building block of computer programming, and are essential for solving complex problems and creating powerful software applications.

RECAP: An algorithm is a set of instructions or a sequence of steps used to solve a problem or perform a specific task in computer programming.

What's System Design?

System design in computer programming is the process of defining the architecture, components, and functionality of a software system, based on the requirements and constraints of the problem being solved. It involves analyzing the problem, identifying the key components and interactions, and designing a system that can meet the desired objectives while taking into account factors such as scalability, maintainability, and security.

System design is an important stage in the software development life cycle, and it lays the foundation for the development and implementation of a successful software system.

The process of system design typically involves the following steps:

1. **Requirements gathering**: The first step in system design is to gather and analyze the requirements of the system. This involves understanding the problem being solved, the users of the system, and the features and functionality required to meet their needs.

2. **Architectural design**: Once the requirements have been gathered, the next step is to define the high-level architecture of the system. This involves identifying the key components of the system and how they will interact with each other.

3. **Detailed design**: With the high-level architecture in place, the next step is to design the individual components of the system in more detail. This involves defining the data structures, algorithms, and interfaces that will be used to implement each component.

4. **Implementation**: After the detailed design is complete, the system can be implemented using a programming language or development platform. This involves writing code, integrating different components, and testing the system to ensure that it works as expected.

5. **Testing and validation**: Once the system has been implemented, it must be thoroughly tested and validated to ensure that it meets the

requirements and performs as expected. This involves a range of testing techniques, including unit testing, integration testing, and system testing.

6. **Maintenance**: Finally, once the system is deployed, it will require ongoing maintenance to keep it up-to-date and to fix any issues that arise over time.

RECAP: system design is a critical stage in the software development process that helps to ensure that the software system being built is effective, efficient, and meets the needs of its users.

Understanding APIs

An API (Application Programming Interface) is a set of protocols and tools for building software applications. It allows for communication between different software systems, providing a way for different applications to interact with each other and exchange data. API is important to modern computer programming because it enables developers to create new applications by reusing existing components and systems, reducing the time and effort required to build new applications from scratch, and facilitating the integration of different applications and services.

Think about it like this: an API can be compared to the recipe for making the pizza. Just like how a recipe outlines the ingredients and steps needed to make a delicious pizza, an API outlines the specifications and protocols for building software applications, allowing different components to communicate and work together effectively like the different ingredients in a pizza recipe.

You probably come in contact with APIs all the time. Ever order Uber or Lyft?

The app uses the API to communicate with the transportation company's database to retrieve information such as the location of drivers, fare prices, and availability. This allows the app to provide the user with real-time updates and information, such as the estimated time of arrival for the driver and the cost of the ride.

Furthermore, there are different types of APIs including Web APIs, Library APIs, Operating System APIs, and Database APIs. Each type serves a different purpose and has different specifications and functionalities. At a glance:

- **Web API** is a type of API that allows communication between a client and server over the internet, usually through HTTP (HyperText Transfer Protocol) requests. Web APIs are commonly used to build modern web applications and mobile apps, as they allow for the transfer of data and functionality between the front-end and back-end of the application.

- **Library API** is a set of rules, protocols, and routines that developers can use to access functionality or data within a software library. The API provides a way for developers to interact with the library without having to know how it is implemented, making it easier to build applications that use the library's functionality.

- **System API** is a type of API that provides access to the underlying operating system services, allowing software to interact with and control the functionality and performance of the system. It is used to interact with and control the operating system's functions, including system calls, file and memory management, and process management. System APIs are typically used by system-level software, such as drivers, operating systems, and other low-level system components.

- **Database API** is a set of programming interfaces that provide access to a database management system's functionality. It allows developers to interact with databases, perform operations such as creating, reading, updating, and deleting data, and manage the underlying data storage system in a standardized way.

Database APIs are used to build applications that interact with databases, and can be specific to a particular database management system or be designed to be database-agnostic.

RECAP: An API (Application Programming Interface) is a set of protocols, routines, and tools for building software and allowing communication between different systems, making it a crucial component in modern computer programming for seamless integration and data exchange between applications.

What's "Open Source" Mean?

Open Source refers to a collaborative approach to software development where the code behind a program is openly shared and freely available for others to contribute to and build upon. It's a way for the tech community to work together, sharing knowledge and expertise to create better software for everyone, and it's the driving force behind some of the most innovative and successful technology companies in the world.

The opposite of Open Source is "Closed Source" or Proprietary. This means that the source code of a software product is not publicly available and is only accessible to the company or individual who created it.

The Open Source Initiative (OSI) is a non-profit organization dedicated to promoting the use and distribution of open source software. It was founded in 1998 with the goal of promoting open source as a viable and sustainable development model for software. The OSI works to educate the public about open source, to advocate for its use in both the public and private sectors, and to provide a standard for open source licenses. It also provides a certification program for open source licenses, ensuring that they meet the organization's criteria for open source software.

RECAP: Open source refers to a type of software license that allows the source code to be freely available to the public, allowing anyone to inspect, modify, or distribute the code.

What's a Framework?

A framework is a pre-written set of code that provides a structure for building applications. It contains a collection of libraries, templates, and tools that simplify the development process and help ensure consistency in the design and functionality of the code. A framework provides developers with a starting point and a set of guidelines to follow, so they can focus on writing the unique, custom code that makes their application unique. The existence of frameworks is to make the development process more efficient, faster, and easier, by providing a solid foundation that can be built upon, reducing the amount of repetitive and redundant code that needs to be written.

RECAP: A framework is a pre-written codebase that offers a structured foundation for application development, streamlining the process and promoting code consistency, while enabling developers to focus on creating custom, unique functionality.

Deep Diving Into OPP Back-End Languages

To quickly review, there are plenty of back-end languages. They can be divided into Object-Oriented Programming and Functional Programming. In OOP, the focus is on objects and their interactions, while in FP, the focus is on functions and their inputs and outputs.

In OOP, objects are modeled as instances of classes and are used to represent real-world entities. These objects have their own data, also known as attributes or properties, and behaviors, also known as methods. OOP also emphasizes the use of inheritance and polymorphism, where objects can be derived from other objects, and objects of different types can be treated as objects of a common type.

Some common and widely used OOP languages include:

- **Java** is used for building enterprise-level applications and mobile applications for Android.

- **Python** is used for a wide range of applications from web development to machine learning and scientific computing.

- **Golang**, or GO, is a statically typed, concurrent programming language designed for fast and efficient network communication and system development

- **Scala** is a modern, statically-typed, multi-paradigm programming language that incorporates both object-oriented and functional programming features and runs on the Java Virtual Machine.

- **C** is a low-level programming language that provides developers with direct access to computer memory and other system resources.

- **C#** is used for building Windows desktop applications, video games, and web applications.

- **.NET**, or also referred to as .NET Core, is a free, open-source, cross-platform framework for building modern applications for web, desktop, mobile, gaming, IoT, AI, and machine learning.

- **C++** is a high-performance, statically typed, multi-paradigm programming language with a focus on system programming, object-oriented and functional programming.

- **Objective-C** is an object-oriented, high-level programming language used for developing applications for Apple platforms, including macOS and iOS.

- **Ruby** is designed for productivity and simplicity, often used for web development and scripting purposes.

- **PHP** is a server-side scripting language used for web development and can be embedded into HTML.

- **Swift** is a general-purpose programming language developed by Apple for iOS, iPadOS, macOS, watchOS, and tvOS development.

- **Kotlin** is a modern, statically typed, cross-platform programming language that is concise, expressive, and interoperable with Java, designed to improve the development of Android applications.

- **Node.js** is Javascript that runs as a server-side language! It allows developers to build scalable, high-performance network applications using non-blocking I/O model.

RECAP: These languages follow the OOP paradigm, which focuses on organizing code into objects that contain both data and behavior. This allows for better modularity and code reusability, making it easier to maintain and expand upon code over time.

Java

Java is a high-level, object-oriented programming language that is designed to be portable and secure, allowing developers to write code once and run it on any platform. It works by compiling source code into an intermediate form called bytecode[9], which is then

---

[9] Bytecode is a compiled code in a form that can be executed by a virtual machine, rather than directly by the computer's hardware. It is a machine-readable representation of code that has been compiled from a higher-level programming language such as Java, and its purpose is to provide a platform-agnostic way of executing code. The Java virtual machine (JVM) interprets the bytecode and executes it on the target platform. This allows Java applications to be written once and run on any device that has a JVM installed,

executed by the JVM. Java's popularity stems from its versatility, scalability, and robustness, making it an ideal choice for a wide range of applications, from enterprise systems to mobile applications.

Java has several editions and variations that cater to different needs and applications. Each edition of Java is designed to meet specific needs and requirements, and developers can choose the one that best suits their project.

Some of the most common ones include:

Java Standard Edition (Java SE)

This is the core Java platform for building standalone and web-based applications. It is the basic version of the Java platform and is used for developing desktop applications, mobile applications, and embedded systems. It provides a wide range of libraries, tools, and APIs for developing applications and has a large developer community. Java SE is typically used when you need a general-purpose, cross-platform programming language that can run on any device that has a Java Virtual Machine (JVM) installed. This makes it ideal for developing applications that need to run on multiple platforms, such as Windows[10], Mac[11], Linux[12], and Solaris[13], among others.

---

regardless of the underlying hardware or operating system.

When people say "Java," this is what they are talking about nearly all the time.

RECAP: Java SE (Java Standard Edition) is a widely-used platform for developing and running Java applications on desktops, servers, and other devices.

---

[10] Windows is an operating system developed by Microsoft that is widely used on personal computers and laptops. It provides a graphical user interface, support for various hardware and software applications, and features such as file management, network connectivity, and security.

[11] macOS (previously Mac OS X, and later OS X) is a series of graphical operating systems developed and marketed by Apple Inc. for their Macintosh line of personal computers. It is based on the Unix operating system and provides a user-friendly interface, desktop environment, and various features such as multiple desktops, window management, and application management. MacOS also includes built-in applications for tasks such as web browsing, email, media playback, and office productivity.

[12] Linux is a free and open-source operating system, based on Unix, that is widely used in servers, desktops, and mobile devices. Linux is known for its stability, security, and flexibility, and it is favored by many developers and system administrators for these reasons. It is highly customizable and has a large community of developers who create and maintain various applications, tools, and distributions (versions) of the operating system.

[13] Solaris is a Unix operating system originally developed by Sun Microsystems, which was later acquired by Oracle Corporation. It is widely used for enterprise-level applications, network services, and cloud computing due to its stability, scalability, and security features. Solaris is also known for its support of advanced technologies such as virtualization, storage, and network management.

Java Enterprise Edition (Java EE)

This edition is designed for developing large-scale, multi-tiered, scalable, and secure network applications. It is a more advanced version of Java that includes a number of additional features and technologies specifically geared towards enterprise applications, such as servlets, JSPs, EJBs, and JMS. If you are developing an enterprise-level application that requires these advanced features, then J2EE may be a better choice for you than regular Java. However, if you are building a smaller or more simple application, then regular Java may be a better fit. If you hear someone say, J2EE, or J-double-E, then they are most likely referring to Java Enterprise Edition.

RECAP: Java Enterprise Edition (Java EE) is a platform for developing and running scalable, distributed, and secure enterprise applications using Java.

Java Micro Edition (Java ME)

This edition is targeted towards resource-constrained devices such as mobile phones, smart cards, and set-top boxes. It affords developers platform independence; Java ME applications can run on a wide variety of devices, regardless of their underlying hardware and operating system. This makes it possible to develop applications that can reach a large audience without needing to be rewritten for each individual device.

Additionally, many embedded devices have limited resources, such as limited memory and processing power. Java ME is designed to work within these constraints, enabling developers to create applications that are optimized for these devices.

Subsequently, Java ME provides a rich set of APIs and tools for developing applications, making it relatively easy to create applications that are both functional and user-friendly.

Lastly, Java ME includes a number of security features that are designed to protect devices and applications from unauthorized access and use.

RECAP: Java Micro Edition (Java ME) is a platform for developing software applications for resource-constrained devices such as mobile phones and smart cards using Java.

JavaFX

This is a Java-based platform for building rich, cross-platform graphical user interfaces (GUIs)[14] for desktop

---

[14] What is a GUI?

GUI stands for Graphical User Interface. It is a type of user interface that allows users to interact with digital devices or software applications through graphical elements such as icons, buttons, windows, and menus, rather than through text commands.

GUIs are designed to be user-friendly and intuitive, enabling users to perform tasks and access information with minimal effort. They

and mobile applications. It provides a rich set of libraries and tools for designing, developing, and deploying applications across desktop, web, and mobile platforms.

JavaFX offers several key features that make it a popular choice for building modern, engaging user interfaces. These include support for 2D and 3D graphics, advanced animation and multimedia capabilities, and a rich set of UI controls and layouts. It also includes a powerful scene graph API that enables developers to create complex graphical scenes and user interfaces.

JavaFX is designed to be easy to use and highly customizable. It integrates seamlessly with other Java technologies, including the Java Development Kit (JDK), and is built on top of the Java Virtual Machine (JVM). This means that JavaFX applications can run on any platform that supports Java, including Windows, macOS, Linux, and mobile devices.

In addition to its graphical capabilities, JavaFX includes a number of other features that make it a useful

---

typically feature visual elements that represent real-world objects or concepts, such as folders, documents, and file icons.

GUIs are used in a wide range of devices and applications, including desktop and mobile operating systems, web browsers, video games, and multimedia applications. They provide a visually-rich and interactive way for users to interact with digital devices and software applications, making it easier and more enjoyable to perform tasks, access information, and communicate with others.

platform for building rich, immersive applications, including support for web services, databases, and other back-end technologies. Overall, JavaFX is a powerful and flexible framework for building modern, cross-platform applications with advanced graphics and multimedia capabilities.

RECAP: JavaFX is for building rich, cross-platform GUIs for desktop and mobile applications.

Android

The Android programming language is primarily Java, which is an object-oriented programming language. Java is used to write Android applications, as well as the Android operating system itself.

In addition to Java, the Android platform also supports the use of other programming languages, such as Kotlin and C++. Kotlin is a modern, statically-typed programming language that runs on the Java Virtual Machine (JVM) and is fully supported by the Android platform. C++ is a powerful, low-level programming language that is often used for developing performance-critical components of Android applications, such as game engines and image processing algorithms.

Java, Kotlin, and C++ are all popular choices for developing Android applications, and each has its own strengths and weaknesses. Java is a mature, widely-used language that has a large ecosystem of libraries and tools, making it a good choice for developing a wide range of Android applications. Kotlin is a modern, concise language that is interoperable with Java and can help developers write more concise and readable code. C++ is a powerful language that can provide high performance and low-level control, but can be more difficult to work with than Java or Kotlin.

RECAP: Android Java is a programming language used to write applications for the Android operating system, based on the Java programming language and optimized for mobile devices.

Summary of Java

Java is a popular and widely-used programming language that was first introduced by Sun Microsystems in the mid-1990s. It is an object-oriented programming (OOP) language that is designed to be platform-independent, meaning that Java programs can run on a wide range of devices and operating systems.

In object-oriented programming, everything is treated as an object, which can be thought of as a self-contained unit of code that contains both data and behavior. Objects are used to model real-world concepts and relationships between them, making it easier to write modular, reusable, and maintainable code.

Java is an important language in the context of OOP because it was one of the first programming languages to fully embrace the object-oriented paradigm. It provides a rich set of features that make it easy to write object-oriented code, including classes, objects, inheritance, polymorphism, and encapsulation.

Classes in Java are the building blocks of objects, providing a blueprint for creating objects of a particular type.

Objects created from these classes contain data in the form of fields and behavior in the form of methods.

Inheritance allows new classes to be based on existing classes, inheriting their fields and methods, and adding new functionality.

Polymorphism allows objects of different types to be treated as if they are the same type, making it possible to write code that works with a wide range of objects.

Encapsulation helps to keep the implementation details of an object hidden, providing a clear separation between the object's interface and implementation.

Additionally, there are also several reasons why you might choose to use Java for a particular project, such as:

- Platform independence: Java is designed to be platform-independent, meaning that Java programs can run on a wide range of devices and operating systems. This can make it a good choice for projects that need to be deployed on multiple platforms.

- Performance: Java is often praised for its performance, particularly when it comes to running large, enterprise-level applications.

- Large enterprise applications: Java is a popular choice for large enterprise applications, where scalability, security, and reliability are important considerations.

- Static typing: Java is a statically-typed language, which means that variables must be declared with a specific type. This can help catch errors earlier in the development process, and make code easier to understand and maintain.

RECAP: Java's support for object-oriented programming makes it a powerful and flexible language for developing complex applications. Its platform-independence, large ecosystem of libraries and tools, and strong community support also make it a popular choice for building a wide range of applications, from desktop and web applications to mobile apps and enterprise software.

Python

Python is a high-level programming language that is used for a wide range of applications, from scientific computing and data analysis to web development and automation. It is an OOP language, meaning that it is designed to allow developers to create software applications using a set of objects that interact with each other.

Python's support for OOP is an important aspect of its design. Like other OOP languages, Python allows developers to create classes, which are the blueprints for objects. These classes define the attributes and methods of an object, and can be used to create multiple instances of the object with different values for their attributes.

Python's syntax is known for being clean and easy to read, making it a popular language for beginners as well as experienced developers. Its support for OOP concepts such as inheritance, polymorphism, and encapsulation make it a powerful language for creating complex software applications that are easy to maintain and extend.

Inheritance allows a new class to be based on an existing class, inheriting its attributes and methods, and adding new functionality. This helps to reduce code duplication and makes it easier to create reusable code. Polymorphism allows objects of different classes to be treated as if they are the same type, making it possible to write more flexible and modular code. Encapsulation allows the internal details of an object to be hidden from the outside world, making it easier to maintain and update the code.

There are several reasons why you might choose to use Python for a particular project:

- **Ease of use**: Python has a reputation for being easy to learn and use, with a simple and clean syntax that is often praised for its readability. This can make it a good choice for beginners or for projects where development time is a key consideration.

- **Large ecosystem of libraries**: Python has a large and active community of developers, which has created a vast ecosystem of libraries and tools for a wide range of applications. This can make it easier to find and use the right tools for a particular project.

- **Data analysis and scientific computing**: Python is particularly well-suited to data analysis and scientific computing, with powerful libraries such as NumPy, Pandas, and SciPy that make it easy to work with large datasets and perform complex calculations.

- **Web development**: Python has a number of popular frameworks, such as Django and Flask, that make it easy to build web applications quickly and efficiently.

- **Rapid prototyping**: Python's ease of use and large ecosystem of libraries make it a good choice for rapid prototyping, where the goal is to quickly create a working prototype that can be refined and improved over time.

RECAP: Python is a popular, high-level programming language that is widely used for web development, scientific computing, and data analysis.

NumPy

NumPy (short for "Numerical Python") is a popular Python library that is used for scientific computing and data analysis. It provides support for large, multi-dimensional arrays and matrices, as well as a wide range of mathematical and statistical operations that can be performed on these arrays.

NumPy is a fundamental library in the Python scientific computing ecosystem, and it is used by a wide range of other libraries and tools, such as Pandas, Matplotlib, and SciPy. It provides a powerful set of features for performing mathematical and scientific operations, such as linear algebra, Fourier transforms, and random number generation.

NumPy's array object is a key feature that sets it apart from other numerical libraries in Python. The array object is an efficient container for large amounts of numerical data, and it provides a wide range of indexing and slicing operations that make it easy to work with multi-dimensional data. NumPy also includes a large set of functions for performing basic operations on arrays, such as element-wise addition, subtraction, multiplication, and division.

RECAP: NumPy is an essential library for anyone working with scientific computing or data analysis in Python. Its support for large, multi-dimensional arrays, and its extensive set of mathematical and statistical functions make it a powerful tool for analyzing and manipulating data.

Pandas

Pandas is a popular open-source data analysis and manipulation library for the Python programming language, designed to make working with "relational" or "labeled" data both easy and intuitive.

It provides a powerful and flexible set of data structures and functions that allow for the manipulation, cleaning, and analysis of structured data, such as data in CSV or Excel files, SQL[15] databases, or even scraped from the web.

Pandas provides features such as data alignment, merging, filtering, and reshaping that are commonly used in data analysis and makes it possible to easily transform and visualize large datasets.

Pandas is a valuable tool for anyone working with data in Python and has become a fundamental library in the data science ecosystem.

RECAP: Pandas is a popular Python library used for data manipulation and analysis, providing data structures and

---

[15] SQL (Structured Query Language) is a programming language that is used to manage and manipulate relational databases. It is used to create, read, update, and delete data in databases, as well as to define the structure and relationships of the data in the database. SQL is a standard language that is widely used in the development of software applications and for data analysis and reporting.

functions for working with structured data, such as tables, time series, and relational databases.

SciPy

SciPy is a popular open-source library for scientific computing in Python, providing a wide range of functions for optimization, signal processing, linear algebra, statistics, and more. It is built on top of NumPy and integrates with other scientific libraries in the Python ecosystem to provide a powerful set of tools for scientific computing and data analysis.

It is built on top of NumPy and is often used in conjunction with other scientific computing libraries, such as Matplotlib and Pandas.

RECAP: SciPy is a popular Python library for scientific and technical computing that provides a wide range of algorithms and functions.

Django

Django is a popular web framework for Python that is designed to make it easy to build web applications quickly and efficiently. It provides a high-level and robust set of tools and libraries that make it easy to create and manage web applications, including features such as URL routing, database modeling, templating, and user authentication.

At a high level, Django works by following the Model-View-Controller (MVC) architectural pattern, with some variations. In Django, this pattern is often referred to as Model-View-Template (MVT), where the Model represents the data and database structure, the View handles the presentation and interaction with the user, and the Template provides the HTML structure for the web pages.

Here's a brief overview of the key components of a Django web application and how they work together:

- **Models**: Django provides an Object-Relational Mapping (ORM) layer that allows you to define your database schema in Python code. This makes it easy to work with databases and data structures, without having to write SQL code directly.

- **Views**: In Django, a view is a Python function that takes an HTTP request and returns an HTTP response. Views are responsible for handling user requests and interacting with the database and other components of the application to generate an appropriate response.

- **Templates**: Templates provide the HTML structure and layout for the web pages that are generated by the application. Django provides a templating language that makes it easy to create dynamic HTML pages that can be customized based on user input and database queries.

- **URL routing**: URL routing in Django maps URLs to the appropriate view function, allowing users to navigate through the application and access different parts of the site.

Overall, Django provides a powerful set of tools and libraries for creating web applications quickly and efficiently, while following best practices for software development and web design. Its modular architecture and robust features make it a popular choice for a wide range of web development projects.

RECAP: Django is a high-level Python web framework that simplifies the process of building web applications by providing a robust set of tools and libraries for common tasks.

Flask

Flask is a lightweight and popular web framework for Python that is used for developing web applications quickly and easily. It provides a simple and flexible set of tools and libraries that make it easy to build web applications, and is often used for small to medium-sized projects where simplicity and flexibility are key.

At a high level, Flask works by providing a set of core features, such as URL routing, templating, and user authentication, which can be easily extended and customized using a wide range of third-party libraries and plugins.

Here's a brief overview of the key components of a Flask web application and how they work together:

- **Routes**: In Flask, routes are defined using Python decorators that map URL patterns to view functions. When a user requests a URL that matches a route, Flask calls the associated view function to generate a response.

- **Views**: Views in Flask are Python functions that take an HTTP request and return an HTTP response. Views are responsible for handling user requests, interacting with the database and other components of the application, and generating a response.

- **Templates**: Templates in Flask provide the HTML structure and layout for the web pages that are generated by the application. Flask uses the Jinja2 templating engine to render dynamic HTML pages that can be customized based on user input and database queries.

- **Extensions**: Flask provides a simple and flexible extension system that allows developers to add additional features and functionality to their web applications, such as user authentication, database integration, and caching.

Overall, Flask is a lightweight and flexible web framework that is well-suited for small to medium-sized web applications. Its simplicity and ease of use make it a popular choice for developers who want to build web applications quickly and easily.

RECAP: Flask is a lightweight and flexible web framework for Python that provides a simple and customizable set of tools and libraries for building web applications quickly and easily.

Matplotlib

Matplotlib is a popular plotting library for Python that provides a wide range of tools and functions for creating high-quality visualizations of data. It can be used to create a wide range of plots and charts, including line plots, scatter plots, bar plots, histograms, and more.

Matplotlib is used to create visual representations of data, which can help users to better understand and analyze complex datasets. For example, a data analyst might use Matplotlib to create a line plot showing how the price of a particular stock has changed over time, or a scatter plot showing the relationship between two variables in a dataset.

Matplotlib provides a wide range of customization options, including the ability to change the color, style, and size of plots, as well as to add titles, labels, and annotations. It also provides support for advanced features such as subplots, grids, and 3D plots.

To use Matplotlib, a developer typically imports the library and calls functions to create and customize plots. Matplotlib can be used in conjunction with other Python libraries, such as NumPy, Pandas, and SciPy, to provide a complete toolkit for scientific computing and data analysis.

RECAP: Matplotlib is a powerful and flexible library that is widely used in scientific computing, data analysis, and machine learning.

TensorFlow

Tensorflow bundles together Machine Learning[16] and Deep Learning models[17] and algorithms. It uses Python

---

[16] Machine learning is a subset of artificial intelligence (AI) that involves developing algorithms and models that enable computers to learn and make predictions or decisions based on data, without being explicitly programmed. In other words, machine learning involves training computers to recognize patterns in data, and use those patterns to make predictions or decisions about new data.

There are several types of machine learning, including supervised learning, unsupervised learning, and reinforcement learning. In supervised learning, the computer is trained on labeled data, where the desired output is already known, to predict the output of new

as a convenient front-end and runs it efficiently in optimized C++. Tensorflow allows developers to create a graph of computations to perform. Created by Google, it is used for building and training machine learning models. It provides a wide range of tools and

data. In unsupervised learning, the computer is trained on unlabeled data to identify patterns and relationships in the data. Reinforcement learning involves training the computer through trial-and-error, where it receives feedback based on its actions and uses that feedback to improve its performance.

[17] A deep learning model is a type of machine learning model that is based on deep neural networks, which are artificial neural networks that are composed of multiple layers of interconnected nodes. These models are called "deep" because they have many layers of processing units, which allows them to learn and recognize complex patterns in data.

Deep learning models are particularly well-suited for tasks such as image and speech recognition, natural language processing, and other applications that involve analyzing large and complex datasets. These models can be trained using large amounts of labeled data, which allows them to identify and learn complex patterns in the data. Once the model has been trained, it can be used to make predictions or decisions about new data, based on the patterns it has learned.

There are several types of deep learning models, including convolutional neural networks (CNNs), recurrent neural networks (RNNs), and deep belief networks (DBNs). Each type of model is suited to different types of tasks and data, and may have different architectures and training methods.

Overall, deep learning models are a powerful tool for machine learning, and have been used to achieve state-of-the-art performance on a wide range of tasks, including image recognition, speech recognition, natural language processing, and more.

functions for building and deploying machine learning applications, including support for deep learning, neural networks, and other advanced machine learning techniques.

At a high level, TensorFlow works by creating and manipulating tensors, which are multi-dimensional arrays that can represent data and calculations in a flexible and efficient way. TensorFlow allows developers to define and train machine learning models using a high-level API, while also providing low-level primitives for more advanced customization.

Here are some of the key features and use cases of TensorFlow:

- **Deep learning**: TensorFlow provides support for building and training deep neural networks, which can be used for tasks such as image and speech recognition, natural language processing, and more.

- **Training and deployment**: TensorFlow includes tools for training and deploying machine learning models, including support for distributed training and serving models in production.

- **Visualization and debugging**: TensorFlow provides tools for visualizing and debugging machine learning models, including support for tensorboard, a web-based visualization tool that can be used to monitor the training process and performance of models.

- **Integration**: TensorFlow can be integrated with other popular machine learning libraries and frameworks, including Keras, PyTorch, and scikit-learn, making it easy to incorporate TensorFlow into existing machine learning workflows.

Overall, TensorFlow is a powerful and flexible machine learning framework that is widely used in industry and academia for a wide range of applications, from image and speech recognition to natural language processing and more.

RECAP: TensorFlow provides a rich set of tools and functions for building and training machine learning models, while also being highly customizable and flexible.

Keras

Keras is an open-source deep learning framework that is designed to make it easy to build and train neural networks. It is written in Python, and is tightly integrated with other popular Python libraries for data analysis and scientific computing, such as NumPy, Pandas, and SciPy.

Keras provides a simple and intuitive interface for building and training deep learning models, and supports a wide range of neural network architectures, including convolutional neural networks (CNNs), recurrent neural networks (RNNs), and more. It also includes a number of built-in tools and utilities for data preprocessing, model evaluation, and visualization.

Keras is often used in combination with other Python libraries for deep learning, such as TensorFlow and PyTorch, as it provides a higher-level, more user-friendly interface for building and training neural networks. Overall, Keras is a powerful and flexible tool for deep learning, and is widely used by data scientists, researchers, and developers in a variety of fields.

RECAP: Keras is a popular, open-source deep learning framework written in Python that provides a simple and intuitive interface for building and training neural networks.

PyTorch

PyTorch is an open-source machine learning library that is used for developing and training deep learning models. It is written in Python and is designed to provide a flexible and efficient platform for implementing neural networks, with a strong emphasis on ease-of-use and rapid prototyping.

PyTorch is tightly integrated with Python, and provides a range of high-level abstractions for building and training deep learning models, as well as low-level primitives for customizing the behavior of the network at a granular level. It is often used in research and academia, as well as in industry, for applications such as natural language processing, computer vision, and robotics.

PyTorch is known for its dynamic computation graph, which allows for easy experimentation and modification of the network during the development process. It also provides a range of tools and utilities for data preprocessing, model evaluation, and visualization.

RECAP: PyTorch is a powerful and flexible machine learning library that is widely used in the Python ecosystem for deep learning applications.

Summary of Python

Overall, Python's support for OOP makes it a powerful language for creating complex and flexible software applications. Its clean syntax and large ecosystem of libraries and tools also make it a popular choice for a wide range of applications, from scientific computing and data analysis to web development and automation.

From web development and data analysis to machine learning and artificial intelligence, here are some of the main reasons why you might choose to use Python:

- **Ease of use**: Python has a simple and easy-to-learn syntax, with a focus on readability and simplicity. This makes it an ideal language for beginners, and also makes it easy to write and maintain code for more experienced developers.

- **Versatility**: Python is a general-purpose programming language that can be used for a wide range of tasks, including web development, data analysis, machine learning, artificial intelligence, and more. This makes it a popular choice for developers who need a language that can be used in a variety of contexts.

- **Rich ecosystem**: Python has a large and active community of developers, which has created a rich ecosystem of tools, libraries, and frameworks for a wide range of tasks. This makes it easy to find and use third-party tools and libraries, and can help to speed up development time.

- **Data analysis**: Python is widely used for data analysis and scientific computing, thanks to libraries such as NumPy, Pandas, and Matplotlib, which provide powerful tools for working with data.

- **Machine learning**: Python is a popular language for machine learning and artificial intelligence, with libraries such as TensorFlow, Keras, and PyTorch that provide powerful tools for building and training machine learning models.

RECAP: Python is a high-level programming language that is used for a wide range of applications, from web development to scientific computing and data analysis.

Perl

Perl is a general-purpose programming language that is widely used for tasks such as system administration, web development, and network programming.

Perl was created by Larry Wall in 1987 and has since become a popular language for developing scripts and applications that require text processing, regular expressions, and other tasks that are well-suited to Perl's strengths.

Perl is known for its flexibility, expressiveness, and text processing capabilities, and it has a large community of developers who have contributed to the language's development over the years. Perl code is often concise and expressive, and the language includes a rich set of built-in functions and modules that make it easy to perform many common programming tasks.

An engineer might choose to use Perl for several reasons:

- **Text Processing**: Perl is particularly well-suited for tasks that involve text processing and regular expressions, making it a popular choice for tasks such as log file analysis, data processing, and system administration.

- **Scripting**: Perl is a scripting language that can be used to automate repetitive tasks, which can save time and reduce the risk of errors.

- **Cross-Platform Support**: Perl is a cross-platform language, meaning that Perl scripts can be run on a variety of operating systems, including Windows, macOS, and Unix/Linux.

Perl is also widely used in web development, particularly in the development of CGI scripts[18], and it is often used

---

[18] CGI stands for Common Gateway Interface, which is a standard protocol for allowing web servers to communicate with external

in conjunction with other web development technologies such as HTML, CSS, and JavaScript.

RECAP: Perl is a versatile and popular programming language that is well-suited for tasks such as system administration, web development, and network programming, and it is known for its flexibility, expressiveness, and text processing capabilities.

applications, such as scripts or programs, to generate dynamic web pages.

A CGI script is a program or script that is executed by the web server in response to a user's request for a dynamic web page. When a user requests a page that requires dynamic content, the web server runs the CGI script and passes any required input data to the script. The script then generates the required output, which is sent back to the web server and ultimately displayed to the user in their web browser.

CGI scripts can be written in a variety of programming languages, such as Perl, Python, Ruby, and others. They are often used for tasks such as processing form data, generating dynamic content, and performing other server-side operations that are required to deliver dynamic web pages.

However, due to security concerns and the development of more modern web technologies, the use of CGI scripts has declined in recent years, with many developers now preferring to use other server-side technologies, such as PHP, Node.js, or serverless functions.

Golang (GO)

Go, also known as Golang, is an open-source programming language created by Google that is designed for building efficient, scalable, and reliable software. It is a statically typed language that is designed to be easy to learn and use, and it includes features such as garbage collection, concurrency, and a standard library that makes it easy to build networked and web-based applications.

At a high level, Go works by compiling code into a native executable, which can be run on a wide range of operating systems and platforms, without the need for an interpreter or virtual machine. The language includes a set of powerful tools and libraries for building networked and web-based applications, making it well-suited for building large-scale and high-performance software systems.

There are several reasons why you might choose to use Go for a particular project. Here are a few of the main factors to consider:

- **Performance**: Go is known for its excellent performance, thanks to its efficient memory management, fast garbage collection, and built-in concurrency features. This makes it a good choice for applications that require high throughput and low latency, such as network servers, databases, and other high-performance applications.

- **Simplicity**: Go is designed to be simple and easy to learn, with a clean syntax and a small, focused set of language features. This can make it easier to write and maintain code, especially for smaller projects or for teams with less experience in software development.

- **Concurrency**: Go has built-in support for concurrency, which makes it easy to write programs that can run multiple tasks in parallel. This can be especially useful for applications that need to handle a large number of concurrent connections or requests, such as web servers or streaming services.

- **Scalability**: Go is designed to be highly scalable, with features like goroutines and channels that make it easy to write programs that can run efficiently on multiple processors or in distributed environments.

RECAP: Go, or Golang, is an open-source programming language created by Google that is designed for building efficient, scalable, and reliable software, with features such as garbage collection, concurrency, and a standard library that makes it easy to build networked and web-based applications.

Scala

Scala is a general-purpose programming language that is designed to be highly scalable and efficient. It was first released in 2003 and is a modern programming language that combines the features of object-oriented programming and functional programming.

But Scala... oh you tricky language you... Scala is a multi-paradigm programming language that supports both functional programming (FP) and object-oriented programming (OOP) paradigms.

What?

Yep... it's OOP and FP!

It was designed to combine the best features of both paradigms and provide developers with a flexible and powerful language for building scalable, high-performance applications. In Scala, developers can write code in a purely functional style or in an object-oriented style, or combine the two paradigms as needed, depending on the requirements of the application. This makes Scala a versatile language that can be used for a wide range of applications, from data processing to web development to machine learning.

Additionally, it is particularly well-suited to developing applications that require high concurrency and parallelism, as it has a powerful type system and supports immutable data structures, which make it easier to write code that is safe and reliable.

One of the key benefits of Scala is its ability to integrate with other programming languages and platforms, including Java and the JVM. This makes it a popular choice for developers who need to build applications that can run on different platforms or that require integration with existing codebases.

There are several reasons why you might choose to code an application using Scala:

- **Scalability**: Scala is designed to be highly scalable, which means it can handle large and complex applications more easily than some other programming languages. It is particularly well-suited to developing applications that require high concurrency and parallelism.

- **Performance**: Scala is generally faster than some other programming languages, particularly for applications that require heavy computation or data processing.

- **Type system**: Scala has a powerful and flexible type system, which can help ensure that your code is correct and free of errors.

- **Functional programming**: Scala is a functional programming language, which means it can be easier to write code that is more declarative and easier to reason about than traditional imperative programming.

- **Interoperability**: Scala can be easily integrated with other programming languages and platforms, particularly Java and the JVM, which makes it a popular choice for developing applications that need to run on multiple platforms.

Overall, Scala is a powerful and versatile programming language that is particularly well-suited to developing large and complex applications that require high performance, scalability, and concurrency.

RECAP: Scala is a general-purpose programming language that is designed to be highly scalable, efficient, and interoperable with other programming languages and platforms.

C

C is a general-purpose programming language that was developed in the early 1970s by Dennis Ritchie at Bell Labs. It is a low-level programming language that provides developers with direct access to computer memory and other system resources.

C is a popular choice for developing operating systems, device drivers, and other system-level software, due to its ability to interface directly with computer hardware. It is also used in a variety of other applications, including web development, databases, and scientific computing.

C is a compiled language, which means that source code is translated into machine code that can be executed directly by the computer. It is known for its efficiency and speed, which makes it a popular choice for applications that require high performance.

An engineer might choose to use C for their programming project for several reasons:

- **Low-level access to computer hardware**: C provides direct access to computer memory and other system resources, which is important for developing system-level software and applications that require precise control over computer hardware.

- **High performance**: C is known for its efficiency and speed, making it a popular choice for applications that require high performance.

- **Portability**: C code can be compiled and executed on a wide range of platforms, including Windows, Linux, and macOS, which makes it a versatile choice for cross-platform development.

- **Strong and mature ecosystem**: C has been around for several decades and has a strong and mature ecosystem, with a large and active community of developers, extensive documentation, and many libraries and tools available to help developers get started with the language.

- **Industry use**: C is widely used in a variety of industries, particularly in the development of operating systems, device drivers, and other system-level software.

Overall, C is a powerful and versatile programming language that offers low-level access to computer hardware and is well-suited to building system-level software and other applications that require high performance.

RECAP: C is a low-level, general-purpose programming language that provides direct access to computer memory and is well-suited for developing system-level software and applications that require high performance.

C#

C# (pronounced "C-sharp") is a modern, object-oriented programming language that was developed by Microsoft as part of its .NET framework.

C# is used for a variety of applications, including web development, desktop applications, mobile applications, and game development. It is particularly well-suited to developing Windows applications, as it has strong integration with the Windows operating system and can easily interact with other Microsoft technologies, such as the .NET framework, SQL Server, and Visual Studio.

Some of the key features of C# include its strong type system, its support for object-oriented programming, and its ability to handle complex applications with ease. C# also has a large and active community of developers, which means there are many resources and tools available to help you learn and develop with the language. Reasons why an engineer might choose to code an application in C# include:

- **Strong type system**: C# has a strong and flexible type system, which makes it easier to write code that is reliable and free of errors.

- **Object-oriented programming**: C# is an object-oriented programming language, which means it is well-suited to developing applications that require a high degree of abstraction and modularity.

- **Windows integration**: C# has strong integration with Windows and other Microsoft technologies, which makes it a popular choice for developing Windows applications.

- **Cross-platform development**: C# is also used for cross-platform development through .NET Core, which allows developers to build and run C# applications on multiple platforms, including Windows, Linux, and macOS.

- **Large and active community**: C# has a large and active community of developers, which means there are many resources and tools available to help you learn and develop with the language.

Overall, C# is a powerful and versatile programming language that is widely used in a variety of applications and industries.

RECAP: C# is a modern, object-oriented programming language developed by Microsoft for a wide range of applications, with strong type systems, object-oriented programming support, and Windows integration.

.NET

Okay, let's talk about .NET, or "dot net" as it's pronounced. Developed by Microsoft and released under the MIT License, .NET is a free and open-source software framework that's designed to work across a range of operating systems, including Windows, Linux, and macOS. It's the successor to the .NET Framework, and is primarily developed by Microsoft employees via the .NET Foundation.

There are several reasons why an engineer might choose to code an application in .NET:

- **Cross-platform development**: .NET Core is a cross-platform framework, which means that developers can use it to create applications that run on multiple platforms, including Windows, Linux, and macOS.

- **Strong type system**: .NET has a strong and flexible type system, which makes it easier to write code that is reliable and free of errors.

- **Language support**: .NET supports multiple programming languages, including C#, F#, and Visual Basic, which gives developers the flexibility to choose the language that best suits their needs.

- **Integration with other Microsoft technologies**: .NET has strong integration with other Microsoft technologies, such as SQL Server[19] and Azure[20], which makes it a popular choice for developing Windows applications.

---

[19] SQL Server is a relational database management system (RDBMS) developed by Microsoft. It is used for managing and storing data in a structured format and is widely used in enterprise applications, web applications, and other data-intensive applications.

SQL Server supports the SQL (Structured Query Language) standard and provides features such as transaction processing, concurrency control, data warehousing, and business intelligence. It also offers features for security, backup and recovery, and high availability.

- **Large and active community**: .NET has a large and active community of developers, which means there are many resources and tools available to help you learn and develop with the framework.

- **Performance**: .NET is known for its performance, particularly for applications that require heavy computation or data processing.

SQL Server comes in different editions, including Enterprise, Standard, and Developer, with each edition providing a different set of features and capabilities. It can be deployed on-premises or in the cloud, with Microsoft Azure offering various deployment options for SQL Server.

[20] Azure is a cloud computing platform developed by Microsoft that provides a wide range of cloud-based services and solutions for businesses and individuals. It enables developers to build, deploy, and manage applications and services through a global network of Microsoft-managed data centers.

Azure offers a variety of services, including infrastructure as a service (IaaS), platform as a service (PaaS), and software as a service (SaaS). It includes services for virtual machines, containers, storage, databases, analytics, artificial intelligence, internet of things, and many more.

One of the key benefits of Azure is its scalability and flexibility. It allows businesses to rapidly provision and scale resources up or down as needed, and pay only for what they use. It also offers strong security and compliance features, which are critical for many businesses.

Overall, Azure is a comprehensive and versatile cloud platform that enables businesses to build and deploy a wide range of cloud-based solutions

Overall, .NET is a powerful and versatile framework that is widely used in a variety of applications and industries.

RECAP: .NET is a free and open-source, cross-platform framework for building modern applications, designed to work on Windows, Linux, and macOS.

C++

C++ is a high-level, general-purpose programming language that is widely used in software development, particularly for applications that require high performance and low-level access to computer hardware.

C++ is an object-oriented programming language that allows developers to write efficient, high-performance code by giving them direct control over computer memory and other system resources. It can be used to build a wide range of applications, including operating systems, device drivers, video games, and financial trading systems.

Some of the key features of C++ include its ability to support both high-level and low-level programming, its support for multiple programming paradigms, including procedural, object-oriented, and generic programming, and its ability to be compiled and executed on a wide range of platforms, including Windows, Linux, and macOS.

At a glance, an engineer might choose to use C++ for a programming project for several reasons:

- **High performance**: C++ is known for its performance, making it a popular choice for applications that require fast processing and low-level access to computer hardware.

- **Low-level control**: C++ gives developers direct control over computer memory and other system resources, which can be useful for building applications that require precise control over these resources.

- **Multi-paradigm support**: C++ supports multiple programming paradigms, including procedural, object-oriented, and generic programming, which gives developers the flexibility to choose the approach that best suits their project.

- **Strong and mature ecosystem**: C++ has been around for several decades and has a strong and mature ecosystem, with a large and active community of developers, extensive documentation, and many libraries and tools available to help developers get started with the language.

- **Platform support**: C++ can be compiled and executed on a wide range of platforms, including Windows, Linux, and macOS, which makes it a versatile choice for cross-platform development.

Overall, C++ is a powerful and versatile programming language that is well-suited to building high-performance, system-level applications, and is widely used in industries such as finance, gaming, and aerospace.

RECAP: C++ is a high-performance, statically typed, multi-paradigm programming language with a focus on system programming, object-oriented and functional programming.

Objective-C

Objective-C is an object-oriented programming language that was developed in the 1980s and is commonly used for developing applications for Apple's macOS and iOS operating systems.

Objective-C is a superset of the C programming language, meaning that it adds additional features and syntax for object-oriented programming, such as classes, objects, and methods. It is also compatible with C libraries and can be compiled alongside C code.

Objective-C was the primary programming language used for developing iOS applications prior to the release of Swift, another programming language developed by Apple specifically for app development on their platforms. However, Objective-C is still widely used for maintaining and updating legacy codebases and for developing macOS applications.

Additionally, Objective-C is a superset of the C programming language, meaning that it can be compiled alongside C code and is compatible with C libraries. While doing so, Objective-C supports automatic garbage collection, which means that developers do not have to manually manage memory allocation and deallocation.

Overall, Objective-C is a popular and powerful programming language for developing applications for Apple's platforms, particularly for those interested in developing software for iOS and macOS. Its support for object-oriented programming, compatibility with C libraries, automatic garbage collection, and strong ecosystem make it a popular choice for developers.

RECAP: Objective-C is a popular and powerful programming language for developing applications for Apple's platforms, particularly for maintaining and updating existing codebases.

Ruby

Ruby is a high-level, dynamic, object-oriented programming language that was designed in the mid-1990s by Yukihiro "Matz" Matsumoto. It is known for its focus on simplicity and productivity, as well as its elegant syntax and powerful features, such as dynamic typing, garbage collection, and built-in support for object-oriented programming concepts such as classes, objects, and inheritance.

Ruby is widely used for developing web applications, particularly with the Ruby on Rails web application framework. It is also used for building command-line utilities, desktop applications, and games. Its popularity has led to the development of many libraries and tools to support development in Ruby, making it a versatile and powerful language for a variety of programming tasks.

An engineer might choose to use Ruby for their programming project for several reasons:

- **Web development**: Ruby is commonly used for developing web applications, particularly with the Ruby on Rails web application framework, making it a popular choice for engineers interested in web development.

- **Rapid prototyping**: Ruby is known for its focus on simplicity and productivity, which makes it a good choice for rapidly prototyping applications and testing out new ideas.

- **Object-oriented programming**: Ruby is an object-oriented programming language that supports features such as classes, objects, and inheritance, which can help developers write cleaner and more maintainable code.

- **Metaprogramming**: Ruby supports metaprogramming, which allows developers to write code that modifies or generates other code at runtime, making it a powerful tool for creating flexible and dynamic applications.

Important to note: Ruby and Ruby on Rails are not the same thing. Nope. Sorry, not sorry. Hate to break it to you.

Ruby on Rails (often abbreviated as "Rails") was created by David Heinemeier Hansson (also known as DHH) in 2004.

Rails provides a set of conventions, libraries, and tools that help developers build web applications more quickly and easily. Rails is known for its "convention over configuration" philosophy, which means that the framework makes assumptions about how developers want to structure their applications, reducing the amount of boilerplate code that needs to be written.

Ruby is a programming language, while Rails is a web application framework that is written in Ruby.

In other words, Ruby is the programming language that provides the syntax and features that allow developers to write code, while Ruby on Rails is a set of libraries, tools, and conventions that help developers build web applications more quickly and easily using the Ruby language.

Ruby on Rails provides a set of conventions and best practices that help developers write maintainable and scalable web applications, such as standardized directory structures, helper functions, and object-relational mapping (ORM) tools[21]. It also provides features such

---

[21] Object-relational mapping (ORM) tools are software libraries that allow developers to map objects in object-oriented programming languages to relational databases.

In other words, when using an ORM tool, developers can write code in an object-oriented programming language, such as Ruby, Python, or Java, and the ORM tool will automatically generate the necessary SQL code to create, read, update, and delete data in a relational database. This allows developers to work with databases

as a built-in web server, database migration tools, and an active community that creates many third-party libraries and plugins that extend the functionality of the framework.

RECAP: Ruby is a high-level, interpreted programming language that prioritizes simplicity and productivity. With a syntax that is natural to read and easy to write, it's known for its use in web development and its strong support for object-oriented programming principles.

---

using the same programming concepts and structures that they use to write their application code, making it easier to develop and maintain complex database-driven applications.

ORM tools often provide features such as schema management, transaction handling, and query optimization, which can help developers write cleaner and more efficient database code. Popular ORM tools include ActiveRecord for Ruby on Rails, SQLAlchemy for Python, and Hibernate for Java.

Overall, ORM tools provide a convenient and powerful way to work with relational databases in object-oriented programming languages, making it easier for developers to write database-driven applications.

PHP

PHP is a general-purpose programming language that is widely used for web development, server-side scripting, and command-line scripting. It was originally developed by Rasmus Lerdorf in 1994, and has since evolved into a mature and widely-used language.

Over the years, PHP has undergone a number of significant changes and improvements. Some of the key milestones in PHP's evolution include:

- **PHP 3**: The first widely-used version of PHP, which was released in 1998 and introduced features such as support for external libraries and more advanced server-side scripting capabilities.

- **PHP 4**: Released in 2000, this version of PHP introduced many new features and improvements, including support for object-oriented programming, better performance, and improved error handling.

- **PHP 5**: Released in 2004, this version of PHP was a major upgrade that introduced a number of important new features, including support for more advanced object-oriented programming, improved performance, and better support for XML and web services.

- **PHP 7**: Released in 2015, this version of PHP introduced significant improvements in performance, memory usage, and error handling, making it a faster and more reliable language for web development.

Today, PHP is widely used in web development, particularly for building dynamic web applications and content management systems. It is known for its ease of use, flexibility, and wide support in hosting environments and server software.

RECAP: PHP has evolved over the years from a simple server-side scripting language to a mature and widely-used language for web development, with significant improvements in performance, object-oriented programming, and other areas.

Swift

Swift is a general-purpose programming language developed by Apple for iOS, iPadOS, macOS, watchOS, and tvOS development. But... wait there's more!

Swift is an open-source language, which means that it is available for anyone to use and contribute to. It is known for its ease of use and readability, which makes it a popular choice for both novice and experienced programmers.

Some of the key features of Swift include:

- Type safety and type inference: Swift is designed to be a safe language, which means that it helps prevent common programming errors, such as type mismatches. It also has a powerful type inference system, which can automatically determine the type of a variable based on its context.

- Optionals: Swift introduces the concept of optionals, which are a way to represent values that may or may not be present. This can help prevent errors and improve code safety.

- Generics: Swift supports generics, which are a way to write code that can work with different types of data.

- Closures: Swift includes support for closures, which are a way to write functions that can be passed around as values.

- Automatic memory management: Swift uses automatic memory management, which means that it handles memory allocation and deallocation automatically, helping to prevent common programming errors such as memory leaks[22].

RECAP: Swift is a modern, fast, and safe programming language that is well-suited for developing software for Apple's platforms. Its features, such as type safety, optionals, generics, closures, and automatic memory management, make it a popular choice for many developers.

---

[22] What is a memory leak?

Chances are you've experienced it before. A memory leak is a type of software bug that occurs when a program fails to release memory that it no longer needs, causing the program to consume more and more memory over time. This can eventually lead to the program running out of memory and crashing or slowing down significantly.

Memory leaks occur when a program dynamically allocates memory during runtime, but does not properly release that memory when it is no longer needed. This can happen, for example, when a program fails to free memory after a variable goes out of scope, or when a program creates objects that are not properly deallocated.

Memory leaks can be a serious problem in long-running programs, particularly those that run on resource-constrained systems such as mobile devices or embedded systems. To avoid memory leaks, developers need to be careful to properly manage memory allocation and deallocation, and to use tools such as memory profilers to detect and correct leaks that do occur.

Kotlin

Kotlin is a modern, statically typed, cross-platform programming language that is concise, expressive, and interoperable with Java, Designed to improve the development of Android applications, it's a statically typed programming language that was developed by JetBrains, a software development company, in 2011. It runs on the Java Virtual Machine (JVM) and can also be compiled to JavaScript or native code for specific platforms.

Kotlin was designed to be a modern language that is more concise, expressive, and safe than Java, while also being fully interoperable with Java. It is known for its readability and ease of use, making it a popular choice for Android app development.

Some of the key features of Kotlin include:

- **Null safety**: Kotlin includes null safety features that help prevent null pointer exceptions, which are a common cause of crashes in Java.

- **Interoperability with Java**: Kotlin is fully interoperable with Java, which means that developers can easily use Kotlin alongside existing Java code and libraries.

- **Extension functions**: Kotlin supports extension functions, which allow developers to add new functionality to existing classes without having to subclass them.

- **Higher-order functions**: Kotlin supports higher-order functions, which are functions that can take other functions as parameters or return functions as results.

- **Type inference**: Kotlin has powerful type inference capabilities, which can make code more concise and easier to read.

Now, you might be wondering "Why would I use Kotlin over Java?" and that's a powerful question to be had. Kotlin is generally more concise than Java, which means that you can write the same code with fewer lines of code. This can make your code easier to read and maintain. Kotlin is the preferred language for Android app development, and many developers find that it is easier and more productive to work with than Java.

RECAP: Kotlin is a modern, easy-to-use language that is fully interoperable with Java and is particularly well-suited for Android app development. Its features, such as null safety, extension functions, higher-order functions, and type inference, make it a popular choice for developers who value safety, expressiveness, and readability.

Node.js

All right, all right, all right! Javascript is not just for the Front-End! Let's get acquainted with Node.js, a JavaScript runtime environment that allows developers to run JavaScript code outside of a web browser, making it possible to build server-side applications using JavaScript, with a focus on scalability, high performance, and non-blocking I/O[23].

Node.js is event-driven, and that makes it particularly well-suited for building real-time, data-intensive applications, such as chat applications, online games, and streaming services.

Node.js is built on the V8 JavaScript engine, which was originally developed by Google for use in the Chrome

[23] Tell me more about blocking and non-blocking I/O: Non-blocking I/O (Input/Output) is a programming technique that allows an application to perform other tasks while waiting for I/O operations to complete.

In traditional, blocking I/O, an application will wait for an I/O operation (such as reading data from a file or a network socket) to complete before it can continue executing other code. This can lead to performance problems, particularly in network-based applications, where a large number of connections can cause the application to become unresponsive.

In non-blocking I/O, an application can issue an I/O operation and then continue executing other code while it waits for the operation to complete. When the I/O operation completes, the application is notified and can process the result. This allows an application to handle a large number of I/O operations simultaneously, without blocking the main event loop.

web browser. This makes Node.js particularly fast and efficient, as it can execute JavaScript code at near-native speeds.

Some of the key features of Node.js include:

- **Asynchronous programming**: Node.js uses a non-blocking, asynchronous programming model that allows it to handle large numbers of connections and I/O operations simultaneously, without blocking the main event loop.

- **NPM**: Node.js comes with a built-in package manager called NPM (Node Package Manager) that makes it easy to install and manage third-party libraries and modules.

- **Cross-platform**: Node.js is cross-platform, which means that it can run on a variety of operating systems, including Windows, macOS, and Linux.

- **Event-driven**: Node.js is event-driven, which means that it responds to events such as incoming data, rather than waiting for requests to be processed in a traditional, synchronous way.

While Node.js is a powerful and flexible platform for building server-side applications, it also has some limitations that developers should be aware of:

- **Single-threaded**: Node.js uses a single thread to handle all incoming requests and I/O operations. While this can be an advantage in terms of performance and scalability, it can also limit the ability to handle complex, CPU-bound tasks.

- **Memory consumption**: Node.js can be memory-intensive, particularly when handling large data sets or high numbers of concurrent connections.

- **Lack of standard library**: Unlike other programming languages, Node.js does not have a standard library, which means that developers often need to rely on third-party libraries and modules for common tasks such as cryptography, compression, and file handling.

- **Callback hell**: Node.js uses callbacks to handle asynchronous code, which can lead to complex and difficult-to-read code, particularly in cases where there are multiple nested callbacks.

- **Limited multithreading support**: Node.js does not support true multithreading, which can limit its ability to handle certain types of applications and workloads.

Despite these limitations, Node.js remains a popular and powerful platform for building server-side applications, particularly for real-time, data-intensive applications where performance and scalability are key considerations.

Also, while speaking of Node.js, it would be a mistake not to mention Express.js.

Express.js is a popular open-source web framework for Node.js that provides a set of features and tools for building server-side web applications and APIs. It provides a simple and flexible API for handling HTTP requests, managing routing, and serving static files, and can be easily extended with middleware and third-party modules. Express.js is known for its minimalistic approach, which allows developers to build web applications in a way that best fits their needs and preferences. It is widely used by developers and companies of all sizes for building scalable and high-performance web applications.

RECAP: Node.js is a powerful and flexible platform for building server-side applications in JavaScript, with a focus on scalability, high performance, and non-blocking I/O.

Deep Diving Into FP Back-End Languages

In FP, functions are the main building blocks of programs and are used to perform specific tasks. Functions are treated as first-class citizens, meaning that they can be passed as arguments to other functions and returned as values from other functions. FP emphasizes immutability, where data is not modified once it is created, and the use of higher-order functions, where functions can take other functions as inputs and return functions as outputs.

In a quick summary, OOP focuses on objects and their interactions, while FP focuses on functions and their inputs and outputs. Both approaches have their strengths and weaknesses, and the choice between them often depends on the specific requirements of a project.

Some of the most common and widely-used FP languages include:

Haskell: A purely functional programming language that is known for its powerful type system and support for lazy evaluation.

Lisp: A family of programming languages known for their simple syntax, powerful macros, and support for functional programming.

Clojure: A modern dialect of Lisp that runs on the Java Virtual Machine and emphasizes immutability, concurrency, and composability.

Scheme: A minimalistic dialect of Lisp that is often used for teaching functional programming and programming language theory.

Erlang: A concurrent, fault-tolerant programming language that is used primarily for building distributed systems and real-time applications.

Elixir: A dynamic, functional programming language that runs on the Erlang virtual machine and is known for its scalability, fault-tolerance, and low-latency performance.

OCaml: A functional programming language that supports both imperative and object-oriented programming and is often used for scientific computing and data analysis.

F#: A functional programming language that is designed for the .NET platform and is particularly well-suited for data analysis and scientific computing.

Scala: A multi-paradigm programming language that supports both functional programming and object-oriented programming, and is often used for building high-performance, distributed systems.

These are just a few examples of the many functional programming languages available, and each language has its own strengths and weaknesses depending on the specific requirements of the application being developed.

Scala

Let's tackle Scala first. If you've already read about Scala in the previous section you know that Scala is a multi-paradigm programming language that supports both functional programming (FP) and object-oriented programming (OOP) paradigms. It was designed to combine the best features of both paradigms and provide developers with a flexible and powerful language for building scalable, high-performance applications.

In Scala, developers can write code in a purely functional style or in an object-oriented style, or combine the two paradigms as needed, depending on the requirements of the application. This makes Scala a versatile language that can be used for a wide range of applications, from data processing to web development to machine learning.

In a pure functional style, the program is composed of functions that have no side effects and always return the same result for a given set of input parameters. This makes the code more predictable and easier to reason about, which can help reduce errors and improve the maintainability of the code.

In Scala, functions are first-class citizens, meaning that they can be passed as arguments to other functions, returned as values, and stored in variables, just like any other data type. This allows developers to write code that is more modular and composable, and can be easily reused in different parts of the program.

Scala also supports higher-order functions, which are functions that take other functions as arguments or return functions as values. This enables developers to write code that is more concise and expressive, and can be used to solve complex problems more easily.

Scala's support for immutable data structures and pattern matching is another key feature of the language that makes it well-suited for functional programming. Immutable data structures are data structures that cannot be modified after they are created, which helps prevent bugs and makes it easier to reason about the code. Pattern matching is a powerful feature that allows developers to match on the structure of data and perform different actions depending on the structure of the data.

RECAP: Scala's support for functional programming concepts and features makes it a powerful and flexible language that is well-suited for building scalable, high-performance applications.

Haskell

Haskell is a functional programming language that is designed to be purely functional, meaning that it doesn't allow side effects and mutable state. In Haskell, programs are composed of functions that take input parameters and return output values, and these functions are defined in a way that is modular and composable.

One of the key features of Haskell is its support for lazy evaluation, which means that the program only evaluates an expression when its value is needed. This can help improve performance and memory usage, as the program only evaluates what is necessary to produce the output. Additionally, Haskell has built-in support for higher-order functions, which are functions that take other functions as arguments or return functions as values. This allows developers to write more expressive and concise code, and can be used to solve complex problems more easily.

Another important feature of Haskell is its type system, which is designed to help prevent bugs and improve code correctness. Haskell has a strong and static type system, which means that the types of values are checked at compile-time, and the compiler can detect many common programming errors before the program is run.

Haskell also has built-in support for algebraic data types and pattern matching, which are powerful features that allow developers to express complex data structures and manipulate them in a more natural way. Additionally, Haskell has a rich library ecosystem that provides developers with many useful functions and data structures for building applications.

RECAP: Haskell is a powerful and expressive programming language that is well-suited for building complex, high-performance applications that are correct and maintainable.

Lisp

Lisp is a programming language that is based on the concepts of symbolic computation and list processing. The language is designed to be very flexible and easy to manipulate, and it is often used in artificial intelligence research and development.

One of the key features of Lisp is its use of s-expressions, which are a way of representing code as data. This makes it easy to write code that can manipulate and generate other code, which is a powerful feature that is often used in macros and code generation.

Lisp is also a dynamically typed language, which means that the type of a variable can change at runtime. This can make it easy to write code that is very flexible and can adapt to changing requirements.

Another important feature of Lisp is its support for functional programming. This means that Lisp programs are composed of functions that take inputs and return outputs, and that these functions can be composed and combined in a variety of ways to create more complex behavior.

Lisp is a very flexible and expressive language that is well-suited to certain types of applications, such as artificial intelligence, numerical analysis, and metaprogramming. However, it may not be the best choice for applications that require a lot of performance or that need to interact closely with system-level resources.

RECAP: Lisp is a family of computer programming languages with a distinctive fully parenthesized prefix notation that is widely used for artificial intelligence and computational linguistics research.

Clojure

Enter the Clojurians! Clojure is a modern Lisp dialect that is designed to run on the Java Virtual Machine (JVM) or on other modern runtimes such as JavaScript and the .NET CLR. Clojure is a functional programming language, and like other Lisps, it is based on the concepts of symbolic computation and list processing.

One of the key features of Clojure is its use of immutable data structures, which makes it easy to write programs that are thread-safe and that can scale to multiple processors. Clojure also provides powerful tools for dealing with concurrency, such as software transactional memory (STM), which makes it easy to write concurrent programs that avoid common pitfalls such as deadlocks and race conditions.

Another important feature of Clojure is its emphasis on functional programming. Clojure provides a rich set of high-level functions that can be used to compose and manipulate data, and it supports advanced functional programming concepts such as higher-order functions and lazy evaluation.

Clojure also provides seamless interoperability with Java, which means that developers can easily leverage the vast ecosystem of Java libraries and tools. Clojure code can call Java code, and Java code can call Clojure code, which makes it easy to integrate Clojure into existing Java projects.

Overall, Clojure is a powerful and expressive programming language that is well-suited to building complex, high-performance applications that need to scale to multiple processors and that require a high degree of concurrency. However, Clojure may not be the best choice for applications that need to interact closely with system-level resources or that require a lot of low-level optimization.

RECAP: Clojure is a modern Lisp dialect designed to run on the Java Virtual Machine, emphasizing immutability, functional programming, and seamless interoperability with Java.

Scheme

Scheme is a minimalist dialect of Lisp that is designed to be a simple, elegant, and powerful programming language. Like other Lisps, Scheme is based on the concepts of symbolic computation and list processing, and it provides a rich set of tools for dealing with data and functional programming.

One of the key features of Scheme is its minimalist syntax, which makes it easy to read and write programs. Scheme programs are expressed in terms of lists, and the core of the language is based on a small number of primitive functions and a set of powerful higher-order functions that can be used to compose and manipulate data.

Another important feature of Scheme is its support for first-class continuations, which makes it possible to implement advanced control structures such as coroutines, generators, and cooperative multitasking. Scheme also provides a powerful macro system that allows programmers to extend the language and define their own domain-specific languages.

Overall, Scheme is a powerful and elegant programming language that is well-suited to academic and research applications, as well as for building small to medium-sized programs. However, Scheme may not be the best choice for building large-scale applications, as it lacks some of the features and tools that are provided by more modern languages.

RECAP: Scheme is a minimalist and elegant dialect of Lisp, designed to support functional programming and symbol manipulation.

Erlang

Erlang is a functional programming language that is designed for developing highly concurrent, fault-tolerant, and distributed systems. It provides a powerful set of abstractions for dealing with concurrency and parallelism, and it uses a unique actor model to achieve high levels of scalability and reliability.

Erlang programs are composed of lightweight processes that communicate via message passing, making it easy to build highly concurrent and fault-tolerant systems. The language also provides a number of powerful abstractions for dealing with distributed systems, including transparent distribution, fault-tolerant data storage, and distributed process coordination.

Commonly used for developing large-scale, high-performance, distributed, and fault-tolerant systems, Erlang is used particularly in the areas of telecommunications, messaging, and networking. It has been used to build everything from high-availability phone switches and messaging platforms to massively multiplayer online games and financial trading systems. Erlang's ability to handle massive concurrency, high reliability, and distributed computing makes it particularly well-suited for these types of applications.

Additionally, Erlang has been adopted by several large companies, including Ericsson, WhatsApp, and Goldman Sachs, to build and maintain large-scale, mission-critical systems.

RECAP: Erlang is a functional programming language designed for developing highly concurrent, fault-tolerant, and distributed systems.

Elixir

Elixir is a functional programming language built on top of the Erlang virtual machine. It offers a syntax that is both expressive and concise, making it easy to write and maintain large-scale systems.

Elixir provides a powerful set of abstractions for dealing with concurrency, parallelism, and distributed systems, including lightweight processes, message passing, and fault-tolerant supervision trees. It also has an extensive set of libraries and tools that make it well-suited for building web applications, distributed systems, and real-time systems. There are several reasons why you might choose to use Elixir, including:

- **Scalability and concurrency**: Elixir's concurrency model is based on lightweight processes and message passing, which makes it easy to write highly concurrent and distributed systems that can scale to handle large workloads.

- **Fault-tolerance**: Elixir provides built-in mechanisms for building fault-tolerant systems, such as supervision trees, which can automatically restart processes in the event of a failure.

- **Performance**: Elixir is built on top of the Erlang virtual machine, which is known for its ability to handle massive amounts of concurrency and high availability. This makes Elixir a great choice for building systems that need to be highly performant.

- **Productivity**: Elixir's syntax is expressive and concise, which makes it easy to write and maintain large-scale systems. It also has a rich set of libraries and tools that make it well-suited for building web applications, distributed systems, and real-time systems.

RECAP: Elixir is a powerful and flexible language that combines the best aspects of functional programming and Erlang's battle-tested concurrency and distribution model.

OCaml

OCaml is a functional programming language that is strongly typed and uses type inference to reduce the need for explicit type annotations. It supports features such as pattern matching, first-class functions, and parametric polymorphism, which make it well-suited for building high-level abstractions and expressive data structures.

Additionally, OCaml has a powerful module system that allows for the effective organization and reuse of code, making it a popular choice for building large-scale software systems. The language also has a native code compiler, which can generate highly efficient code for a variety of platforms, making it useful for building high-performance applications.

In OCaml, functions are first-class citizens, meaning that they can be passed as arguments to other functions, returned as values from functions, and assigned to variables. The language also supports a wide range of data types, including tuples, records, variant types, and lists, which can be used to represent complex data structures. Additionally, OCaml has a number of advanced features, such as pattern matching and parametric polymorphism, which make it easy to write expressive and concise code.

RECAP: OCaml is a functional programming language that emphasizes the use of small, modular functions and supports a wide range of data types, advanced features, and expressive and concise code.

F#

Pronounced F-sharp, F# is a functional programming language that is built on top of the .NET framework and emphasizes the use of immutable data structures and pure functions to simplify the development of high-performance, concurrent, and scalable applications.

The language supports a wide range of functional programming features, including type inference, pattern matching, currying, and partial application, and also provides access to the .NET framework libraries and tools, making it a powerful and flexible tool for developing applications on the Microsoft platform.

F# is a functional programming language that is well-suited for developing cloud applications, and it has become increasingly popular in the Azure ecosystem. One of the main reasons for this is that F# integrates seamlessly with the .NET framework, which is the foundation of many Azure services. F# is also a highly expressive and concise language that supports a wide range of programming paradigms, including functional, object-oriented, and imperative programming. This makes it a flexible and powerful tool for developing cloud-based applications, and its strong support for asynchronous programming and data processing makes it particularly well-suited for building highly responsive and scalable systems in Azure.

RECAP: F# is a universal programming language for writing succinct, robust and performant code. F# allows you to write uncluttered, self-documenting code, where your focus remains on your problem domain, rather than the details of programming.

Chapter Seven

What Data Matters?

Welcome to the Data! The data layer in computer programming is crucial because it's where all the important information about a product, user or business is stored. If the data layer isn't properly maintained or accessed, it can lead to a number of problems, including security breaches and unreliable product performance. So, understanding how to properly manage and structure data is critical to creating a successful and secure digital product.

Think of it like this: the data layer is critical to computer programming because it's like the foundation of a building - it holds everything up. Without a solid data layer, the whole system can come crashing down like a house of cards. It's the backbone that supports all the software and services built on top of it. Data is the lifeblood of software, and the data layer is where it all flows. That's why we need to take it seriously and build it with the same rigor and care that we would build any other critical system.

We break this section into a few critical areas including:

- **Databases**: a collection of data that is stored and managed in a computer system.

- **Cache**: a high-speed storage layer that stores frequently accessed data and allows for quick access to data without the need for repeated computation or data retrieval.

- **Search**: a process of finding information from a database or other source based on user-defined criteria or queries.

- **Data Analytics**: the process of examining and interpreting large volumes of data to derive insights and inform decision-making

Databases

In our earlier discussion, we highlighted that web applications are more complex to build than brochure websites as they require personalized information for each user, which is stored in databases. Databases are specialized software used for data storage and retrieval, akin to a spreadsheet, with multiple specialized types available for specific use cases.

Data is the new oil and databases are the refineries that help us extract insights from the vast troves of information we accumulate online, providing valuable competitive advantages to companies and driving innovation across industries.

There are many types of specialized databases developed for different use cases including:

- **Relational databases**: These are the most common type of database, which store data in tables with rows and columns, and use structured query language (SQL) to manage and retrieve data.

- **NoSQL databases**: These databases use different data models than relational databases and do not require a fixed schema, making them flexible for handling unstructured data.

- **Object-oriented databases**: These databases store objects, classes, and methods, which allow for complex relationships and can handle complex data structures.

- **Graph databases**: These databases use graph theory to store, organize, and query data, which is especially useful for complex relationships.

- **Document databases**: These databases store data as documents, typically using JSON or BSON formats, and are useful for storing and managing unstructured data.

- **In-memory databases**: These databases store data in memory for faster processing and can be useful for real-time applications that require fast data access.

Let's tackle some of the most common Databases you will encounter!

SQL

SQL (Structured Query Language, pronounced "sequel") databases work by organizing data into tables, where each table consists of columns and rows. The columns represent the data fields and the rows represent individual records. SQL is a programming language used to manage and manipulate data in these databases. With SQL, users can create, update, and retrieve data from the tables, as well as perform complex queries and aggregate functions on large data sets.

SQL is a programming language designed specifically for managing and manipulating data stored in relational databases, allowing us to access, modify, and extract valuable insights from vast amounts of structured data.

Think of it as a Swiss Army knife for your data, allowing you to sort, filter, and analyze large datasets with ease. It's the backbone of data-driven decision making in the modern digital age. SQL databases are widely used in many applications, including finance, healthcare, e-commerce, and more.

RECAP: SQL, or Structured Query Language, is a programming language used to manage and manipulate relational databases.

MySQL

A MySQL database is a type of relational database management system (RDBMS) that uses the SQL (Structured Query Language) to manage and organize data. It is one of the most popular open-source database systems and is widely used in web development and other software applications.

MySQL databases are used to store and manage data in a structured format that makes it easy to access and manipulate. This data can be anything from customer information, product catalogs, financial data, or any other information that needs to be stored and managed.

MySQL databases are highly scalable, meaning they can handle large amounts of data and multiple users simultaneously. They also have a high degree of flexibility, allowing developers to easily modify and customize the database to suit their specific needs.

RECAP: MySQL is an open-source relational database management system that uses SQL to manage and organize data.

PostgreSQL

PostgreSQL is an advanced open-source relational database management system (RDBMS) that uses and extends the SQL language to provide a powerful and flexible platform for storing, managing, and querying data. It is known for its high performance, scalability, and reliability, and is used by many organizations for mission-critical applications and data processing.

PostgreSQL works by organizing data into tables, which can be related to one another through common fields. Users can then perform SQL queries to retrieve, insert, update, and delete data in the database.

PostgreSQL also supports advanced features such as multi-version concurrency control (MVCC) which allows for simultaneous read and write operations on the same data without conflicts, as well as transaction management and stored procedures, which provide greater control and flexibility in managing data.

RECAP: PostgreSQL is a highly flexible and powerful database system that can handle complex data models and large amounts of data, making it a popular choice for enterprise-level applications and data-intensive projects.

NoSQL

NoSQL (Not Only SQL) is a type of database management system that uses a non-relational approach to storing and managing data.

NoSQL databases work by storing data in a flexible, schema-less format that can easily adapt to changing data structures and data types. This means that data can be stored as key-value pairs, document-based structures, or graph-based structures, among others.

NoSQL databases typically support horizontal scaling, meaning they can be easily distributed across multiple servers, allowing for better performance and reliability in handling large amounts of data. They also often provide high availability and fault tolerance, with built-in replication and backup features that can help prevent data loss or downtime.

One of the main advantages of NoSQL databases is their flexibility and scalability, which allows for faster development cycles and more agile data management. They are also well-suited for handling unstructured or semi-structured data, such as social media data or IoT sensor data, which may not fit neatly into a traditional relational database schema.

However, NoSQL databases may not be the best fit for all use cases, and may require more specialized skills or tools to work with. Additionally, the lack of a rigid schema can make it more difficult to maintain data consistency or enforce data validation rules, and complex queries may be more challenging to write and optimize.

RECAP: NoSQL is a type of database management system that uses a non-relational approach to storing and managing data, providing flexibility and scalability for handling unstructured or semi-structured data.

MongoDB

MongoDB is a NoSQL document-oriented database that stores data in a JSON-like format called BSON (Binary JSON).

MongoDB works by organizing data into collections, which are made up of documents. Documents are self-contained data structures that contain all the information needed for a particular piece of data, including fields and values.

MongoDB's querying language, MongoDB Query Language (MQL), is designed to be flexible and powerful, allowing users to perform complex queries on data using a variety of operators and functions.

MongoDB supports several advantages, including:

- Scalability: MongoDB is designed to scale horizontally, allowing for the addition of more servers to handle increased data volumes and user traffic.

- Flexibility: MongoDB's document-oriented data model allows for greater flexibility in storing and managing data, making it easier to handle unstructured and semi-structured data.

- High Availability: MongoDB supports replication and sharding, which can provide high availability and fault tolerance in case of server failures.

- Performance: MongoDB's use of in-memory processing and indexing can provide faster query performance compared to traditional relational databases.

- Overall, MongoDB is a popular choice for applications that require a flexible and scalable database system that can handle large amounts of unstructured data.

RECAP: MongoDB is a popular NoSQL document-oriented database system that stores and retrieves data in flexible, JSON-like documents.

Cassandra

Cassandra is a distributed, highly scalable NoSQL database system designed to handle large amounts of structured and unstructured data across many commodity servers, while providing high availability and fault tolerance.

Cassandra works by distributing data across multiple nodes in a cluster, using a peer-to-peer architecture. Each node in the cluster is responsible for a portion of the data, and data is replicated across multiple nodes for fault tolerance.

Cassandra also supports automatic data partitioning and distribution, which allows it to scale horizontally by adding more nodes to the cluster as needed. It also supports tunable consistency, allowing developers to trade off consistency for availability or vice versa, depending on their specific needs.

Some advantages of Cassandra include its ability to handle large amounts of data, its high availability and fault tolerance, its flexible data model, which can handle structured and unstructured data, and its support for tunable consistency and automatic data distribution.

RECAP: Cassandra is a powerful database system that is well-suited for applications with large amounts of data and high availability requirements, such as IoT systems, social media platforms, and e-commerce applications.

Cosmos DB

Cosmos DB is a globally distributed, multi-model database service provided by Microsoft Azure. It is designed to provide fast and reliable access to data, no matter where in the world it is located.

Cosmos DB works by distributing data across multiple regions and providing automatic failover capabilities to ensure high availability and disaster recovery. It supports multiple data models, including document, key-value, graph, and column-family, giving developers the flexibility to choose the most appropriate model for their data.

Cosmos DB also supports multiple APIs, including SQL, MongoDB, Cassandra, Gremlin, and Azure Table Storage, allowing developers to use familiar tools and interfaces to interact with the database. It also provides automatic indexing, enabling high-performance queries and real-time analytics.

Some of the advantages of Cosmos DB include its global scalability, high availability, low latency, and multi-model and multi-API support. It is designed for applications that require high performance and low latency, such as real-time IoT, gaming, and e-commerce applications, as well as big data and analytics workloads.

RECAP: Cosmos DB is a powerful and flexible database service that provides developers with the tools and capabilities they need to build fast and reliable applications at a global scale.

Couchbase

Couchbase is a NoSQL, distributed, multi-model database system that is designed to handle large amounts of data and provide fast access to that data in real-time.

Couchbase works by using a distributed architecture, where data is automatically distributed across multiple nodes in the database cluster, ensuring that data is always available even if some nodes fail. The database can be scaled horizontally by adding more nodes to the cluster, which allows for greater capacity and performance as the amount of data and users grows.

Couchbase also supports a flexible data model that allows developers to store and retrieve data in a variety of ways, including document-based storage, key-value storage, and query-based access. This flexibility allows developers to choose the best data model for their specific needs, making it easier to build applications that can handle complex data structures and use cases.

Some of the advantages of using Couchbase include its high performance, scalability, and flexibility. Its distributed architecture and memory-centric design allow it to handle high volumes of data with low latency, making it well-suited for real-time applications and big data projects. Couchbase also supports ACID transactions, providing data consistency and reliability, and its flexible data model and query language allow for rapid development and iteration.

RECAP: Couchbase is a powerful database system that is designed to handle the demands of modern, data-intensive applications, and it provides developers with the tools and flexibility they need to build scalable and responsive applications.

Firestore

Firestore is a cloud-hosted NoSQL document database that is part of the Google Cloud Platform. It is designed to store and manage large amounts of unstructured data, and is optimized for real-time updates and scalability.

Firestore works by storing data in documents, which can contain key-value pairs, arrays, and nested objects. These documents are organized into collections, which can be queried and filtered using a variety of parameters.

One of the main advantages of Firestore is its real-time synchronization capabilities. It uses websockets to enable real-time updates to documents, so any changes made by one user are immediately reflected in the database and can be seen by other users who are viewing the same data.

Another advantage of Firestore is its scalability. It is designed to handle large amounts of data and can automatically scale up or down to meet changing demand. It also supports offline data access, allowing applications to continue functioning even when a user loses connectivity.

In addition, Firestore supports a wide range of programming languages and platforms, including web, mobile, and server-side applications, making it a versatile and flexible option for developers. It also integrates seamlessly with other Google Cloud Platform services, such as Cloud Functions and Firebase Authentication.

RECAP: Firestore is a powerful and flexible database system that offers real-time synchronization, scalability, and a range of other features that make it well-suited for a wide variety of applications and use cases.

Redis

Redis is an open-source, in-memory data structure store that can be used as a database, cache, and message broker.

Redis works by storing data in RAM rather than on disk, which makes it incredibly fast and efficient. It uses a key-value data model, which means that data is stored as a set of key-value pairs, and users can perform operations such as adding, retrieving, and deleting data using the keys.

Redis supports a wide range of data types, including strings, hashes, lists, sets, and sorted sets, which makes it a versatile tool for managing and manipulating data. It also supports advanced features such as pub/sub messaging, which allows users to send messages between clients, and Lua scripting, which enables users to execute custom scripts within Redis.

One of the biggest advantages of Redis is its speed and performance. Since it stores data in RAM, it can deliver lightning-fast response times, making it ideal for use cases that require low latency and high throughput. It also supports high availability through replication and automatic failover, which ensures that data is always accessible and resilient to failures.

Another advantage of Redis is its flexibility and ease of use. It can be used as a standalone database, as a cache layer in front of a database, or as a message broker for real-time applications. Its simple API and extensive documentation make it easy to integrate into existing applications and start using right away.

Overall, Redis is a powerful and versatile tool for managing and manipulating data, with speed, performance, and flexibility being its primary advantages.

RECAP: Redis is a fast, flexible, and powerful data store that can provide significant performance advantages over traditional disk-based databases and caching solutions, particularly for applications that require real-time data processing and high throughput.

DynamoDB

DynamoDB is a fully managed NoSQL database service provided by Amazon Web Services (AWS). It is designed to provide high scalability and performance with low latency and high availability.

DynamoDB works by storing data in tables that are partitioned across multiple servers to provide high performance and scalability. Each table consists of items, which are essentially key-value pairs, and each item can have multiple attributes. DynamoDB also supports document data models through its Document API.

One of the key advantages of DynamoDB is its ability to scale automatically based on demand. It supports both horizontal scaling through partitioning and vertical scaling through provisioned throughput capacity. This means that users can adjust the database capacity to handle any level of traffic without experiencing any downtime.

Another advantage of DynamoDB is its low latency and high availability. It achieves this by replicating data across multiple availability zones within a region. This ensures that even if one zone goes down, data is still available from another zone.

RECAP: DynamoDB is a highly scalable and performant NoSQL database service that is ideal for applications that require low latency, high availability, and high scalability. It is commonly used for web applications, mobile applications, gaming, ad tech, and many other use cases where real-time data processing and storage are critical.

Cache

As previously noted, Cache (or caching) is a high-speed storage layer that stores frequently accessed data and allows for quick access to data without the need for repeated computation or data retrieval.

But what is it really?

Cache, my friends, is like the VIP room of a club where your favorite computer processor goes to chill out with the most frequently needed data. It's a small, super-fast memory space, right next to the processor, that stores information your machine is gonna need pronto. You see, processors are the Brad Pitts of the computer world - they're fast, sexy, and expensive. So, you want to keep them busy and not let them waste time waiting for slower components like main memory.

Now, how does this VIP room work? It's all about the bouncers - clever algorithms that predict which data is gonna be the star of the show next. When the processor needs something, it checks the cache first. If it's there, that's a cache hit, baby! And the party goes on. But if it's not (a cache hit), we call that a cache miss. And then the processor has to go to the main memory, which is like waiting in line for a drink at the bar - not cool.

Cache is important to computation because, without it, our processors would be stuck in the slow lane. By having the cache right next to them, we're cutting the time it takes to access data significantly. And that, my friend, is how you turbocharge your computer's performance. It's like going from a scooter to a Bugatti Veyron in the computing world.

So, cache is crucial, and it's all about speed, efficiency, and keeping your processor from twiddling its digital thumbs. Next time your computer is blazing through tasks, remember to raise a glass to cache, the unsung hero of the computing world.

RECAP: Cache is a small, ultra-fast memory space adjacent to the processor that temporarily stores frequently used data, dramatically boosting the computer's performance by reducing access time.

Memcache

Alright, buckle up, because we're about to dive into the wild world of Memcache. Picture this: you're at a fancy dinner party, but instead of small talk about the latest binge-worthy show or the inflated price of avocado toast, you're dropping knowledge bombs about Memcache. Because who doesn't love a good caching conversation, am I right?

So, what the hell is Memcache? It's like the VIP room at a swanky club, but for data. It's an in-memory caching system that helps you access your frequently used data at lightning speed. This means less time spent waiting for data retrieval, and more time spent looking like a rockstar in your business meetings.

Now let's talk about how it works. Memcache is like the world's most efficient bouncer – it keeps the party going by quickly and efficiently giving you access to the data you need most. The cache stores key-value pairs, and when you ask it for something, it checks if it's got it in its memory. If it does, it'll hand it over faster than a New York minute. If not, you'll have to go to the back of the line and get it from the slower, less exclusive database. Memcache uses a Least Recently Used (LRU) algorithm to decide which data gets the boot when it needs to make room for new data.

But why does any of this matter? Well, it's all about efficiency, my friend. Just like nobody wants to wait in line for the bar at a hot new nightclub, developers don't want to waste time waiting for data retrieval. By cutting down the time it takes to access frequently used data, Memcache helps web applications run like Usain Bolt on rocket fuel. It's crucial for scaling web apps and keeping them performing at peak levels.

In a world where people have the attention span of a caffeinated goldfish, nobody's got time for slow-loading websites or applications. That's where Memcache comes in – the unsung hero, the VIP bouncer, the guy who keeps the party going all night long.

So next time you're chatting with your friends over a glass of pinot noir, remember – Memcache is where it's at.

RECAP: Memcached is a high-performance, distributed memory caching system, primarily used to speed up dynamic database-driven websites and applications by caching data in RAM to reduce the number of times an external data source, like a database or API, needs to be read. It's essentially a simple key-value store, allowing rapid access to data based on a unique key, significantly reducing latency and improving overall system performance.

Ehcache

Well, my friends, let me tell you about Ehcache, the Gucci of Java-based caching systems. It's an open-source, in-memory cache that's become one of the go-to options for folks looking to optimize their applications. Just like how Amazon ruthlessly optimizes for their customers, Ehcache strives to ensure that your applications run as efficiently as possible.

The magic of Ehcache lies in its ability to store data in memory, so that future requests for the same data can be retrieved much faster than if they were fetched from the primary data source. It's like the bouncer at a fancy club who knows your name and lets you in without waiting in line. This kind of caching strategy is just pure genius for reducing latency and enhancing the overall performance of your application.

Now, let's delve into how this bad boy works. Ehcache uses a simple key-value store system. When you request data from the cache, Ehcache looks for the corresponding key in its memory. If the key is present, boom, you've got yourself a cache hit, and the data is quickly returned. But, if the key isn't found, we have what we call a cache miss. In this case, the application fetches the data from the primary source, stores it in the cache, and returns it to the user. Think of it like the efficient, data-fetching ninja that it is.

So why is Ehcache important to computation? It's all about optimization, baby. In a world where we're all trying to make a digital dent, the companies that succeed are those that manage to deliver exceptional performance without breaking the bank. Just like how

Apple's sleek design and efficiency have made it a titan of industry, Ehcache's ability to improve an application's response time, reduce the load on primary data sources, and decrease costs associated with scalability make it a key player in the realm of computation.

To sum it up, Ehcache is that beautiful, elegant solution that'll take your application's performance to the next level. If you're looking to strut your stuff in the world of computation, Ehcache is your ticket to the VIP section.

RECAP: Memcached is an open-source, high-performance, distributed memory object caching system that is primarily used to speed up dynamic database-driven websites by caching data and objects in RAM. It reduces the number of times an external data source, such as a database or API, needs to be read, thus minimizing latency and increasing throughput.

Redis

Redis, my friends, is an open-source, in-memory data structure store that wears many hats. It's a database, a cache, and a message broker all rolled into one sleek package. Now, you might be thinking, "Big whoop, another database. What's the fuss about?" Well, hold onto your hats, because Redis is a freaking rocket ship in the world of data management.

How does it work? Well, Redis is all about speed and flexibility. It stores data in memory, not on disk, which means it's lightning fast compared to traditional databases. Think of it like Usain Bolt racing your grandma. Redis doesn't just store your everyday key-value pairs; it supports strings, lists, sets, sorted sets, and even more data structures. This versatility makes it a rockstar in the realm of real-time applications.

So, why is Redis so damn important to computation? Simply put, it's a game-changer for scaling and performance. In today's world, we want things done yesterday. Ain't nobody got time for slow-loading applications or data bottlenecks. Redis steps up to the plate, letting developers build high-performance, scalable apps that can handle millions of requests per second without breaking a sweat.

But wait, there's more! Redis is also clutch for real-time analytics, message queuing, and caching. Seriously, this thing is like the Swiss Army knife of databases. With Redis, you can shave precious milliseconds off your response times, making your users happier than a toddler with an ice cream cone.

So, to wrap this up, Redis is the Lamborghini of databases, the real MVP of in-memory data storage. It's important to computation because it helps developers build insanely fast, scalable applications that can take the digital world by storm. If you're not using Redis, it's time to level up, my friends.

RECAP: Redis (Remote Dictionary Server) is an open-source, in-memory data structure store that can be used as a database, cache, and message broker. It supports various data structures such as strings, hashes, lists, sets, and provides high availability, replication, and automatic partitioning, making it ideal for real-time applications requiring high performance and low latency.

Apache Ignite

Ladies and gentlemen, let me introduce you to Apache Ignite, a high-octane, high-performance, in-memory computing platform that's designed to supercharge your applications with lightning-fast speed. Think of it like giving your applications a masterclass in digital steroids.

So how does this bad boy work? Picture this: your applications need to access and store data, right? The traditional way is to use disk-based storage, which is slower than a '90s dial-up modem. But Apache Ignite is different. It uses in-memory storage, which is like Usain Bolt sprinting through your data instead of a snail crawl. That's because in-memory storage keeps data on RAM, giving you ultra-low latency and sky-high throughput.

Apache Ignite is like the Swiss Army Knife of data processing. It comes equipped with a data grid, a SQL engine, a compute grid, a service grid, and even a machine learning library. All those components work in unison to ensure your data processing is smoother than a freshly waxed surfboard.

Now, you're probably thinking, "Great, but why should I care?" Well, let me tell you, in today's data-driven world, speed is the name of the game. Companies are constantly fighting to stay ahead of the curve, and Apache Ignite is like a secret weapon that gives you that competitive edge.

Need to process massive amounts of data in real-time? Apache Ignite has you covered. Want to build highly scalable, fault-tolerant systems that can take a punch and keep going? Look no further. Apache Ignite is the heavyweight champ in the world of in-memory computing.

In conclusion, Apache Ignite is more than just a tool; it's a game-changer in the computation world. It's here to make sure your applications don't just run – they soar, like a majestic eagle. And in the digital age, that's not just an advantage; it's a necessity. So, if you're looking to leave your competitors in the dust, Apache Ignite is your one-way ticket to victory.

RECAP: Apache Ignite is an open-source, high-performance, integrated and distributed in-memory platform for computing and transacting on large-scale data sets in real-time. It provides powerful capabilities such as a distributed database, computing across distributed data, and machine learning and AI capabilities, enabling rapid processing and analysis of large amounts of data.

Hazelcast

Alright, so buckle up and let me take you on a ride through the land of Hazelcast, a platform that's crushing it in the distributed computing game. Think of Hazelcast as the LeBron James of the computing world, a powerhouse that's always a step ahead and changing the way we manage data.

Now, at its core, Hazelcast is a distributed, in-memory data grid. I know, I know - it sounds like some Silicon Valley buzzword, but it's legit. Imagine you've got a bunch of computers, each with a piece of data. Hazelcast is the boss that comes in and tells them, "Hey, let's work together to get the job done!" It's like the ultimate team player, making sure everybody's on the same page, sharing data, and doing their part.

One of the key things Hazelcast does is it stores data in memory, rather than on disk. Think of memory as a supercharged sports car while disk storage is your grandma's station wagon. Data access in memory is way faster, and that's what makes Hazelcast a game changer for applications where speed is king. We're talking financial services, e-commerce, IoT - you name it, Hazelcast is there, flexing its muscles and delivering the goods at breakneck speeds.

Now, the secret sauce that makes Hazelcast tick is its ability to scale horizontally. That means as you throw more computers into the mix, Hazelcast just gets better and better, like a fine wine or a well-aged scotch. It's got this super cool feature called data sharding that splits data into smaller chunks and spreads them across the grid. This not only makes the system more efficient, but also more resilient. If one node goes down, no problemo - Hazelcast's got your back, ensuring your data is safe and sound.

So, why is Hazelcast important to computation? Three words, my friend: speed, scalability, and reliability. In a world where data is the new oil, and we're churning out zettabytes of the stuff like there's no tomorrow, it's crucial that we have a system that can keep up. And that's where Hazelcast steps up to the plate, delivering a jaw-dropping, mind-blowing performance that leaves its competitors in the dust.

In short, Hazelcast is like the love child of Usain Bolt and a Swiss army knife - it's lightning-fast, versatile, and gets the job done, no matter what you throw at it. The future of computation is all about distributed systems, and Hazelcast is the poster child for what's possible in this brave new world. So, if you're looking to level up your data game, it's time to get on the Hazelcast train and buckle in for the ride of your life.

RECAP: Hazelcast is an open-source in-memory data grid solution that enables high-speed data processing by storing and managing data across distributed systems in memory. It excels in use cases requiring low latency, scalability, and resilience, and is often used for caching, microservices architectures, and real-time data analytics.

Couchbase

Alright, listen up folks. I'm about to drop some knowledge on you about Couchbase, and you're gonna wanna pay attention, because this bad boy is shaking things up in the world of databases like a boss.

Couchbase, my friends, is a NoSQL database, but not just any NoSQL database—it's a distributed, multi-model, high-performance beast that's perfect for web, mobile, and IoT applications. It's like the CrossFit athlete of databases: lean, mean, and ready to take on the competition.

Now, let's break down how this sucker works. Couchbase is all about scalability and performance. It uses a flexible data model, which means it can store data in JSON format, making it easy for developers to work with. It's got a built-in caching layer, because, you know, speed is the name of the game. And it's got this nifty thing called Cross Datacenter Replication (XDCR), which allows it to replicate data across multiple data centers—think of it as a virtual world tour, but for your data.

But, wait, there's more! Couchbase has got this wicked-cool query language called N1QL (pronounced "nickel"), which is SQL-like and allows developers to work with JSON documents just as if they were working with traditional relational databases. It's like giving SQL a makeover and sending it out to party in the NoSQL world.

So, why is Couchbase important to computation? Well, my friends, we're living in a world where data is the new oil, and Couchbase is like a high-performance sports car that can guzzle that oil and go from zero to sixty in no time. It enables businesses to build massively scalable applications with lightning-fast performance, giving them the edge they need to survive in the digital economy. It's the kind of technological innovation that separates the winners from the losers, the sharks from the minnows, the titans from the also-rans.

To sum it up, Couchbase is a game-changer in the database space, providing speed, flexibility, and scalability that few competitors can match. If you're looking to build the next killer app or revolutionize your industry, Couchbase might just be the secret sauce you need. And that, ladies and gentlemen, is why you should be paying attention to this bad boy.

RECAP: Couchbase is a high-performance, NoSQL database engine designed to deliver scalability and flexibility for managing unstructured and semi-structured data. It offers features such as memory-first architecture, distributed design, and easy scalability, making it well-suited for web, mobile, and IoT applications requiring fast access to data and real-time analytics.

Aerospike

Alright, kiddos, gather 'round. Let's have a chat about this badass technology called Aerospike. Picture this: you're dealing with big data, I mean seriously massive amounts of data, and you need a solution that's faster than Usain Bolt and more reliable than your grandma's cooking. That's where Aerospike swoops in, like a superhero in the tech world.

Aerospike, my friends, is a NoSQL database. And no, that doesn't mean it's anti-SQL. It simply stands for "Not Only SQL." Aerospike is designed to handle large-scale, high-performance, real-time applications. You want speed? You got it. Consistency? Check. Scalability? Hell yeah.

So how does this magical piece of technology work? Aerospike has a secret sauce called the Hybrid Memory Architecture. Sounds like something straight out of a sci-fi flick, doesn't it? But it's all too real, my friends. This architecture combines the best of both RAM and SSDs, so you get lightning-fast access to your data with a price tag that won't leave your wallet weeping.

But wait, there's more. Aerospike is also a distributed database. Picture a synchronized swimming team - it works together seamlessly, across multiple nodes, to ensure you've got data redundancy and fault tolerance. If one node goes down, it's no biggie. The others have got its back.

Now, why is Aerospike important to computation? We live in a world where data is king, and businesses are clamoring for ways to process and analyze that data faster than ever before. Aerospike is like a secret weapon, empowering companies to deliver real-time, personalized experiences to their customers. We're talking finance, e-commerce, telecommunications - it's a game-changer, folks.

In conclusion, Aerospike is the Usain Bolt, the Serena Williams, the LeBron James of databases. It's fast, reliable, and built for the big leagues. And in a world where every millisecond matters, Aerospike is a heavyweight contender that's not to be underestimated.

RECAP: Aerospike is a high-performance, distributed NoSQL database that is optimized for providing low latency and high throughput for read/write operations on large-scale data. It's built to handle real-time big data workloads, offering robust features for managing, scaling, and handling data across multiple servers and locations with strong consistency and reliability.

GridGain

Let me introduce you to the sensational world of GridGain, a robust, scalable, and powerful in-memory computing platform that's making waves in the realm of big data and high-performance computing. You see, in this era of digital gold rush, businesses are constantly juggling enormous amounts of data, and our good friend GridGain here, is the secret sauce that's making data processing faster than Usain Bolt.

So how does this data processing superstar work? Well, I'm glad you asked. GridGain leverages the power of Apache Ignite, an open-source, in-memory computing platform, to provide a distributed, massively parallel processing framework. It's like a room full of Einsteins working together on a single problem, processing data at breakneck speed. By storing data in-memory, GridGain reduces the need to read and write from slowpoke disk storage, boosting performance like a Tesla Roadster on ludicrous mode.

Now, you might be wondering why this high-flying, data-crunching machine is so vital to the world of computation. Let me tell you, my friends, GridGain is a game-changer. In today's cutthroat business environment, companies need real-time insights and lightning-fast decision-making. GridGain swoops in like a superhero and enables these enterprises to handle massive amounts of data with ease, giving them the agility of a Silicon Valley startup even when they're more like a lumbering, old-world behemoth.

In short, GridGain is the secret weapon that businesses need to stay relevant in this fast-paced, data-driven world. It's like adding rocket fuel to your data processing engine, and who wouldn't want that?

RECAP: GridGain is a high-performance, integrated and distributed in-memory computing platform built on Apache Ignite that allows for massive data processing and real-time analytics. It provides powerful capabilities including data grid, compute grid, machine learning, and more, designed to tackle complex computations and process large volumes of data with speed and scalability.

Search

Alright, buckle up, because we're about to dive into the sexy world of search software. Picture this: you're in a room packed with billions of documents, and you're looking for that one piece of information that'll skyrocket your business or give you the ultimate edge. That's where search software comes into play, like a digital bloodhound sniffing out the clues in this massive haystack of data.

So, let's break it down. Search software is the badass digital tool that enables you to find the most relevant piece of information in a vast ocean of data. These tools use algorithms, which are like recipes for finding the juiciest, most mouth-watering morsels of information, and indexing, a process that's essentially like creating a giant, uber-organized library of all the data that's out there.

Now, how do these puppies work? There's no one-size-fits-all answer, but let's focus on the big kahuna: text-based search. It starts with the search software crawling and indexing the content, like an army of data-hungry spiders. Then, when you type your query, the software kicks into high gear, matching your keywords to the indexed content, and then ranking the results based on relevancy. It's like having a super-efficient personal assistant who knows where to find everything you could ever want.

But why, you ask, is search software so crucial to computation? Well, my friend, we're living in an era of information overload. We're drowning in data, and without search software, we'd be lost at sea, struggling to find that life-saving nugget of wisdom. These tools empower us to make sense of the chaos, to find the needle in the haystack, and to turn the raw, untamed power of data into actionable insights that drive innovation and success. It's like a high-octane fuel for the engine of human progress.

In conclusion, search software is the unsung hero of the digital age. It's the secret sauce that keeps us from drowning in a sea of information, and it's a vital component of the computational ecosystem that powers our world. So the next time you type a query into Google or search for a file on your computer, take a moment to appreciate the magic of search software – the digital bloodhound that sniffs out the answers you need and makes our modern world possible.

RECAP: Search in software refers to the ability to input queries or keywords into a system to locate specific information or data. It relies on algorithms, often leveraging indexing and pattern matching, to quickly sift through vast amounts of data and provide relevant results.

Why is Search a Key Feature

Search is a key feature of business because it enables efficient and effective discovery of information, products, and services that are critical to the success of any organization. Here are some reasons why:

- **Enhanced user experience**: Providing a robust search capability on a business's website or platform can greatly enhance the user experience by making it easier for customers and employees to find what they need quickly and easily.

- **Increased efficiency**: With search, employees can quickly find the information they need to perform their jobs, reducing the amount of time spent searching through documents or contacting colleagues for assistance.

- **Competitive advantage**: Having a comprehensive search feature can give a business a competitive edge by making it easier for customers to find and purchase products or services, and providing a better overall user experience.

- **Improved decision-making**: With access to relevant and timely information through search, business leaders can make better decisions based on data-driven insights.

- **Cost savings**: By making it easier to find information, search can reduce the need for manual processes or redundant data entry, which can lead to cost savings and increased productivity.

In summary, search is a key feature of business because it enhances user experience, increases efficiency, provides a competitive advantage, improves decision-making, and saves costs.

Apache Solr

Apache Solr is a raging bull in the world of search platforms. It's like the LeBron James of search – powerful, versatile, and ready to dunk on the competition. Born out of the Apache Lucene project, Solr is an open-source, full-text search engine that lets you query large volumes of data at scale like a boss.

Now, let's break it down. Solr is built on top of Lucene, which is the engine behind the madness. It's got all the swagger you need: indexing, search, and analysis capabilities that make it a rock star in the text search game. Solr struts its stuff by providing additional infrastructure around Lucene, like a distributed search, fault tolerance, and a swanky REST-like API that's easier to use than a NutriBullet blender.

To understand how Solr works, picture yourself at an epic party where everyone's trying to find their soulmate. Solr is like the all-knowing host who knows the ins and outs of everyone's likes, dislikes, and deepest desires. When someone asks Solr to find their perfect match, it dives into its well-organized index (the little black book of data) and surfaces the best options based on the query.

Solr's importance to computation is like the importance of a Rolex on a Wall Street trader's wrist — it's a status symbol that screams efficiency and performance. As the world becomes increasingly data-driven, Solr steps up to the plate, helping businesses and organizations make sense of their data and deliver relevant information with lightning speed. It's the kind of tech that gets you ahead in the game.

In summary, Apache Solr is the search platform hero we never knew we needed. It's fast, flexible, and downright sexy when it comes to handling large-scale data. So, if you're looking to up your search game, Solr is the answer. Just remember, with great power comes great responsibility. Use it wisely, my friends.

RECAP: Apache Solr is a powerful, open-source search platform built on Apache Lucene, often used for enterprise search and analytics use cases. It offers robust text search capabilities, distributed searching, faceted search, and real-time indexing, enabling developers to create sophisticated, high-performance search applications with complex data relationships.

Amazon CloudSearch

This is an absolute beast of a service. Now, let me tell you something: Jeff Bezos and his army of e-commerce wizards over at Amazon have managed to make our lives simultaneously better and worse by putting everything we could possibly want at our fingertips. But Amazon isn't just about selling us stuff; it's also in the business of helping us find stuff. Enter Amazon CloudSearch, a fully managed search service that you can just plug and play to make your applications more powerful and your users less frustrated.

How does this bad boy work? Well, it's all about building a search index. You feed it your data, and it does the rest—auto scaling, monitoring, and patching—so you can sip on a Pellegrino while your application lets users find exactly what they're looking for. Amazon CloudSearch is equipped with powerful text processing and search capabilities, meaning it supports things like free text search, faceted search, and even geospatial search. And if you want to get fancy, you can customize your search configurations like a boss.

Now, why is Amazon CloudSearch important to computation? First off, we're living in an era where data is the new oil, and if you can't find what you're looking for in this ocean of data, you're basically on a one-way trip to Loserville. Having a robust search functionality is crucial to making sense of the endless digital cacophony we've created. Amazon CloudSearch helps companies and developers build a smarter, more efficient search experience, and that, my friends, is like giving your users a first-class ticket to Success Town.

So, to sum it up, Amazon CloudSearch is the result of the relentless pursuit of customer satisfaction by the Bezos Brigade. It lets you build powerful search applications without breaking a sweat, making sense of the data madness and elevating your user experience to stratospheric heights.

RECAP: Amazon CloudSearch is a scalable, fully managed search service provided by Amazon Web Services that enables developers to easily integrate fast and highly customizable search functionality into their applications. It offers features such as faceted search, geospatial search, and customizable ranking, handling all the complexity of running and scaling a search platform, so developers can focus on enhancing their applications.

Graylog

Let me introduce you to the marvelous world of Graylog, a tool that is nothing short of a rockstar in the realm of log management and data analysis. The sheer brilliance of Graylog lies in its ability to process and analyze the massive streams of data generated by modern computing systems. Think of it as the "Nirvana" of centralized logging, where it offers a cohesive, accessible, and visually appealing platform to dig deep into the mysteries of data.

At its core, Graylog is like the conductor of a grand symphony, elegantly orchestrating log data from various sources in real-time. It leverages the power of Elasticsearch, MongoDB, and a little magic from the Graylog server itself to bring data to life in ways that would leave the Einsteins of the world utterly flabbergasted.

Now, let's get down to the nitty-gritty of how Graylog works. You see, it all starts with the log data being sent to Graylog from multiple sources. Graylog then processes and enriches this data with its own secret sauce, which includes the use of extractors and pipelines. The data is then stored in Elasticsearch, a potent search engine and analytics platform, giving Graylog the power to run complex queries, create custom dashboards, and generate alerts that would make Tony Stark envious.

So, why is Graylog important to computation? Well, in this digital era, we're generating data at an unprecedented scale, and with great power comes great responsibility. Graylog provides organizations with the ability to monitor and analyze their systems and applications like never before, allowing them to detect anomalies, troubleshoot issues, and make data-driven decisions with the panache of a Silicon Valley mogul.

In essence, Graylog is the James Bond of the log management world – suave, sophisticated, and powerful. It's an indispensable asset in the high-stakes game of managing complex computing systems, ensuring that we continue to push the boundaries of what's possible and leave our mark on the digital frontier.

RECAP: Graylog is an open-source log management and analysis platform that allows you to aggregate, process, and analyze vast amounts of machine data from various sources in a centralized location. It offers powerful search capabilities, alerting functions, and data visualization tools, providing insights that can help with debugging, compliance, security investigations, and performance analysis.

Splunk

Splunk, in essence, is like the Sherlock Holmes of data analysis. It's an American company, founded in 2003, that delivers software for searching, monitoring, and analyzing machine-generated big data, all in real-time. They're focused on making that data both accessible and useful for businesses, so they can get insights and make better decisions. Think of it as the James Bond of software, sifting through data with suave precision.

Now, let's get to the "how." Splunk has this thing called the "Indexer," which is the engine that turns data into pure insight. It ingests raw data and indexes it into events, basically making it searchable. They've also got this nifty thing called "Search Heads" that let you query the indexed data. You can create real-time dashboards, alerts, and reports with this stuff. In short, Splunk takes raw, untamed data and turns it into something you can use, like unleashing a pack of data-hungry hounds to sniff out the clues you need.

So why does Splunk matter in computation, you ask? Well, my friend, in this era of big data and digital transformation, organizations have more data than they know what to do with. It's like being stranded in a sea of information, and without a good way to make sense of it all, you're just treading water. Splunk acts as a life raft, helping businesses navigate through the data deluge and gain valuable insights. It's crucial for cybersecurity, IT operations, and application management, among other things. In other words, Splunk is like the swiss army knife of data analysis.

In conclusion, Splunk is a vital tool for organizations looking to unlock the full potential of their data. By providing a platform for real-time analysis, monitoring, and searching, Splunk enables businesses to harness their data and make informed decisions. It's the secret sauce that separates winners from losers in today's data-driven world. So, if you're looking to up your game, you'd better get acquainted with Splunk, amigo.

RECAP: Splunk is a powerful software platform used for searching, analyzing, and visualizing the machine-generated data gathered from various sources across an organization's IT infrastructure. It transforms big data into insights for IT and business operations, enhancing performance, security, and compliance.

ElasticSearch

It's time to drop some wisdom bombs about this rad piece of technology called ElasticSearch. Picture this: you've got a mountain of data, and you need to find that one golden nugget of info, right? ElasticSearch is your ticket to ride that data wave like a boss.

ElasticSearch is an open-source, distributed search engine built on top of the Java-based library, Apache Lucene. Think of it as your personal jet-ski for navigating oceans of data at breakneck speed. It's optimized for searching and analyzing gobs of structured and unstructured data in real-time. Can I get an amen for real-time analytics?

Now, let's get down to the nitty-gritty of how this bad boy works. ElasticSearch is all about scale, resilience, and speed. It uses a distributed architecture that allows it to scale horizontally by spreading data across multiple nodes. And it's got this thing called "sharding," which lets it break data down into smaller chunks for faster searching. Oh, and did I mention it's got built-in replication for fault tolerance? Yeah, this thing is a beast.

But why should you care? Why is ElasticSearch important to computation? Well, my friends, we live in an era where data is the new oil. Data drives everything, from business decisions to consumer behavior. And ElasticSearch is like the supersonic jet that helps you find that sweet, sweet data nectar and make sense of it all.

ElasticSearch is a critical tool for businesses that want to stay agile, adaptive, and ahead of the competition. It helps you unlock the power of big data, spot trends and patterns, and make data-driven decisions that can skyrocket you to the top. And in today's cutthroat business world, if you're not leveraging the power of data, you might as well be paddling upstream without a paddle. You get the picture.

So there you have it, my data disciples. ElasticSearch is the bee's knees of search engines, the epitome of data prowess. It's how we tame the wild beast of information overload and ride the data wave like the digital rock stars we are. Now go forth and conquer, you data-driven dynamos!

RECAP: Elasticsearch is a highly scalable, open-source search and analytics engine that allows you to store, search, and analyze large volumes of data in near real-time. Built on Apache Lucene, it excels at full-text search, has powerful APIs, and can handle structured and unstructured data, making it a go-to solution for many diverse use cases ranging from log and event data analysis to distributed search for large-scale enterprise applications.

Data Analytics

Ladies and gentlemen, boys and girls, let's talk about data analytics for web technologies, and why it's the Beyoncé of the digital age. Oh yes, this is important, so perk up your ears and listen.

Data analytics for web technologies is all about collecting, analyzing, and interpreting information from your online presence. It's like having a backstage pass to your own digital concert. You get to know who's visiting, what they're doing, and how they're engaging with your website or app. It's a treasure trove of insights that lets you fine-tune your digital experience like a maestro.

Now, why is it so crucial to application design? Think of data analytics as the magic wand that turns your app into the unicorn of the digital world. It helps you understand your users' behavior, preferences, and pain points, and that's like gold. By leveraging these insights, you can create a user experience that's more addictive than an episode of Game of Thrones.

So how does data analytics discover and summarize useful information? Picture yourself as a digital Sherlock Holmes, uncovering patterns and trends in the data. With sophisticated tools and techniques like data mining, machine learning, and statistical analysis, you'll start connecting the dots like a pro.

Why is Data Analytics a Key Feature of Web Technologies?

Let's explore why data analytics is the secret sauce that takes web technologies from "meh" to "mind-blowing." In a world where digital presence is the new black, and every brand is fighting for attention, data analytics swoops in like a superhero to save the day.

Here are some compelling reasons why data analytics is a key feature of web technologies:

1. **Understanding user behavior:** As any savvy business person knows, knowledge is power. Data analytics enables you to dive deep into your users' minds, discovering their likes, dislikes, and everything in between. It's like having a crystal ball that reveals how users interact with your website or app, helping you create a user experience that's as satisfying as a perfectly brewed cup of coffee.

2. **Personalization:** In this era of digital revolution, personalization is the name of the

game. With data analytics, you can tailor content, offers, and recommendations to specific user segments or even individuals. This creates a feeling of "This was made just for me," increasing engagement, loyalty, and the chances of conversion. It's like having a digital concierge that knows your users better than they know themselves.

3. **Performance optimization**: Data analytics gives you the ability to identify the weak spots in your website or app, so you can optimize performance and deliver a seamless user experience. Think of it as a digital fitness coach that helps you tone and shape your online presence to achieve peak performance.

4. **Informed decision-making**: By leveraging data analytics, you can make data-driven decisions that are based on cold, hard facts, rather than gut feelings or intuition. This empowers the developer, engineer, and architects.

What Do We Mean By "Processing Data"?

Processing data refers to the manipulation and transformation of raw data into a format that is more useful and meaningful for a specific purpose. This involves performing various operations on the data, such as sorting, filtering, aggregating, calculating, and analyzing, using specialized software or programming tools.

Data processing can involve different stages, including data input, data validation and cleaning, data transformation, and data output. The ultimate goal of processing data is to extract valuable insights, trends, and patterns from the data, which can be used to inform decision-making, improve efficiency, and drive innovation in various fields such as business, science, healthcare, and education.

How Do We "Handle" Data?

There are several technologies that are all designed to handle large volumes of data in distributed environments and provide support for real-time and batch processing, machine learning, and other advanced analytics use cases. There are several popular frameworks for distributed storage and processing of large data sets on computer clusters. Here are some examples:

- **Hadoop**: Hadoop is an open-source framework that provides distributed storage and processing of large data sets. It consists of two main components: Hadoop Distributed File System (HDFS) for storage and MapReduce[24] for

---

[24] Behold! Let me tell you about MapReduce. It's a programming model and a software framework used for processing large data sets

processing. Hadoop has been widely used for big data analytics and is known for its scalability, fault tolerance, and cost-effectiveness.

- **Apache Spark**[25]: Spark is an open-source distributed computing framework that provides

---

in a distributed computing environment.

So, imagine you have a giant pile of data, like terabytes or even petabytes of data. How do you process all that data in a reasonable amount of time? That's where MapReduce comes in.

The basic idea behind MapReduce is to divide the data into small chunks and distribute them across a cluster of computers. Each computer then processes its chunk of data independently and sends the results back to a central computer for aggregation.

Now, let me break that down for you. The "map" function takes in a set of data and converts it into a set of key-value pairs. The "reduce" function takes in the output of the map function and combines the values with the same key.

What does this mean for you? It means you can process massive amounts of data quickly and efficiently. And it's not just for tech companies or data scientists, either. MapReduce is used in a variety of industries, from finance to healthcare to retail.

In summary, MapReduce is a powerful tool for processing large data sets in a distributed computing environment. It divides the data into small chunks and processes them independently, making it fast and efficient. So if you're dealing with big data, you better get to know MapReduce.

[25] What is The Apache Foundation?

Allow me to introduce you to the Apache Foundation—a non-profit organization that's like the fairy godmother of open-source

an interface for programming entire clusters with implicit data parallelism and fault tolerance. Spark is designed to support various workloads, including batch processing, streaming, SQL queries, and machine learning. Spark is known for its speed and ease of use, and it can run on various cluster managers, including Hadoop YARN[26], Apache Mesos[27], and Kubernetes[28].

---

software projects. Officially known as the Apache Software Foundation (ASF), it was established in 1999 and has been making open-source magic ever since.

The ASF provides a vibrant ecosystem for open-source projects to thrive. It offers resources, infrastructure, and guidance to help projects grow and flourish. Think of it as a greenhouse for open-source innovation, nurturing the seedlings of tomorrow's software solutions.

Additionally, the ASF believes that great ideas should rise to the top, regardless of their origin. By fostering an inclusive and meritocratic environment, the Foundation ensures that the best ideas and contributions get the recognition they deserve. It's like hosting an open-mic night for software developers, where everyone gets a chance to shine.

The Apache Foundation encourages collaboration between developers from diverse backgrounds and organizations. This melting pot of ideas and expertise fuels innovation and helps create better, more robust software. It's like hosting a global potluck dinner, where everyone brings their unique flavors to the table.

Many Apache projects have become the gold standard in their respective domains, like Apache HTTP Server, Hadoop, and Cassandra. The Foundation's commitment to quality and excellence has raised the bar for open-source software development.

- ~~Apache Flink: Flink is an open-source~~

²⁶ I just learned about Hadoop... but what is Hadoop Yarn?

So, you know Hadoop, right? It's the open-source software framework that provides distributed storage and processing of large data sets. Well, YARN is short for Yet Another Resource Negotiator, and it's a major component of Hadoop.

Think of YARN as the traffic cop for Hadoop. It manages all the resources on a cluster, including memory, CPU, and disk space. But that's not all, folks. YARN also handles scheduling and resource allocation for different applications running on the cluster.

Now, why is YARN such a big deal? Well, it allows Hadoop to support a wide variety of workloads beyond just MapReduce, which is what Hadoop was originally designed for. YARN enables Hadoop to support other distributed computing frameworks, such as Apache Spark and Apache Flink.

YARN also provides fault tolerance and scalability, allowing Hadoop clusters to handle massive amounts of data. And it's all open source, so anyone can use it and contribute to it.

So there you have it, folks. YARN is the unsung hero of the Hadoop ecosystem, managing all the resources and enabling Hadoop to support a wide range of workloads. And that's why it's such a big deal.

²⁷ Tell me more about Apache Mesos.

It's a distributed systems kernel that abstracts CPU, memory, storage, and other compute resources away from machines in a cluster.

In plain English, it's a powerful tool that lets you manage computer resources across a bunch of machines in a cluster. Think of it like a traffic cop for your computer servers - it helps to allocate resources to different applications as needed, without causing traffic jams or accidents.

distributed data processing framework that Mesos was built with scalability and fault-tolerance in mind, meaning it can handle large clusters of machines and recover from failures without disrupting service. It's also highly flexible, allowing you to run different types of applications side by side, whether it's containers, virtual machines, or good old-fashioned software.

So, why should you care about Mesos? Well, if you're running a large-scale operation with lots of machines, you need a way to manage all those resources efficiently. Mesos is designed to help you do just that. It lets you optimize resource utilization, improve application performance, and ensure high availability, all in a single, easy-to-use platform.

In short, Mesos is the glue that holds your computer cluster together, and it does it all with ease and flexibility.

28 What on earth is Kubernetes?

Well, let me tell you, it's a container orchestration platform that's taking the tech world by storm.

Think of it like a conductor of a symphony orchestra. Kubernetes manages and coordinates containers, which are like the individual instruments in the orchestra, to ensure they're all playing in harmony. It makes sure your applications are running smoothly, and if one container fails, it automatically replaces it with a new one.

Why is Kubernetes so hot right now? Well, it's incredibly scalable and can handle millions of containers across multiple nodes. Plus, it's open-source, which means anyone can use it and contribute to its development.

But what does that mean for you? Well, if you're running a large-scale application, Kubernetes can help you deploy, manage, and scale it with ease. It also provides a platform-agnostic way to manage your applications, so you can run them anywhere, whether it's in the cloud or on-premises.

provides low latency, high throughput, and fault tolerance. Flink is designed for streaming and batch processing, and it supports various programming languages, including Java, Scala, and Python. Flink provides built-in support for stateful streaming, complex event processing, and machine learning.

- **Apache Storm**: Storm is an open-source distributed real-time stream processing system that provides fault-tolerance and scalability. Storm is designed for processing high-volume, high-velocity data streams, and it provides a simple programming model based on spouts and bolts. Storm can integrate with various data sources and sinks, including Apache Kafka [29] and Hadoop HDFS.

Now, I know what you're thinking. "But Brian, isn't Kubernetes complicated to use?" Sure, it can be a bit daunting at first, but there are plenty of resources out there to help you get started. And once you get the hang of it, you'll wonder how you ever managed without it.

So, there you have it. Kubernetes is the conductor of the container orchestra, making sure your applications run smoothly and scale effortlessly. It's a game-changer for large-scale application development, and it's not going anywhere anytime soon.

[29] Kafka? What's Apache Kafka?

Okay, so picture this: you have a ton of data. And I mean a ton. It's coming in from all different sources, at all different speeds, and in all different formats. How do you make sense of it all? Enter

- **Apache Cassandra**: Cassandra is an open-source distributed NoSQL database that provides high availability, fault tolerance, and scalability. Cassandra is designed to handle large volumes of structured and unstructured data, and it provides a flexible data model based on a key-value store. Cassandra supports various data access patterns, including random reads and writes, range scans, and full-text search.

- **Apache HBase**: HBase is a NoSQL database that is designed for storing and retrieving large volumes of structured data in real-time. It is

Apache Kafka.

Apache Kafka is an open-source, distributed streaming platform that lets you manage all that data in real-time. It's like a giant, high-speed conveyor belt for data, delivering it from its source to its destination at lightning-fast speeds.

But that's not all. Kafka is also designed to be highly scalable and fault-tolerant, meaning it can handle massive amounts of data and keep going even if something goes wrong. It's like the superhero of data management.

Now, you might be wondering, "Brian, how does Kafka actually work?" Great question. Kafka is built on a pub/sub model, which means data is organized into topics, and each topic has multiple publishers and subscribers. This allows for multiple streams of data to be processed in parallel, without any bottlenecks.

And here's the best part: Kafka can integrate with all sorts of other data management systems, like Hadoop, Spark, and Flink. So if you're already using those systems, Kafka can fit right in and make your life even easier.

built on top of Hadoop and provides support for random access to data.

Overall, these frameworks provide powerful tools for processing and analyzing large data sets in a distributed computing environment. They provide various features, including fault tolerance, scalability, and support for various programming languages and workloads.

Hadoop

Hadoop, the godfather of big data processing! Allow me to break down its role in data analytics like a boss.

Hadoop is an open-source framework that was designed to store and process massive amounts of data in a distributed computing environment. It plays a pivotal role in the world of data analytics by enabling companies to harness the true potential of their data. Here's how Hadoop flexes its muscles in data analytics:

- **Scalability**: Hadoop can handle data in biblical proportions, thanks to its distributed storage system, HDFS (Hadoop Distributed File System). It lets you scale up or down as needed, simply by adding or removing nodes. It's like having an elastic waistband for your data storage—snug, secure, and ready to adapt.

- **Cost-effectiveness**: Traditional data storage and processing systems can cost an arm and a leg, but Hadoop is the Robin Hood of the data world. Its open-source nature and ability to work with commodity hardware make it an affordable option for organizations of all sizes. Hadoop lets you store and process data without breaking the bank.

- **Fault tolerance**: Hadoop has your back when it comes to data reliability. Its distributed architecture ensures that data is replicated across multiple nodes, so if one node fails, the show goes on. Hadoop is like the superhero who keeps your data safe, even in the face of adversity.

- **Processing power**: With its data processing engine, MapReduce, Hadoop can process vast amounts of data in parallel, significantly reducing processing time. It's like having a fleet of Ferraris to navigate the data highway, getting you to your destination faster than ever.

- **Flexibility**: Hadoop doesn't discriminate when it comes to data. Structured, unstructured, or semi-structured—Hadoop can handle it all.

Apache Spark

Let me tell you about Apache Spark. This is a big data processing framework that is designed to handle massive amounts of data with speed and ease. Think of it as a supercharged engine for your data analytics needs. Spark allows you to process data in real-time and supports various workloads, including batch processing, streaming, SQL queries, and machine learning. It's like having a Swiss Army Knife for your data needs.

Now, why should you care about Apache Spark? Well, it enables you to process and analyze data faster and more efficiently than ever before. With Spark, you can extract valuable insights from your data that can help you make better business decisions and gain a competitive edge in your industry. Plus, it's open-source, so it's cost-effective and flexible.

So, if you're looking to process and analyze large amounts of data with speed and ease, Apache Spark is the way to go. It's a game-changer in the world of big data analytics.

RECAP: Apache Spark is an open-source, distributed computing system that provides an interface for programming entire clusters with implicit data parallelism and fault tolerance. It's widely used for big data processing and analytics, offering robust capabilities for data ETL, SQL queries, machine learning, and stream processing within a single unified framework.

Apache Flink

We're gonna talk about Apache Flink - a real-time data processing framework that's taking the tech world by storm.

Now, Flink is like a superhero that can handle huge amounts of data with lightning-fast speed. It's designed for streaming and batch processing, which means it can process data as it comes in, and also work with large data sets that are stored offline.

Think about it this way - Flink is like a personal assistant that can handle all your data needs. It can help you sort through vast amounts of information, analyze it, and give you insights in real-time. That means you can make decisions faster, and stay ahead of the competition.

But that's not all, folks! Flink is also highly flexible and can work with a variety of programming languages. So, whether you're a Java, Scala, or Python expert, Flink's got your back.

In short, Apache Flink is a powerful tool that can help businesses process and analyze large data sets in real-time, and make data-driven decisions faster.

RECAP: Apache Flink is an open-source, unified stream and batch processing framework designed for big data computations. It excels at processing vast amounts of data in real-time with high speed and reliability, making it ideal for applications that require real-time analytics, machine learning, and event-driven applications.

Apache Storm

Let's talk about Apache Storm. This is a piece of software that helps process high-volume data streams in real-time. Think about it like this, you've got a ton of data coming in from different sources, like social media feeds, website traffic, or weather sensors. That's a lot of information to handle, right?

Well, Apache Storm is like the ultimate traffic cop for all that data. It takes in all the information and sorts it out, so you can make sense of it all. It does this by breaking the data down into tiny pieces, like puzzle pieces, and then passing them through different processing stages. These stages could include filtering out certain types of data, calculating metrics, or storing the information in a database.

The coolest thing about Apache Storm is that it's really fast and can handle a massive amount of data without breaking a sweat. It's designed to be fault-tolerant, which means that if one processing stage fails, the rest of the system can keep running. This makes it a really reliable tool for handling large-scale data streams in real-time.

So, in a nutshell, Apache Storm is like the ultimate data superhero, helping you make sense of massive amounts of information quickly and reliably. It's a powerful tool for businesses and organizations that need to keep track of real-time data and make informed decisions based on that information.

RECAP: Apache Storm is an open-source, real-time computation system that allows for processing of large volumes of high-velocity data. It's designed for distributed computing, providing robust reliability and scalability, making it ideal for applications requiring real-time analytics, online machine learning, continuous computation, and more.

Apache Cassandra

Imagine you have a ton of data that you need to store and retrieve quickly. That's where Apache Cassandra comes in.

It's an open-source distributed database management system that's designed for storing and retrieving large volumes of structured and unstructured data with high availability and low latency.

Now, what does that mean? It means that if you're a business with a lot of data, like a big retailer or a financial institution, you can use Apache Cassandra to store all of that data in a way that makes it easy to access and use. Plus, it's scalable and can handle massive amounts of data, so you don't have to worry about it slowing down as you grow.

And let's be real, in today's world, data is everything. You need to be able to quickly access and analyze your data in order to make smart decisions and stay competitive. Apache Cassandra makes that possible.

So there you have it, folks. Apache Cassandra is a powerful tool that helps businesses store and retrieve large volumes of data quickly and easily. It's like having a supercharged database that can handle anything you throw at it.

RECAP: Apache Cassandra is a highly scalable, distributed NoSQL database designed to handle large amounts of data across many commodity servers, providing high availability with no single point of failure. It offers robust support for clusters spanning multiple datacenters, with asynchronous masterless replication allowing low latency operations for all clients.

Apache HBase

Let me tell you about Apache HBase. It's a NoSQL, column-oriented database management system built on top of the Hadoop Distributed File System (HDFS).

What does that mean for you? Well, it means HBase is a powerful tool for storing and retrieving large amounts of structured data in real-time. Think of it like a giant Excel spreadsheet, but on steroids.

HBase is designed to handle petabytes of data, and it can do so while maintaining high availability and low latency. It's also highly scalable, meaning you can add more nodes to the cluster as your data grows.

Now, I know what you're thinking. "But Brian, how is HBase different from other databases?" Great question, my friend. HBase is built for random access to data, meaning you can easily retrieve specific rows and columns of data without having to scan through the entire database.

In short, if you're dealing with massive amounts of data and need a database that can handle it all in real-time, Apache HBase is the way to go. It's fast, scalable, and designed for random access to data. And that's what I call a win-win-win.

RECAP: Apache HBase is a highly scalable, open-source, distributed database system designed to store and process large volumes of data across clusters of commodity servers. It's a part of the Apache Software Foundation's Hadoop project and built on the Hadoop Distributed File System (HDFS), providing BigTable-like capabilities for Hadoop, hence offering a fault-tolerant way of storing large quantities of sparse data.

Chapter Eight

What Infrastructure Does?

Let's talk about the infrastructure layer of a web application. Think of it as the backbone, the underlying foundation that supports the entire operation.

This layer consists of hardware and software components that work together to provide the necessary resources for the web application to function. These components include servers, storage devices, networking equipment, operating systems, and databases.

Now, I know what you're thinking. "Brian, why is the infrastructure layer so important?" Well, my friend, it's simple. The infrastructure layer directly affects the performance and reliability of the web application.

If the servers are slow, the storage is limited, or the network is unreliable, the web application will suffer.

This can result in slow load times, errors, crashes, and other issues that will drive users away.

That's why it's crucial to have a robust infrastructure layer that can handle the demands of the web application. This means having enough servers to handle the traffic, enough storage to store the data, and a reliable network to connect everything together.

In summary, the infrastructure layer is the foundation of a web application. It consists of hardware and software components that provide the necessary resources for the web application to function.

What Makes Up The Infrastructure of a Web App?

This is the backbone of any web app, the plumbing that keeps everything running smoothly.

At its core, the infrastructure layer is made up of servers, databases, and networks. These are the foundational components that enable a web application to function.

First up, we have servers. These are the machines that host the web application and handle incoming requests. They can range from physical machines to virtual servers in the cloud, and they're responsible for processing user requests, serving up content, and handling any backend processing that needs to be done.

Next, we have databases. These are the repositories where all the data for the web application is stored. Databases can come in many different flavors, but the most common ones are relational databases like MySQL or PostgreSQL, or NoSQL databases like MongoDB or Cassandra. The type of database used depends on the needs of the application and the data being stored.

Finally, we have networks. These are the connections between all the different components of the infrastructure layer. Networks enable data to flow between servers and databases, and they ensure that everything is communicating with each other properly.

So, there you have it! The infrastructure layer is the foundation of any web application, and it's made up of servers, databases, and networks. These are the building blocks that enable web applications to function and serve up content to users all over the world.

Server

Let's talk about servers in the infrastructure layer. Now, servers are the backbone of any digital infrastructure. They are the hardware components that provide computing power, storage, and networking resources to support various applications and services.

Think of servers like the workhorses of the internet. They handle all the heavy lifting, from serving web pages and processing transactions to storing data and running applications. Without servers, we wouldn't have the fast, reliable, and scalable digital services we rely on every day.

Now, servers can come in different forms, from physical machines to virtual servers and cloud-based instances. But regardless of the form factor, servers are essential for building a robust and scalable infrastructure layer that can handle the demands of modern digital services.

In short, servers play a critical role in the infrastructure layer by providing the necessary computing, storage, and networking resources to support various digital services. Without them, we wouldn't have the fast and reliable digital experiences we've come to expect.

RECAP: A server is a powerful computer that provides data, services, or resources to other computers, known as clients, over a network. It's designed to process requests and deliver data to other computers over a local network or the internet, playing a key role in the functioning of everything from websites to email, file sharing, and streaming.

Virtualization

Let's talk about virtualization. It's the act of creating a virtual version of something, like a computer, a server, or a network. It's like creating a digital version of a physical thing.

So, why is virtualization important? Well, it allows you to do more with less. Instead of having to buy a bunch of physical servers or computers, you can create virtual versions of them and run multiple virtual machines on a single physical machine. This means you can save money on hardware, reduce energy costs, and increase efficiency.

Virtualization also makes it easier to manage your resources. You can allocate resources like memory, storage, and processing power to each virtual machine as needed, and you can easily move virtual machines between physical machines without having to worry about compatibility issues.

But wait, there's more! Virtualization also makes it easier to test and develop new software. Instead of having to set up a bunch of physical machines for testing, you can create virtual machines that mimic different environments and configurations. This allows you to test your software in a controlled environment without having to worry about damaging your physical machines.

So, there you have it, folks. Virtualization is like creating a digital version of a physical thing, and it allows you to do more with less, manage your resources more efficiently, and test and develop software more easily. It's a win-win-win.

RECAP: Virtualization is a technology that allows for the creation of simulated, or "virtual," resources, such as servers, storage devices, network resources, and operating systems, from a single physical hardware system. It enables multiple software environments to coexist and operate independently on the same physical computer, thereby improving efficiency, scalability, and reducing costs.

Life Before Virtualization

Before virtualization, hosting providers had to work a lot harder to deliver their services. Back in the day, hosting providers had to rely on physical servers to host their clients' websites and applications.

This meant that hosting providers had to manage a lot of hardware, from the servers themselves to the storage, networking, and power infrastructure. It was a real pain in the you-know-what.

And when a client needed more resources, like additional CPU or RAM, the hosting provider would have to physically add new hardware to the server, which could take a lot of time and money. It was like building a new house every time someone needed a bigger living room.

But then came virtualization, and everything changed. Virtualization allowed hosting providers to create multiple virtual machines on a single physical server, with each VM running its own operating system and applications. This meant that hosting providers could offer more flexible and scalable services, without having to deal with all the hardware headaches.

With virtualization, hosting providers could quickly provision new resources to clients on the fly, without having to physically add new hardware. And if a client's needs changed, hosting providers could simply adjust the resources allocated to their VMs, instead of having to rebuild the entire server from scratch.

So, in short, virtualization made life a lot easier for hosting providers. It allowed them to offer more flexible, scalable, and cost-effective services to their clients, without having to manage all the hardware themselves. And that, my friends, is what we call progress.

Types of Virtualization

There are several types of virtualization, each with its own unique tricks up its sleeve. Let's dive into the key types:

- **Server virtualization**: This is the Houdini of the virtualization world, making multiple virtual servers appear out of thin air using just one physical server. Server virtualization relies on a hypervisor, which divides the physical server's resources among the virtual machines, maximizing efficiency and reducing costs.

- **Storage virtualization**: Picture this as a masterful illusion, where multiple storage devices are pooled together and presented as a single, unified storage resource. Storage virtualization simplifies management, optimizes resource utilization, and makes data migration a breeze.

- **Network virtualization**: Abracadabra! Network virtualization transforms the physical network infrastructure into a flexible, software-based entity. This type of virtualization allows for the creation of multiple virtual networks on a single physical network, enabling better resource management, isolation, and security.

- **Application virtualization**: Imagine a world where applications can run independently of the underlying operating system—enter application virtualization. By encapsulating an application in a virtual container, it can be executed without installing it on the user's device. This reduces compatibility issues, simplifies application management, and enhances security.

- **Desktop virtualization**: Desktop virtualization, also known as Virtual Desktop Infrastructure (VDI), is like having a digital doppelgänger for your computer. It separates the desktop environment, including the operating system and applications, from the physical device and stores it on a remote server. Users can access their virtual desktops from any device, providing flexibility, centralized management, and improved security.

So, there you have it—the wondrous world of virtualization, where technology works its magic to make the impossible possible.

Containers

Imagine you're packing for a trip, and you need to organize all your stuff efficiently. You don't want your shoes squished up against your clothes, and you don't want your toiletries spilling everywhere. That's where containers come in.

In the world of tech, containers are like virtual boxes that allow you to organize and package up all the components of an application, like code, libraries, and dependencies. Think of them as little compartments that keep everything in its place, and make it easy to move the application from one environment to another, like from a developer's laptop to a production server.

Containers are lightweight, which means they don't require a lot of resources to run, and they're also highly portable. That makes them a popular choice for companies that want to build and deploy applications quickly and efficiently.

Now, I know what you're thinking. "But Brian, how are containers different from virtual machines?" Well, my friend, while virtual machines emulate an entire computer system, including an operating system, containers only package up the application and its dependencies. That means they're much more efficient and faster to deploy than virtual machines.

So there you have it, folks. Containers are like virtual boxes that make it easy to organize and move applications from one environment to another. They're lightweight, highly portable, and efficient.

RECAP: Containers are stand-alone, lightweight packages of software that include everything needed to run an application: the code, a runtime, libraries, environment variables, and system tools. They provide a consistent and reproducible environment across different stages of development and deployment, ensuring that the application runs the same way, irrespective of the underlying host system.

Types of Containers

Containers are all the rage these days. And as someone who's always ahead of the curve, I can tell you that there are several types of virtual containers out there that you need to know about.

First, we've got Docker containers. Docker is the big daddy of virtual containers and it's what most people think of when they hear the term. Docker containers are lightweight and portable, which means you can move them between environments without any fuss. Plus, Docker has a huge community of users and developers, which means you've got lots of resources available to you.

Next up, we've got Kubernetes containers. Kubernetes is a container orchestration platform that makes it easier to manage Docker containers at scale. With Kubernetes, you can automate deployment, scaling, and management of containerized applications. It's a powerful tool that's become a must-have for many organizations.

Then there's LXC (Linux Containers). LXC is an operating system-level virtualization method for running multiple isolated Linux systems (containers) on a single control host. It's a lightweight option that's great for running multiple instances of the same application.

Last but not least, we've got OpenVZ containers. OpenVZ is a container-based virtualization technology for Linux. It uses a single Linux kernel to run multiple isolated virtual environments, which makes it efficient and lightweight. OpenVZ is great for running multiple applications on a single server, without any of them interfering with each other.

Docker

Docker—the game-changing technology that has taken the software world by storm. Docker is an open-source platform designed to automate the process of developing, deploying, and running applications inside lightweight, portable containers. Think of it as a genie that grants your wish for a hassle-free, consistent environment across development, testing, and production stages.

But what does Docker do, and how does it work its magic? Let's find out:

- **Containerization**: Docker's main trick is containerization. A Docker container packages an application, along with its dependencies, libraries, and runtime environment, into a neat little box. This ensures that the application runs consistently, no matter where it's deployed. It's like packing your suitcase for a trip, with everything you need neatly organized and ready to go.

- **Isolation**: Docker containers are isolated from each other and the host system, which means they run independently without interfering with one another. This minimizes conflicts and enhances security. It's like having your own private cabin on a cruise ship—cozy, secure, and undisturbed.

- **Lightweight and efficient**: Unlike traditional virtual machines that require a full operating system for each instance, Docker containers share the host OS's kernel. This makes them significantly lighter and faster, so you can run more containers on the same hardware. It's like traveling light, leaving the bulky baggage behind.

- **Portability**: Docker containers can run on any platform that supports Docker, which makes moving applications between environments a breeze. It's like having a universal travel adapter that fits any socket, anywhere in the world.

- **Version control and collaboration**: Docker uses images to create containers. These images can be version-controlled and shared with others, fostering collaboration and ensuring everyone is on the same page. It's like having a shared recipe book that everyone can access, contribute to, and learn from.

RECAP: Docker is an open-source platform that automates the deployment, scaling, and management of applications by encapsulating them into containers. These containers package up an application with everything it needs, such as libraries and system tools, enabling it to run consistently on any machine, thereby enhancing portability and simplifying software development.

Kubernetes

Kubernetes, also known as K8s is the maestro that orchestrates the complex symphony of containerized applications. Born in the hallowed halls of Google and later donated to the Cloud Native Computing Foundation (CNCF)[30], Kubernetes is an open-source

---

[30] What is the CNCF?

Simply put, it's an open-source software foundation that was created to advance the development and adoption of cloud-native computing technologies. In other words, they want to help companies build and run scalable, resilient, and portable applications in the cloud.

Now, you might be thinking, "Brian, what's the big deal? We already have cloud computing, why do we need cloud-native computing?" Well, my friends, cloud-native computing takes it to the next level. It's all about building applications that are designed to run in the cloud from the ground up. This means they're more efficient, more flexible, and more reliable than traditional applications.

The CNCF is home to some of the most exciting projects in the tech world, including Kubernetes, Prometheus, and Envoy. These are all open-source projects that are designed to help companies

container orchestration platform that automates the deployment, scaling, and management of containerized applications.

So, what does Kubernetes do? Let me break it down:

Deployment: Kubernetes ensures that your application is deployed seamlessly across a cluster of machines, taking care of the nitty-gritty details so you can focus on what matters—your application.

Scaling: Kubernetes can scale your application up or down based on demand, like a skilled conductor adapting the tempo of a performance to captivate the audience.

Load balancing: Kubernetes distributes the incoming traffic among your application's instances, ensuring that no single container bears the brunt of the workload. It's

---

build and run cloud-native applications.

So, why should you care about the CNCF? Because it's the future of computing, folks. As more and more companies move to the cloud, they're going to need to adopt cloud-native technologies to stay competitive. And the CNCF is leading the way.

In summary, the CNCF is the go-to organization for anyone who wants to build and run cloud-native applications. They're pushing the boundaries of what's possible in the cloud, and they're doing it in an open, collaborative way. So, if you're not paying attention to the CNCF, you're missing out on the future of computing, my friends.

like a skilled choreographer ensuring that every dancer has a chance to shine.

Self-healing: Kubernetes is like a digital superhero, constantly monitoring the health of your application and taking action when things go awry. If a container fails, Kubernetes replaces it with a healthy one, ensuring that the show goes on.

But how does Kubernetes work its magic? Let's dive into its inner workings:

- **Cluster**: A Kubernetes cluster is a set of machines, called nodes, that run containerized applications. A cluster can have multiple nodes, providing high availability and fault tolerance.

- **Nodes**: Nodes are the worker machines that run containerized applications. They can be physical or virtual machines, and they're managed by the control plane. A node has a container runtime (e.g., Docker) to run containers and the kubelet agent to communicate with the control plane.

- **Control Plane**: The control plane is a set of components that manage the overall state of the cluster. It includes:

    o **API Server**: The central point of communication for the cluster, exposing the Kubernetes API. It processes and validates

REST requests and updates the etcd store with the desired state.

- **etcd**: A distributed key-value store that holds the configuration data and the state of the cluster.

- **Controller Manager**: Runs various controllers responsible for maintaining the desired state, such as the replication controller, which ensures the desired number of replicas for a given application.

- **Scheduler**: Assigns newly created pods to nodes based on resource availability, user-defined constraints, and other factors.

- **Pods**: The smallest and simplest unit in Kubernetes, a pod represents a single instance of a running application. It can contain one or more containers that share the same network namespace, allowing them to communicate via localhost.

- **Services**: A Kubernetes service is an abstraction that defines a set of pods and a policy to access them.

This is to say, think of it like this, folks: you're at a fancy restaurant, and you're trying to order some food. The waiter takes your order and brings it to the kitchen, where the chef prepares your meal. Now, the chef is working hard in the kitchen, but you don't need to know or care about that. All you care about is getting your food when it's ready.

Well, in a Kubernetes cluster, you have pods that are running your application code, just like the chef in the kitchen. And a Kubernetes service is like the waiter that brings your food to the table. It provides a stable IP address and DNS name for a set of pods, so that clients can access them without needing to know anything about the underlying infrastructure.

So, there you have it, folks. Kubernetes services are like waiters in a fancy restaurant, providing a stable and reliable way for clients to access your application code without needing to know anything about the underlying infrastructure. And that's how Kubernetes makes it easy to manage and scale your containerized applications.

RECAP: Kubernetes, often referred to as K8s, is an open-source platform designed to automate deploying, scaling, and managing containerized applications. It provides a framework to run distributed systems resiliently, scaling horizontally, providing load balancing, orchestrating storage, and more.

LXC

Linux Containers are like those Russian nesting dolls, you know? The ones where you have a big doll, and inside that, you have a smaller doll, and so on? Only in this case, the dolls are actually applications.

See, Linux Containers are a way to package up software applications so that they can run anywhere, on any machine, without any fuss or bother. It's like putting your app in a box and carrying it around with you wherever you go.

But here's the real kicker: Linux Containers are incredibly lightweight. They don't weigh down your system, they don't take up a lot of space, and they don't require a lot of resources to run. That means you can have a lot of different applications running on a single machine, without any of them getting in each other's way.

And that, my friends, is why Linux Containers are such a big deal. They make it easier and more efficient to run all kinds of software applications, from the simple to the complex, from the desktop to the cloud. And they do it all without breaking the bank or causing you any headaches.

So, in summary, Linux Containers are like those Russian nesting dolls, only for applications. They're lightweight, efficient, and incredibly useful for anyone who needs to run a lot of different applications on a single machine. And that's why you should care about Linux Containers, my friends.

RECAP: Linux Containers (LXC) is an open-source lightweight virtualization technology that allows the creation and management of isolated Linux virtual environments on a single host. It works at the operating system level, enabling multiple Linux distributions to run simultaneously on the same hardware while maintaining a high level of isolation between containers.

OpenVZ

This is a virtualization technology that's used to create multiple virtual environments on a single physical server. Think of it like a digital hotel, where you have one physical building, but many virtual rooms.

Now, what makes OpenVZ unique is that it's based on containerization. What does that mean? It means that each virtual environment created by OpenVZ is completely isolated from the others. Think of it like having multiple Tupperware containers, each with its own food inside. If something goes wrong with one container, the others are still safe and sound.

And let me tell you, folks, this technology is fast. Because each virtual environment is isolated, there's no need for a full-blown operating system to be installed in each one. That means less overhead and faster performance. And in today's world, where speed is king, that's a big deal.

RECAP: OpenVZ is a server virtualization solution that allows for the creation and management of multiple isolated, secure

Linux containers (also known as VPSs) on a single physical server. These containers behave much like a stand-alone server but share system resources, such as kernel, hardware, and network, offering efficient utilization, high performance, and easy scalability.

Serverless

Step right up and witness the marvels of the serverless world—a paradigm shift that's transforming the way we build and deploy applications.

When we say something is "serverless," we're not talking about a world without servers (plot twist!). Instead, we're referring to a cloud computing execution model where the cloud provider dynamically manages the allocation of resources and servers for you. It's like having an invisible army of servers at your command, ready to scale up or down as needed.

In a serverless architecture, you only pay for the actual compute time and resources consumed by your application, instead of pre-allocating server capacity. This on-demand approach results in cost savings, improved scalability, and reduced operational overhead.

Serverless computing is often associated with Functions as a Service (FaaS), where developers can write and deploy individual functions or pieces of code that are triggered by specific events. Some popular serverless platforms include AWS Lambda, Azure Functions, and Google Cloud Functions.

In summary, serverless is a cloud-based wonderland that frees developers from the burden of server management and allows them to focus on what they do best—creating game-changing applications that delight users and leave the competition in the dust.

RECAP: Serverless computing is a cloud computing model where the cloud provider dynamically manages the allocation and provisioning of servers. This allows developers to focus on building applications without worrying about server management, infrastructure scaling, or capacity planning.

The Serverlessness of the Cloud

Well, buckle up folks because we're about to talk about the wild world of serverless technologies!

First off, let's clarify what we mean by "serverless". This doesn't mean there are no servers involved (that would be impossible), but rather that the server management and infrastructure is handled by a third-party cloud provider. This means developers can focus on writing code rather than managing servers.

So, what are some examples of serverless technologies? Let's start with AWS Lambda, which is one of the most popular. Lambda allows developers to run code without having to provision, scale, or manage servers. It supports a variety of programming languages and can be used for a wide range of applications, from simple webhooks to complex data processing pipelines.

Next up, we've got Google Cloud Functions, which is Google's serverless offering. Like Lambda, Cloud Functions allows developers to write code without worrying about the underlying infrastructure. It supports a variety of triggers, including HTTP requests and Cloud Pub/Sub[31] events, and integrates seamlessly with other Google Cloud services.

Another option is Microsoft Azure Functions, which is Microsoft's serverless offering. Azure Functions supports a variety of programming languages and integrates with a wide range of Azure services. It also

---

[31] What is Pub/Sub?

Oh, Cloud Pub/Sub, the beating heart of Google Cloud's data streaming capabilities! This is a service that allows you to ingest and distribute messages of all shapes and sizes at lightning-fast speeds. It's like having your very own digital postal service that can handle an endless stream of letters, packages, and parcels without breaking a sweat.

Now, let me break it down for you. Cloud Pub/Sub is essentially a messaging service that helps you decouple your applications and services. You can think of it as a middleman that ensures seamless communication between all the different components of your cloud-based infrastructure. Whether it's sending notifications, processing events, or sharing data between different services, Cloud Pub/Sub has got you covered.

But what really sets Cloud Pub/Sub apart from other messaging services is its scalability and reliability. This thing can handle millions of messages per second without breaking a sweat. And even if there are hiccups along the way, Cloud Pub/Sub will ensure that your messages get delivered to their intended recipients without fail.

offers built-in monitoring and debugging tools to help developers troubleshoot their code.

But wait, there's more!

We've also got serverless databases, like Amazon DynamoDB and Google Cloud Firestore. These databases scale automatically and allow developers to focus on writing queries rather than managing the underlying infrastructure.

In conclusion, serverless technologies are a game-changer for developers who want to focus on writing code rather than managing servers. AWS Lambda, Google Cloud Functions, and Microsoft Azure Functions are just a few examples of the many serverless offerings available.

RECAP: Serverless computing is a cloud-computing model where the cloud provider dynamically manages the allocation and provisioning of servers, freeing developers from server management duties. This allows developers to focus on building their applications' core functionality, while the infrastructure, including computing resources and scaling, is handled automatically by the cloud provider.

AWS Lambda

Hey there, let me tell you about AWS Lambda. It's a serverless computing service provided by Amazon Web

Services (AWS), which means that you don't have to worry about managing servers or infrastructure.

Think of it like a pay-as-you-go service that allows you to run your code without the need to provision or manage servers. That's pretty cool, right?

So how does it work? Well, you write your code, upload it to Lambda, and then Lambda automatically provisions and scales the infrastructure needed to run your code. And the best part? You only pay for the computing time that you actually use.

That's why AWS Lambda is perfect for running small, event-driven functions in response to events like changes to a database or an incoming email. You can run your code in response to these events without having to pay for a full-time server.

AWS Lambda supports various programming languages, including Node.js, Python, Java, and C#. It also integrates with other AWS services, like Amazon S3 and Amazon DynamoDB.

In summary, AWS Lambda is a serverless computing service that allows you to run your code without having to worry about servers or infrastructure. It's perfect for running small, event-driven functions in response to events like changes to a database.

RECAP: AWS Lambda is a serverless computing service provided by Amazon Web Services, allowing developers to run their code without having to manage servers. It automatically scales and monitors your applications, only charging for the compute time when the code is running, making it cost-effective and efficient.

Google Cloud Functions

In short, Cloud Functions is a serverless compute platform that lets you run event-driven code in response to triggers such as HTTP requests, changes to data in a database, or the uploading of a file to a storage bucket.

Think of it like a virtual assistant that automatically performs tasks for you without you having to lift a finger. With Cloud Functions, you can focus on writing the code that powers your application, while Google takes care of the underlying infrastructure and scaling.

Now, I know what you're thinking, "Brian, what does all of that tech jargon mean for the average person?" Simply put, it means that Cloud Functions can help you build more efficient, scalable, and responsive applications.

For example, if you're building a web application and want to process user input in real-time, you can use Cloud Functions to automatically execute code every time a user submits a form or makes a request. This can help you save time and resources by reducing the need for manual intervention and enabling you to focus on developing the core features of your application.

Overall, Google Cloud Functions is a powerful tool that can help you streamline your development process and build better applications. So, whether you're a seasoned developer or just starting out, it's definitely worth checking out.

RECAP: Google Cloud Functions is a serverless, event-driven computing service offered by Google Cloud Platform that allows developers to design and connect cloud services with code. It enables the creation of single-purpose, stand-alone functions that respond to cloud events without the need to manage a server or a runtime environment, enhancing productivity and scalability.

Microsoft Azure Functions

Now, you might be wondering, what the heck is Azure Functions? Well, let me tell you, it's a serverless computing platform that allows developers to build, deploy, and scale event-driven functions.

So, what does that mean? Think of it like a bunch of little robots that are programmed to do specific tasks, and they only wake up when they're needed. Azure Functions allows developers to create these little robots, or functions, that run in response to events such as a new file being uploaded or a database update.

One of the coolest things about Azure Functions is that you only pay for the time your function runs, not for the time it's idle. So, if your function only runs for a few seconds, that's all you pay for. This makes it an extremely cost-effective way to run your applications.

Another great thing about Azure Functions is that it integrates with a wide variety of other Microsoft services and tools, such as Azure Event Grid, Azure Cosmos DB, and Visual Studio. This makes it easy to build and deploy your functions, and to integrate them into your existing workflows.

In short, Microsoft Azure Functions is a powerful serverless computing platform that allows developers to build, deploy, and scale event-driven functions in a cost-effective and efficient manner.

RECAP: Microsoft Azure Functions is a serverless computing service that allows you to run event-triggered pieces of code without having to explicitly provision or manage infrastructure. It enables developers to build, deploy, and scale applications quickly and efficiently, supporting a variety of programming languages such as C#, JavaScript, Python, and more.

Amazon DynamoDB

So, what is it?

Well, simply put, DynamoDB is a fully managed NoSQL database service offered by Amazon Web Services (AWS).

Now, I know what you're thinking. "Brian, what's so special about it?" Great question. Here's the deal: DynamoDB is designed for high scalability, performance, and availability. It can handle any amount of data and any level of traffic, without any degradation in performance.

Plus, DynamoDB is fully managed, which means you don't have to worry about the operational aspects of running a database. AWS takes care of all the heavy lifting, so you can focus on building your applications.

One of the coolest things about DynamoDB is its flexible data model. It supports both document and key-value data models, which means you can store and retrieve any type of data, whether it's structured or unstructured. Plus, it integrates with other AWS services, like Lambda and API Gateway, so you can build powerful serverless applications with ease.

But, of course, with great power comes great responsibility. DynamoDB can get expensive if you're not careful, and there's a bit of a learning curve when it comes to its query language. But overall, if you're looking for a scalable, high-performance, fully managed NoSQL database, DynamoDB is definitely worth considering.

RECAP: Amazon DynamoDB is a fully managed, multi-region, multi-active, durable database with built-in security, backup and restore, and in-memory caching for internet-scale applications. As a NoSQL database service, it provides fast and predictable performance with seamless scalability, making it a great choice for mobile, web, gaming, ad tech, IoT, and many other applications.

Google Cloud Firestore

Alright, let me tell you about Google Cloud Firestore. It's a fully managed, cloud-native NoSQL document database that's designed to store and sync data for client and server-side development.

Now, what does that mean? Well, think of it as a tool for developers to store and manage data in the cloud. Firestore is highly scalable, meaning it can handle large amounts of data and traffic without breaking a sweat.

It's also highly flexible, allowing developers to store and retrieve data in various formats, including structured, semi-structured, and unstructured data. Plus, Firestore supports real-time data synchronization, which means any changes made to the database are immediately reflected across all connected clients.

Firestore also provides a simple and intuitive API that developers can use to easily interact with the database. And it's fully integrated with other Google Cloud services, such as Cloud Functions and Firebase, making it a powerful tool for building serverless applications.

RECAP: Google Cloud Firestore is a flexible, scalable NoSQL cloud database that's designed to store and sync data for client- and server-side development. It offers live synchronization, offline support, and robust querying, making it an ideal solution for building collaborative, real-time applications across various platforms.

Web Servers

Web servers are the computers that store and serve up the web pages you see when you're browsing the internet.

Think of it like this: when you type in a website address or click on a link, your browser sends a request to the web server asking for the page. The web server then processes that request, retrieves the page from its storage, and sends it back to your browser, all in a matter of milliseconds.

Web servers can handle thousands, if not millions, of requests at once, and they're constantly working to keep the internet running smoothly. Without them, we wouldn't have access to the vast amount of information and services that we rely on every day.

But web servers aren't just for serving up web pages. They can also handle other types of data, like images, videos, and files. And they can run applications and scripts, like e-commerce platforms or social media networks.

Now, there are many different types of web servers out there, but some of the most popular include Apache HTTP, Nginx, and Microsoft IIS. They all have their strengths and weaknesses, but what they have in common is their crucial role in making the internet work.

RECAP: Web servers are specialized systems that deliver content or services to end users over the internet, typically processing requests to access webpages. They receive HTTP requests from clients (like web browsers), process these requests, and then send back the appropriate HTTP responses, which often contain the requested webpage, images, or other resources.

Apache HTTP Server

Well, Apache HTTP Server, also known as Apache, is a popular open-source web server software. It's like the bouncer outside of a nightclub, making sure that only authorized users get access to the content inside.

Apache has been around since the mid-1990s and has become one of the most widely used web server software out there. It's like the elder statesman of the web server world, providing stability and reliability for millions of websites around the world.

Now, let me give you a little history. Apache was created by a group of developers who wanted to make a web server that was free and open-source. They named it after the Native American tribe Apache, who were known for their strength and resilience.

And just like the Apache tribe, Apache HTTP Server is a force to be reckoned with. It's powerful, flexible, and can handle a high volume of traffic with ease. It's like the muscle car of web servers, packing a punch and getting the job done quickly.

But what really sets Apache apart is its modularity. It's like a toolbox filled with different components that can be customized and combined to create a web server that fits your specific needs. Whether you need to serve static files, run a dynamic website, or handle multiple domains, Apache has the tools you need.

So there you have it, Apache HTTP Server in a nutshell. A trusted and reliable web server software that's been around for decades, powering millions of websites worldwide. It's like the wise old owl of the web server world, offering stability and flexibility for all your web hosting needs.

RECAP: Apache HTTP Server, commonly referred to as Apache, is an open-source, cross-platform web server software that's known for its flexibility and power. It serves as the backbone for a vast portion of the internet, enabling websites to host and serve content to users across the globe.

Nginx

Ah, Nginx! One of the most powerful and widely used web servers out there. This thing is like the Swiss Army Knife of web hosting. It's fast, efficient, and can handle a huge amount of traffic without breaking a sweat.

Nginx was developed to address the limitations of traditional web servers like Apache. It uses an event-driven, asynchronous architecture[32] that allows it to

---

[32] Well, buckle up, folks, because we're about to talk about event-driven, asynchronous architecture. And let me tell you, it's not just some fancy buzzword. It's a game-changing approach to building software systems that can help businesses operate more efficiently, and I'm here to break it down for you in plain English.

So, what does event-driven, asynchronous architecture actually mean? Well, it's a way of building software systems that are designed to handle events or messages in an asynchronous manner. In other words, when something happens, like a customer placing an order or a server going down, the system can react quickly and efficiently, without waiting for a response.

Now, you might be thinking, "Okay, that sounds great, but what's the big deal?" Well, the big deal is that event-driven, asynchronous architecture allows for greater scalability, reliability, and responsiveness in software systems. By breaking down complex processes into smaller, more manageable components, businesses can build systems that can handle a high volume of events with ease.

Plus, because the system can handle events asynchronously, it can operate in a non-blocking manner, which means it doesn't get bogged down waiting for a response. This can lead to faster processing times, lower latency, and a better overall user experience.

handle a large number of connections at once, without the overhead of creating a separate thread for each one. This means it can process requests faster and with fewer resources than other servers.

But that's not all. Nginx is also highly configurable and flexible, with a wide range of modules and plugins available that can be used to extend its functionality. It can be used as a reverse proxy, load balancer, and even a caching server, making it an incredibly versatile tool for web developers and system administrators alike.

And let's not forget about its security features. Nginx has built-in protection against DDoS[33] attacks and can

---

But don't just take my word for it. Some of the world's most successful tech companies, like Amazon, Netflix, and Airbnb, have adopted event-driven, asynchronous architecture to build scalable and responsive systems. And if it's good enough for them, it's definitely worth considering for your business.

So, there you have it, folks. Event-driven, asynchronous architecture is a powerful tool for building efficient and scalable software systems. And if you're not already thinking about how to incorporate it into your tech stack, well, you might be missing out on a game-changing approach to software engineering.

[33] A DDoS attack, or Distributed Denial of Service attack, is a nasty little trick that malicious actors use to disrupt the normal functioning of a website or online service.

Here's how it works: imagine you're trying to get into a club, but the bouncer won't let you in. So you start calling up all your friends and telling them to come to the club too, and to keep trying to get in even if they get turned away. Pretty soon, the line to get into the club is so long that nobody can get in or out, and the club shuts

be configured to use SSL/TLS encryption[34] to secure

---

down for the night. That's basically what a DDoS attack does to a website or online service - it floods it with so much traffic that it can't handle it all, and it crashes or becomes inaccessible.

Now, why would someone do something like this? Well, sometimes it's just for kicks - you know, like a bunch of teenage vandals spray-painting graffiti on a wall. But more often than not, it's because the attacker has a grudge against the website or the company behind it. Maybe they're angry about something the company did, or they want to extract some kind of ransom or other concession. Or maybe they're just trying to make a name for themselves as a hacker.

Whatever the reason, DDoS attacks are a real pain in the neck for anyone who runs a website or online service. They can cause all kinds of headaches, from lost revenue to damage to a company's reputation. So if you ever find yourself on the receiving end of one of these attacks, my advice is to hunker down and get ready for a long night. Because it's going to be a bumpy ride, folks.

[34] We're about to talk about SSL/TLS encryption. Now, SSL/TLS stands for Secure Sockets Layer/Transport Layer Security, and it's essentially a way to keep your online communications safe from prying eyes.

Here's how it works: when you connect to a website that uses SSL/TLS, your browser and the website's server agree on a set of encryption algorithms to use. These algorithms scramble your data as it travels over the internet, making it unreadable to anyone who might be trying to intercept it.

Now, you might be thinking, "But Brian, why do I need encryption? I'm not doing anything shady online." Well, let me tell you, my friend, it's not just about protecting your own data. Encryption also helps to protect the integrity of the internet as a whole.

Think about it: if someone can intercept your communications and

connections to your website. It's a tough nut to crack, and that's exactly what you want in a web server.

So, there you have it. Nginx is fast, flexible, and secure. It's a powerhouse of a web server that can handle anything you throw at it.

RECAP: Nginx is a powerful, open-source software used as a web server, reverse proxy, load balancer, and HTTP cache. Its key features include high performance, stability, rich feature set, simple configuration, and low resource consumption, making it a popular choice for serving web content.

Microsoft IIS

Oh, Microsoft IIS. Let me tell you, it's like the silent but deadly ninja of the internet world. I mean, it's not as well-known as some of the other big players out there, but it's definitely got some moves.

So, for those of you who aren't familiar, IIS stands for Internet Information Services. It's a web server software developed by none other than the mighty Microsoft.

tamper with them, they could potentially cause all kinds of havoc. They could steal your personal information, spread malware, or even manipulate the news or social media to spread fake information.

So, if you want to keep your online communications safe and help maintain the integrity of the internet, look for that little padlock icon in your browser's address bar. That means you're using SSL/TLS encryption, and you can browse with confidence.

And let me tell you, Microsoft knows a thing or two about dominating a market.

But back to IIS. Essentially, it's a piece of software that runs on a Windows server and allows you to host websites and applications. And it's not just any old web server software, oh no. IIS has some serious chops.

First of all, it's super reliable. I mean, we're talking 99.9% uptime here. And when you're running a website or application, that kind of reliability is crucial. You don't want your site to go down every time someone sneezes.

Secondly, IIS is highly scalable. You can start with a small site and easily expand it to handle thousands of users. And trust me, when your business starts blowing up, you're going to need that kind of scalability.

But perhaps the best thing about IIS is how well it integrates with other Microsoft products. I mean, we're talking seamless integration here. If you're already using Windows servers and other Microsoft products, IIS is a no-brainer.

RECAP: Microsoft Internet Information Services (IIS) is a flexible, secure, and manageable web server from Microsoft that is used to host websites and web applications. It supports HTTP, HTTPS, FTP, FTPS, SMTP and NNTP protocols, and provides a unified interface for managing your web applications efficiently.

Load Balancers

Alright, folks, let's talk about load balancers. Now, a load balancer is essentially a traffic cop for your website or application. You see, when you have a website or application that's getting a lot of traffic, it can start to slow down or even crash under the weight of all those users. That's where a load balancer comes in.

Think of it like this: imagine you're at a concert and there's only one entrance to the venue. You can imagine the chaos that would ensue as everyone tries to get in at once. But if you have multiple entrances, each with its own bouncer, things can move much more smoothly. That's essentially what a load balancer does. It distributes incoming traffic across multiple servers, so that no single server gets overwhelmed.

Now, there are a few different types of load balancers. You've got your hardware load balancers, which are physical devices that sit in front of your servers and do the balancing for you. Then you've got your software load balancers, which are essentially just pieces of software that you install on your servers to do the same thing.

So there you have it, folks. Load balancers are the traffic cops that keep your website or application running smoothly, and they come in both hardware and software varieties. Keep that in mind the next time you're dealing with a high-traffic situation.

RECAP: A load balancer is a device or service that acts as a reverse proxy, distributing network or application traffic across a number of servers to enhance both the availability and the responsiveness of applications. It ensures no single server bears too much demand, thereby preventing potential network congestion or server failures, leading to a more efficient, reliable and robust service.

Types of Load Balancers

As you know, in today's hyper-connected world, websites and applications have to handle a massive amount of traffic. And if you don't have the right infrastructure in place, that can lead to slow page load times, dropped connections, and unhappy customers.

Enter load balancers. These bad boys distribute incoming traffic across multiple servers to ensure that no single server gets overwhelmed. And let me tell you, there are a few different types to choose from.

First up, we've got **hardware load balancers**. These are physical devices that sit in front of your servers and distribute traffic based on predefined rules. They're fast, reliable, and can handle massive amounts of traffic without breaking a sweat. But they can also be expensive and require specialized knowledge to set up and maintain.

Next, we've got **software load balancers**. These are programs that run on your servers and perform the same task as hardware load balancers. They're generally more affordable than their hardware counterparts and can be easier to set up and configure. But they may not be as scalable or as reliable in some situations.

Finally, we've got **cloud load balancers**. These are load balancers that are hosted in the cloud, often as part of a larger cloud infrastructure. They can be very flexible and scalable, and are often easy to set up and use. But they can also be more expensive than other types of load balancers, and may require some specialized knowledge to use effectively.

Here are a few examples:

- **NGINX**: This is a powerful open-source web server that also includes load balancing capabilities. It's highly configurable and can handle a wide variety of workloads.

- **HAProxy**: Another popular open-source load balancer, HAProxy is known for its high performance and reliability. It's often used for mission-critical applications where uptime is crucial.

- **Apache Traffic Server**: This is an open-source caching and proxying server that also includes load balancing capabilities. It's designed for high performance and can handle a large number of requests.

- **Microsoft Application Request Routing (ARR)**: This is a software load balancer that's specifically designed to work with Microsoft's IIS web server. It can be configured to handle a variety of different workloads.

- **F5 BIG-IP**: This is a commercial load balancer that's often used for large-scale deployments. It's highly configurable and can handle a wide variety of workloads.

Operating Systems

Let's talk about operating systems. If you're not familiar with the term, an operating system (or OS) is essentially the software that manages your computer's hardware and provides a platform for other applications to run on top of. It's the foundation upon which everything else rests.

Now, when it comes to examples of operating systems, there are a few that immediately come to mind. One of the oldest and most well-known is Unix. Unix was developed back in the 1970s by some smart folks at Bell Labs, and it's still in use today. In fact, many modern operating systems, like Linux and macOS, are based on Unix.

Speaking of Linux, that's another popular operating system worth mentioning. It's open-source, which means the source code is freely available and can be modified by anyone. This has led to a vast array of different "flavors" of Linux, each with their own unique features and capabilities.

And of course, we can't forget about Microsoft Windows. This is probably the most widely-used operating system in the world, especially when it comes to personal computers. It's been around since the 1980s, and has gone through many different iterations over the years.

So there you have it, folks. Operating systems are the unsung heroes of the tech world, quietly working behind the scenes to make all of our devices run smoothly. Whether you're using Unix, Linux, Windows, or something else entirely, you can thank your lucky stars that someone out there put in the hard work to create an OS that's stable, reliable, and easy to use.

RECAP: An operating system (OS) is a critical software that manages all hardware and software resources of a computer, serving as an intermediary between users and the computer hardware. It provides essential functionalities such as running applications, managing files and devices, providing user interface, and ensuring security and stability of the overall system.

Unix

Unix is a rockstar of an operating system, my friend. It's like Mick Jagger or Bono, legendary and still going strong after all these years.

Unix was born in the late 60s, in the midst of the hippie movement and the rise of counterculture. It was created by some of the brightest minds in computer science, and it quickly became the backbone of the internet and a cornerstone of modern computing.

What makes Unix so special, you ask? Well, for starters, it's incredibly robust and reliable. Unix systems are known for their stability and security, which is why they're widely used in industries like finance, healthcare, and government.

But Unix is also flexible and adaptable. It's like a chameleon, able to morph into whatever form it needs to suit the needs of different users and applications. That's why it's been able to evolve and stay relevant for over 50 years.

Now, I know what you're thinking. Unix is old school, right? But let me tell you, my friend, it's still as relevant as ever. In fact, many of the technologies we use today, like the internet and cloud computing, are built on top of Unix.

So if you want to understand the roots of modern computing and get a glimpse into the future, you better get familiar with Unix. It's a true OG, and it's not going anywhere anytime soon.

This OG has evolved into different flavors or distributions. Here are some of the different types of Unix:

Solaris: Developed by Sun Microsystems, Solaris is a Unix-based operating system that was specifically designed for servers and workstations.

HP-UX: HP-UX is a Unix-based operating system that is used on Hewlett Packard Enterprise servers. It is designed for high-performance computing and is commonly used in large enterprises.

AIX: Developed by IBM, AIX is a Unix-based operating system that is used on IBM's Power Systems servers. It is designed for enterprise-level applications and provides advanced security features.

BSD: Berkeley Software Distribution (BSD) is a Unix-based operating system that was developed at the University of California, Berkeley. It is known for its reliability, scalability, and advanced networking capabilities.

RECAP: UNIX is a powerful, multi-user and multitasking operating system that originated in the 1970s, designed to provide a simple, stable, and secure environment for software development and execution. It's highly portable, which means it can run on various hardware platforms, and it's the foundation for many modern operating systems, including Linux and MacOS.

Linux

Alright folks, let's talk about Linux. Linux is an operating system that has been around for quite some time and has become increasingly popular over the years.

So, how does it work? Well, unlike other operating systems, Linux is open-source, which means that it is freely available for anyone to use, modify and distribute. This is what makes Linux so special and unique.

Linux operates on a command line interface, which can be a bit intimidating for beginners, but it allows for greater flexibility and control. The user can access and manipulate every aspect of the system through these commands.

Now, you might be thinking, "why should I care about Linux?" Well, Linux is used in a wide range of applications, from servers to smartphones. It's secure, efficient, and customizable. And did I mention that it's free?

In fact, Linux has become so popular that it's even used by tech giants such as Google, Amazon, and Facebook.

So, if you're looking to up your tech game, Linux might just be the way to go.

Well, when it comes to Linux, there are a lot of different distributions (or "distros" for short) to choose from. Each distro has its own unique characteristics and target audience.

Let's start with some of the more well-known distros:

Ubuntu: One of the most popular distros, known for its user-friendliness and ease of installation.

Debian: Another popular distro, known for its stability and reliability.

Fedora: Developed by Red Hat[35], Fedora is known for being cutting-edge and innovative.

---

[35] Alright, let's talk about Red Hat. Red Hat is a company that's been around since the mid-90s and has become one of the biggest names in the world of enterprise software.

At its core, Red Hat is all about open-source software. They offer a wide range of products and services based on open-source technologies, including the popular Red Hat Enterprise Linux operating system.

Red Hat is known for its strong commitment to the open-source community and for being a major contributor to many open-source projects. They believe that the power of open-source software comes from collaboration and community involvement.

But Red Hat isn't just about software. They also offer a range of services and support options for their products, including training,

CentOS: Based on Red Hat Enterprise Linux[36], CentOS consulting, and technical support. This makes them a popular choice for businesses and organizations looking for reliable, enterprise-grade software solutions.

In fact, Red Hat has become so popular that it was acquired by IBM in 2018 for a whopping $34 billion. That's a pretty big deal, folks.

So, whether you're a developer, a business owner, or just someone interested in the world of open-source software, Red Hat is definitely a name to know. They're a major player in the industry and are showing no signs of slowing down anytime soon.

[36] Ah, Red Hat Enterprise Linux. Now there's a distro that's worth talking about.

Red Hat Enterprise Linux, or RHEL for short, is a powerful and robust operating system designed for use in enterprise environments. It's known for its rock-solid stability, security, and performance, which is why it's often used in mission-critical applications.

RHEL is based on the open-source Fedora project, but it's specifically designed for enterprise use with a focus on security, reliability, and support. In fact, Red Hat provides world-class support for RHEL, including software updates, security patches, and technical support.

One of the key features of RHEL is its support for a wide range of hardware architectures, from x86 to ARM to IBM Power Systems. This makes it a flexible and versatile option for a variety of different use cases.

But what really sets RHEL apart is its focus on security. RHEL includes a number of advanced security features, such as SELinux, which provides enhanced security controls, and System Security Services Daemon (SSSD), which simplifies authentication and identity management.

is a stable and secure distro often used for servers.

Arch Linux: A lightweight and customizable distro that's popular among experienced Linux users.

Mint: Based on Ubuntu, Mint is known for its sleek interface and user-friendly design.

openSUSE: Another stable and reliable distro often used for servers.

There are many other distros out there as well, each with its own unique set of features and target audience. Some are designed specifically for certain purposes, like Kali Linux for security testing, while others are more general-purpose distros like Manjaro.

So, whether you're a seasoned Linux user or just starting out, there's a distro out there for everyone.

In summary, Linux is an open-source operating system that operates through a command line interface, providing users with greater flexibility and control. It's secure, efficient, customizable, and used by some of the biggest names in tech. So, if you haven't already, give Linux a try and see what all the fuss is about.

So, if you're looking for a powerful and reliable operating system for use in an enterprise environment, look no further than Red Hat Enterprise Linux. It's the gold standard when it comes to enterprise Linux.

RECAP: Linux is an open-source operating system, based on Unix, that was created by Linus Torvalds in 1991. It's widely known for its high stability, robustness, and flexibility, making it a staple for servers, embedded systems, and increasingly, as a desktop OS.

Windows

Ah, Windows. Now we're talking about something that's a little more familiar to the average user.

Windows is an operating system developed by Microsoft and is one of the most widely-used operating systems in the world. It's been around for decades and has gone through many iterations, from Windows 3.1 to Windows 10.

Unlike Linux, Windows is a proprietary operating system, which means that it's owned and controlled by Microsoft. This has its pros and cons. On the one hand, Microsoft can ensure that Windows is easy to use and works seamlessly with other Microsoft products. On the other hand, this means that users have less control over the inner workings of the operating system.

Windows has a graphical user interface, which makes it easy for beginners to navigate. It also has a wide range of applications available, from productivity tools to games.

However, Windows has had its fair share of issues over the years. Security vulnerabilities and system crashes have plagued the operating system at times. And let's not forget the infamous Windows Vista, which was widely criticized for its slow performance and compatibility issues.

But despite its flaws, Windows remains a popular choice for many users, especially in the corporate world. And with the latest versions of Windows, Microsoft seems to be making strides to address some of the issues of the past.

In summary, Windows is a proprietary operating system developed by Microsoft that has a graphical user interface and a wide range of applications available. While it has had its fair share of issues over the years, it remains a popular choice for many users, especially in the corporate world.

RECAP: Windows is a popular operating system developed by Microsoft Corporation that is primarily used on personal computers and servers. It's renowned for its graphical user interface, a vast array of software compatibility, and its central role in personal and business computing environments worldwide.

Mac OS

Ah, Mac OS, one of the most iconic operating systems out there. Let's dive into what makes it so special.

Mac OS is the operating system developed by Apple, and it's designed specifically for use on Apple's line of Macintosh computers. What sets it apart from other operating systems is its unique user interface, which is sleek, intuitive, and user-friendly.

But Mac OS isn't just about looks. It's also known for its stability, security, and performance. It's built on a Unix-based foundation, which makes it a reliable and efficient system.

And let's not forget about the Apple ecosystem. With Mac OS, you have access to a wide range of exclusive apps and features that you won't find on other operating systems. Plus, if you have other Apple devices like an iPhone or iPad, you can easily integrate them into your workflow for a seamless experience.

But what really makes Mac OS stand out is the attention to detail that Apple puts into every aspect of the system. From the way the icons bounce when you open an app to the way the system transitions between tasks, every detail is carefully crafted to provide a delightful user experience.

RECAP: macOS is the proprietary operating system developed by Apple for their Mac lineup of computers, known for its sleek design and intuitive user interface. It boasts a robust architecture, strong security measures, seamless integration with other Apple devices and services, and is highly optimized for creative workflows, making it a popular choice among professionals in fields such as design, video editing, and music production.

iOS

Alright, let's talk about iOS. iOS is the mobile operating system developed by Apple, and it's what powers all of their mobile devices, including the iPhone and iPad.

Now, what makes iOS so special? Well, for starters, it's incredibly user-friendly and intuitive. The interface is sleek and well-designed, making it easy to navigate and use.

iOS is also known for being incredibly secure. Apple has put a lot of effort into making sure that their devices are protected against viruses, malware, and other security threats. This is one of the reasons why iOS is often preferred by businesses and other organizations.

But iOS isn't just for work – it's also great for play. There are over two million apps available on the App Store, covering everything from gaming to productivity to social networking. And thanks to the powerful hardware that Apple puts in their devices, these apps run smoothly and quickly.

Of course, there are some downsides to iOS as well. One of the biggest is the closed nature of the platform. Apple tightly controls what apps are allowed on the App

Store, which can be frustrating for developers and users alike.

RECAP: iOS is Apple's mobile operating system that powers devices like the iPhone, iPad, and iPod Touch. Known for its user-friendly design, robust security features, and smooth integration with other Apple products, it hosts a vast ecosystem of apps available through the Apple App Store.

Android

Let's talk about the Android operating system. Android is a mobile operating system that was developed by Google and has become the most popular mobile OS in the world.

So, what makes Android so great? Well, for starters, it's open-source, which means that anyone can access and modify the source code. This has led to a wide range of devices that run Android, from smartphones to tablets to smart TVs and even some cars.

Android is known for its flexibility and customization options, allowing users to tailor their devices to their specific needs. It also has a huge app store, with over 2.8 million apps available for download.

But it's not just about the apps. Android also has a robust security system, with features like app permissions and Google Play Protect to keep your device and data safe.

Another advantage of Android is its integration with Google services. This includes Google Maps, Gmail, Google Drive, and more. It also means that Android devices are often the first to receive updates for these services.

Now, I know some people might be concerned about privacy with Google services, but Android allows users to control their privacy settings and opt out of data collection if they choose.

In summary, Android is an open-source mobile operating system developed by Google that offers flexibility, customization, a huge app store, robust security, and integration with Google services. It's no wonder Android has become the most popular mobile OS in the world.

RECAP: Android is an open-source mobile operating system developed by Google, designed primarily for smartphones and tablets, but also used in other devices such as smart TVs and wearables. It provides a rich ecosystem of apps, customization options, and integration with Google services, making it one of the most popular and widely used mobile platforms worldwide.

Security

Let's talk about the importance of security in web technologies. Now, I know some people might be thinking, "why do we need to worry so much about security?" Well, let me tell you, security is critical when it comes to web technologies.

First and foremost, security helps protect user data. We all know how much personal information we share online these days, from credit card numbers to social security numbers. Without proper security measures in place, this data is vulnerable to hackers and cybercriminals.

But it's not just about protecting user data. Security is also important for protecting websites and web applications themselves. Cyber attacks like DDoS attacks can take down entire websites and cost businesses millions of dollars.

In addition, security is becoming increasingly important for compliance with laws and regulations. For example, the General Data Protection Regulation (GDPR) in the European Union requires companies to take certain security measures to protect user data, and failure to comply can result in hefty fines.

Now, some might argue that investing in security is too expensive or that it's too complex to implement. But the truth is, investing in security is an investment in the long-term success and sustainability of a business. It's a small price to pay compared to the potential costs of a data breach or cyber attack.

In summary, security is critical when it comes to web technologies. It helps protect user data, websites, and web applications, and is increasingly important for compliance with laws and regulations. Investing in security is an investment in the long-term success of a business, and it's not something that should be taken lightly.

Types of Attacks

Well, when it comes to cyber security attacks, there are a lot of different types to be aware of. Here are a few of the most common:

- **Phishing**: This is when attackers send fraudulent emails or messages to try and trick people into providing sensitive information, such as login credentials or financial data.

- **Malware**: Malware is any type of malicious software that is designed to harm or gain unauthorized access to a computer or network. This can include viruses, trojans, and ransomware.

- **DDoS attacks**: Distributed denial of service (DDoS) attacks involve flooding a website or network with traffic in an attempt to overwhelm it and take it offline.

- **SQL injection**: This is a type of attack that targets web applications and databases, where attackers insert malicious code into SQL statements to gain access to sensitive data.

- **Man-in-the-middle attacks**: In these attacks, attackers intercept communications between two parties and can potentially steal or modify the data being transmitted.

- **Password attacks**: These attacks involve attempts to guess or crack passwords in order to gain access to a system or network.

- **Social engineering**: This type of attack involves manipulating people into divulging sensitive information or performing actions that are not in their best interest.

These are just a few examples of the many types of cyber security attacks that are out there. It's important for individuals and businesses to be aware of these threats and take appropriate measures to protect themselves. This can include things like using strong passwords, keeping software up to date, and investing in security software and services.

Prevention

Well folks, when it comes to preventing cyber attacks, there's no silver bullet. Cybersecurity is a complex issue that requires a multi-pronged approach.

First and foremost, education is key. It's important to educate employees and individuals on how to recognize and prevent cyber attacks. This includes things like phishing emails, weak passwords, and social engineering tactics.

Secondly, investing in cybersecurity technology is crucial. This includes firewalls, antivirus software, intrusion detection and prevention systems, and more. It's important to keep these systems up-to-date and regularly test them to ensure they're working properly.

Thirdly, implementing strong access controls and password policies can help prevent unauthorized access to sensitive data. This includes things like multi-factor authentication and regular password changes.

Fourthly, regular backups are important to ensure that data can be recovered in case of a cyber attack or data breach.

Finally, it's important to have an incident response plan in place in case of a cyber attack. This includes things like procedures for containing the attack, communicating with stakeholders, and recovering data.

Now, I know some of you might be thinking that all of this sounds expensive and time-consuming. But the cost of a cyber attack can be far greater than the cost of investing in cybersecurity measures. And in today's digital age, it's not a matter of if you'll be targeted, but when.

So, let's take cybersecurity seriously and invest in education, technology, access controls, backups, and incident response plans to prevent cyber attacks before they happen.

Common Job Titles: Who Does What and When Do They Do It?

There are many job titles in software engineering, and some of the most common ones include:

- Software Developer/Software Engineer
- Front-end Developer
- Back-end Developer
- Full-stack Developer
- DevOps Engineer
- Quality Assurance (QA) Engineer
- Test Automation Engineer
- Mobile Developer
- Data Engineer
- Cloud Engineer
- Technical Architect

- Project Manager
- Scrum Master
- Technical Writer
- UX/UI Designer
- Security Engineer
- Machine Learning Engineer
- Data Scientist
- Infrastructure Engineer
- Site Reliability Engineer (SRE)

Software Developer

Alright, listen up, party people. Gather 'round and let me break down the enigma that is a software developer. Now, imagine this digital realm as the Wild West, a place where creativity and innovation are kings. The software developer? They're like the gunslinger, the sheriffs of this digital frontier.

These code-slinging warriors don't just sit around and daydream about the future; they freakin' build it. They're the architects, the Einsteins, the Picassos of the zeros and ones. They weave together lines of code, creating the software that runs our digital lives – from the apps that let you swipe right on potential soulmates to the algorithms that help you find the perfect pair of shoes online.

Software developers are like the Jedi Knights of our era, wielding their coding lightsabers to battle the dark forces of crappy user interfaces, buggy apps, and painfully slow websites. They innovate, iterate, and dominate the digital landscape, all while staying on top of an ever-evolving world of programming languages, frameworks, and tools.

In a nutshell, my friends, software developers are the badass digital gladiators who turn our wildest dreams into reality. They build the platforms and tools that allow us to navigate this brave new world, and we should be grateful for the power they wield. Because without them, we'd be stuck in a world where smartphones and social media are just figments of our imagination. And, quite frankly, that sounds like a nightmare.

RECAP: A software developer is a professional who creates computer programs and applications to solve specific problems or meet specific needs.

Software Engineer

Next, we're going to talk about the unsung heroes of the digital world - software engineers. These folks are, simply put, the lifeblood of our digital ecosystem. You know, like the mitochondria of the technology cell. They're the ones who turn ideas into reality, code by code, while making sure everything runs as smooth as butter on a bald monkey.

Software engineers are like the Navy SEALs of the tech world - they've got their fingers on the pulse of everything that's cutting-edge and innovative. And let's be honest, they've got the skills to pay the bills. They don't just slap some code together and call it a day. Oh no, my friends. They're the masters of the dark art of coding, diving deep into the nitty-gritty of programming languages, algorithms, and data structures like some sort of coding ninjas.

These digital maestros meticulously craft and maintain software applications that power our lives - from the apps that feed our insatiable desire for instant gratification, to the platforms that keep us connected to our dear Aunt Sally halfway across the world. They're the architects of our digital world, the silent puppeteers who make sure the show goes on without a hitch.

And let's not forget about their adaptability. Software engineers can pivot faster than a yoga instructor on steroids. As the tech landscape evolves, they're continuously learning and growing, making sure they're always at the top of their game. So, the next time you're browsing through your favorite app, take a moment to appreciate these digital warriors who make it all possible. They're not just software engineers, they're the unsung heroes that keep our digital lives humming along.

RECAP: A software engineer is a professional who designs, develops, tests, and maintains software systems and applications.

Front-end Developer

the front-end developer, the digital Picassos of our time, the masters of visual allure, or as I like to call them, the "make-it-pretty wizards." You see, the internet is a stage, and the front-end developer, well, they're the set designer. These folks have an uncanny ability to conjure up a digital experience that captures the imagination and keeps the dopamine surging, my friends.

Now, let's talk shop. Front-end developers are proficient in the holy trinity of web development: HTML, CSS, and JavaScript. HTML, or HyperText Markup Language, is the digital skeleton, the bare bones that lay the foundation for our captivating online experiences. CSS, or Cascading Style Sheets, is the wardrobe department, giving our digital creations that fashionable touch, the colors, the fonts, and the general "je ne sais quoi" that keeps us coming back for more.

Finally, we have JavaScript, the lifeblood of interactivity. It's the puppeteer pulling the strings, breathing life into the digital ether, making websites dance to the tune of user whims. With JavaScript, our front-end sorcerers can craft seamless transitions, snappy animations, and features that keep users engaged in the infinite scroll of the internet.

But wait, there's more! Front-end developers don't just stop there. They're connoisseurs of a veritable smorgasbord of frameworks and libraries. React, Angular, Vue - these are the tools of the trade, and like a Swiss Army knife, they can help create pixel-perfect, responsive web designs that cater to our every digital desire.

So, my dear interlocutor, a front-end developer is an architect of the digital canvas, a curator of interactive art, and a wielder of the technology that turns the mundane into the magical. As we continue our love affair with screens, they are the ones painting the tapestry of our digital lives.

RECAP: A front-end developer is a professional who specializes in designing and coding the user interface of a website or application.

Back-end Developer

Alright, so picture this, my fellow future unicorns: in the business world, we have this thing called a "Back-end Developer." You might be thinking, "What the hell is that?" But bear with me, because I'm about to tell you.

In the digital ecosystem, there's this sexy, mysterious, and alluring thing called the "back end." Now, I'm not talking about a Beyonce-level derriere. No, my friends, this is the technological powerhouse that makes your favorite apps, websites, and platforms purr like a Maserati engine. You know, the kind of stuff that gets your pulse racing and your brain aching for more sweet, sweet innovation.

So, what's the deal with these Back-end Developers? They're like the puppet masters, orchestrating the symphony of code and data that keeps the digital world spinning. They build and maintain the infrastructure, databases, and application logic that power the experiences you love. And guess what? They do it all behind the scenes, like freaking Houdini.

Now, let's talk tech. Back-end Developers are fluent in a plethora of programming languages and frameworks, including but not limited to Python, Java, Ruby, Node.js, PHP, and C#. They tango with databases like MySQL, PostgreSQL, and MongoDB, and they know their way around server-side technologies like Nginx and Apache. Put simply, these code-wielding wizards have a toolset that would make even Batman jealous.

To sum it up, my friends, Back-end Developers are the unsung heroes of the digital age, the puppeteers who make the magic happen. They're the powerhouse that keeps your favorite platforms running smooth as silk, and without them, we'd be lost in a sea of 404 errors and endless loading screens. So, the next time you use an app or website, take a moment to appreciate the genius at work in the shadows, because that's where the real magic lies.

RECAP: A Back-end Developer is responsible for developing and maintaining the server-side of web applications.

Full-stack Developer

Alright, my young padawans, let's talk about this mystical creature in the tech ecosystem, the full-stack developer. Like a digital Swiss Army knife, these tech ninjas have the chops to slice and dice through both front-end and back-end development. They're the SEAL Team Six of coding, with the ability to infiltrate any part of the tech landscape and come out victorious.

Now, let's dive into their arsenal. On the front-end, these maestros of aesthetics and interactivity wield the Holy Trinity of web development: HTML, CSS, and JavaScript. Like the almighty Zeus hurling lightning bolts, they create visually stunning and engaging user experiences that'll leave you drooling for more.

But wait, there's more. They don't just stop at making your digital platforms look like a million bucks; they dive deep into the murky waters of back-end development too. Armed with languages like Python, Ruby, PHP, or Node.js, these code commandos build the scaffolding of the digital universe. They ensure that the engine that drives your website or app is running smoother than a Tesla on autopilot.

Let's not forget about the sacred bond between these two worlds, the APIs. Full-stack developers are the high priests of API integration, conjuring the magic that makes your favorite platforms talk to each other in sweet, sweet harmony.

Finally, we arrive at the pièce de résistance: databases. Like squirrels storing acorns for winter, full-stack developers work with SQL or NoSQL databases to ensure that your precious data is organized, secure, and accessible at a moment's notice.

In summary, full-stack developers are the superheroes of the tech world, armed with an array of technologies and skills to conquer any challenge. From front-end to back-end, and everything in between, these digital warriors have you covered.

RECAP: A full-stack developer is a professional who has expertise in developing both the front-end and back-end components of a software application.

DevOps Engineer

DevOps Engineer, huh? Well, think of them as the mystical, all-powerful unicorns of the tech industry. They're the fearless warriors who ensure the perfect marriage of software development and IT operations.

They're the ones who obliterate the walls of confusion and chaos between developers and IT, creating a harmonious ecosystem where continuous integration, delivery, and deployment live in a sexy tango of productivity and efficiency.

Now, if you want to get into the nitty-gritty, these bad boys and girls work with an arsenal of cutting-edge technologies to make the magic happen. They wield tools like Git, the version control system that's become the gold standard for collaborative coding. Jenkins, Travis CI, or CircleCI, the CI/CD gods, ensuring that code is always being tested, built, and deployed as quickly and safely as possible.

But wait, there's more! These tech aficionados also master containerization platforms like Docker and Kubernetes, which are kind of like the equivalent of Tupperware for your apps. These containerization maestros ensure that applications can run anywhere, anytime, without any ugly surprises.

They don't stop there, though. DevOps engineers are also cloud ninjas, seamlessly moving applications between AWS, Azure, or Google Cloud. They're like the ultimate puppet masters, orchestrating infrastructure as code using tools like Terraform, Ansible, and Chef, automating the heck out of everything.

These modern-day superheroes are armed to the teeth with monitoring and logging tools like Prometheus,

Grafana, ELK, and Datadog, ensuring that all systems are go, and if anything goes sideways, they'll be the first to know.

So, when you encounter a DevOps Engineer, give them a high-five or a respectful nod. They're the unsung heroes of the tech world, the maestros conducting the symphony of code and infrastructure that keeps our digital world spinning round and round. And let's be honest, who doesn't want a unicorn on their team?

RECAP: A DevOps Engineer is a professional who combines development and operations skills to improve software development and deployment processes. They focus on automating and streamlining the entire software delivery pipeline to increase efficiency and speed while maintaining quality.

Quality Assurance (QA) Engineer

A Quality Assurance (QA) Engineer, my friends, is the unsung hero of the tech world. They're the digital gladiators, the code warriors, fighting valiantly to ensure that the software you use doesn't crumble like a stale baguette the moment you lay your hands on it. You see, they play a critical role in the never-ending battle against buggy code and subpar user experiences.

These brave souls dive deep into the labyrinth of software development, scrutinizing every line of code, every feature, and every user interaction like a hawk. They work with a lethal arsenal of testing methodologies—manual, automated, functional, non-functional, the list goes on—leaving no stone unturned, no bug unnoticed.

QA Engineers have a diverse skillset, combining the acumen of a detective, the curiosity of a scientist, and the resilience of a marathon runner. They master the art of communication to collaborate with developers, product managers, and other stakeholders, ensuring that the digital experience is as smooth as a fine Bordeaux.

Now, let's talk tech. These code-warriors wield a variety of weapons in their never-ending quest for software excellence. Tools like Selenium, JIRA, TestRail, and Jenkins become an extension of their very being. They're well-versed in programming languages such as Java, Python, and Ruby, as well as markup and scripting languages like HTML, CSS, and JavaScript.

In the end, my friends, a QA Engineer is that invisible force, the ultimate guardian of software quality, tirelessly working behind the scenes to ensure that the digital world remains a safe and reliable place for all its denizens. So, the next time you use an app or software that just works, spare a thought for these uncelebrated heroes of the tech world. They've got your back.

RECAP: A Quality Assurance (QA) Engineer is responsible for ensuring that software products and applications meet the established quality standards through testing and analysis. They work closely with developers and project managers to identify and resolve any defects or issues before the final release of the product.

Test Automation Engineer

Let me introduce you to the high priest of quality assurance, the one and only Test Automation Engineer. Now, don't let the dry title fool you, because these ninjas of the tech world are anything but ordinary.

You see, these test automation wizards are on a quest to ensure that the digital world functions like a Swiss watch – and we all know how those run – with precision, accuracy, and reliability. How do they do it, you ask? By creating and executing automated tests, these savants of software eliminate the need for tedious manual testing, transforming the mundane into a well-oiled machine.

Now, let's talk about their arsenal. These digital gladiators are equipped with an array of weapons in the form of frameworks and tools, and they're not afraid to use them. We're talking about the likes of Selenium, the sleek Aston Martin of web application testing, or JUnit, the trusty Volkswagen of Java-based testing.

Then there are the scripting languages, where these test automation maestros can make Python, Java, or JavaScript dance to their tunes. And let's not forget the pièce de résistance, CI/CD pipelines – continuous integration and continuous delivery – which are the lifeblood of the modern software development process.

So, when you click a button and everything just works, take a moment to appreciate the mastery of the Test Automation Engineer. They're the unsung heroes of the tech universe, keeping our apps running smoothly while we live our digital lives blissfully unaware of the chaos that could have ensued without their expertise.

RECAP: A Test Automation Engineer is responsible for developing and implementing automated tests to ensure the quality of software products. They work closely with software developers and quality assurance teams to design and execute test plans and identify defects.

Mobile Developer

A mobile developer, my friends, is the fearless gladiator in the digital Colosseum, conquering the ever-evolving landscape of the smartphones and tablets that rule our lives. These warriors harness their technical prowess to craft the software masterpieces that infiltrate every crevice of our existence. They're the architects of the dopamine-inducing apps that keep us in a constant state of thumb-swiping euphoria.

These mobile developers, like the Greek gods of yore, wield the power of two distinct realms: the pristine orchards of Apple's iOS, and the sprawling, diverse kingdom of Google's Android. They are fluent in the languages of the gods, such as Swift and Objective-C, for iOS, and Java and Kotlin for Android. They also dabble in the sorcery of cross-platform frameworks like React Native and Flutter, as they bring forth glorious app experiences for the masses to consume.

In the age of digital addiction, these titans of technology also juggle the integration of backend services, because, let's face it, we're all about instant gratification in our hyperconnected world. They work with APIs, databases, and the mysterious cloud to ensure that the flow of data is as smooth as Don Draper in his prime.

So, the mobile developer – equal parts artist and warrior – is responsible for taming the beasts that reside in our pockets and purses, creating the experiences that keep our eyeballs glued to screens and our fingers tapping away in insatiable hunger for more. The mobile developer, ladies and gentlemen, is the conductor of the symphony that is modern life.

RECAP: A Mobile Developer is a software developer who specializes in creating applications for mobile devices such as smartphones and tablets. They are responsible for designing, building, and testing mobile applications to ensure they meet the needs and requirements of users.

Data Engineer

Ah, so you want to know about data engineers? All right, buckle up, my friend. Data engineers are the unsung heroes of the digital realm, the stealth ninjas who tirelessly work behind the scenes, orchestrating the data symphony that powers our world. In an age where data is the new oil, these badass maestros are the ones refining it, ensuring it flows seamlessly through the pipes of today's technology.

Now, let's get real about the technologies these data wizards work with, shall we? Data engineers play with a dizzying array of tools and platforms, ensuring that big, sexy data can be ingested, transformed, and stored in the most elegant and efficient way possible.

First and foremost, they've got to know their way around databases, both SQL and NoSQL. Think PostgreSQL, MySQL, Oracle, MongoDB, and Cassandra. These are the playgrounds where data engineers frolic, wrestling data into submission.

Next up, we've got the ETL (Extract, Transform, Load) process, which is like CrossFit for data. Tools like Apache NiFi, Talend, and Informatica help them whip data into shape, transforming it from raw, unruly gibberish into something our data-hungry systems can digest.

Data engineers also have a special love affair with big data technologies. Hadoop and Spark are the power couple of the big data universe, with data engineers mastering the art of distributed processing and fault-tolerant systems.

When it comes to storage, data engineers are the Marie Kondo of organizing your digital life. They skillfully navigate cloud platforms like AWS, Azure, and Google Cloud, implementing storage solutions that spark joy in the hearts of data scientists everywhere.

And last but not least, these data wranglers also dabble in programming languages like Python, Scala, and Java, using them to write the scripts that orchestrate the grand ballet of data.

In summary, data engineers are the glorious, behind-the-scenes puppeteers of the data-driven world. They are the champions that work with a plethora of technologies to ensure data is flowing freely and efficiently, ultimately enabling businesses to thrive and survive in our digital age.

RECAP: A Data Engineer is a professional who designs, builds, and maintains the infrastructure necessary to support the collection, storage, and processing of large volumes of data. They are responsible for creating and optimizing data pipelines, ensuring data quality, and enabling efficient data analysis by Data Scientists and Analysts.

Cloud Engineer

Alright, my friends, buckle up because we're diving into the exhilarating world of Cloud Engineers – the swashbuckling tech-savvy individuals who keep the internet's backbone up and running. Yeah, that's right:

these are the unsung heroes behind the cloud computing revolution.

Picture this: a Cloud Engineer is like the DJ at a party, making sure everything runs smoothly, and everyone gets their fix of digital beats. They're responsible for designing, managing, and maintaining the infrastructure that powers the digital economy. Without these maestros, your Netflix binges and seamless food delivery experiences would be nothing but a pipe dream.

Now, let's talk shop. Cloud Engineers work with a smorgasbord of technologies to make the magic happen. They've got their hands in the proverbial cookie jar of cloud platforms like Amazon Web Services (AWS), Microsoft Azure, and Google Cloud Platform (GCP). These titans of the tech industry have locked horns in a battle for cloud supremacy, and our fearless Cloud Engineers are right there in the trenches.

And what's a Cloud Engineer without their trusty toolkit? Well, my friends, they're well-versed in an array of programming languages like Python, JavaScript, and Go. They're also skilled in managing databases, like MySQL, PostgreSQL, and MongoDB, and they juggle various DevOps tools, like Docker, Kubernetes, and Terraform, like a boss.

So, there you have it, the Cloud Engineer – the rockstar of the digital age, spinning up virtual machines and orchestrating container deployments. They're the unsung heroes that keep the cloud humming along and our digital lives running smoother than a fresh jar of Nutella. Cheers to the Cloud Engineers, the maestros of the digital revolution!

RECAP: A Cloud Engineer is a professional who designs, develops, and manages the infrastructure and services of cloud-based computing systems. They ensure the cloud environment is secure, scalable, and efficient, while also optimizing cost and performance.

Technical Architect

Behold the Technical Architect! The Yoda, the Dumbledore, the (dare I say) Master Shifu of the tech world. This mystical creature of the digital realm is the one who weaves the strategy, the vision, and the structure of technology systems. They're the intellectual love child of a software developer, a system engineer, and a business savant. These tech virtuosos are the masterminds behind the cutting-edge tech infrastructures that power today's digital juggernauts.

So, what technologies do these magicians of the digital realm work with? Well, let me tell you, they're like DJs, spinning a diverse playlist of tracks to create a symphony of technological harmony. They're well-versed in cloud computing, dealing with the likes of AWS, Azure, and Google Cloud. They're up to their eyeballs in APIs, databases, and messaging systems. Let's not forget their intimate relationship with programming languages like Python, Java, and JavaScript. And, of course, they're no strangers to microservices, containers, and serverless architecture.

In a world ruled by digital empires, the Technical Architect is the unsung hero, playing the role of the puppet master, orchestrating the dance of code and hardware that keeps the wheels of innovation turning. So, next time you marvel at the latest technological breakthrough, spare a thought for the Technical Architect – the badass who made it all possible.

RECAP: A Technical Architect is a professional who designs and oversees the implementation of technical solutions for complex problems or projects. They ensure that the technology used meets the business requirements and objectives, and aligns with industry best practices and standards.

Project Manager

Hold onto your seats because we're about to dive into the wild world of Project Managers. Picture this: the love child of a Swiss Army knife and a human octopus, with the juggling skills of a circus performer. That's right, we're talking about the unsung heroes of the business world, the maestros of mayhem, the champions of chaos – Project Managers.

In a nutshell, a Project Manager is the person who takes charge of a project's execution, from conception to completion. They're the ones who bring order to the pandemonium, ensuring that all the moving pieces work in harmony, and that everyone's on track, on budget, and on time. Think of them as the business equivalent of an orchestra conductor, waving their baton of badassery to create a symphony of success.

Now, you may be wondering, "Brian, what kind of techno-wizardry does a Project Manager use to keep the chaos at bay?" Well, my curious compadre, they have a whole arsenal of tools at their disposal. From collaboration platforms like Slack or Microsoft Teams, which allow for real-time communication and file sharing, to project management software like Trello, Asana, or Basecamp, which help them break down projects into tasks and monitor progress like a hawk with night-vision goggles.

In addition, Project Managers also wield the mighty powers of Gantt charts, spreadsheets, and other data visualization tools to keep stakeholders informed and dazzled by their progress. They're always on the lookout for new technologies that can streamline their processes, cut down inefficiencies, and ultimately make their lives – and the lives of their team members – a little less like a rollercoaster and a little more like a well-oiled machine.

RECAP: A project manager is responsible for planning, executing, and closing projects, while ensuring they are completed on time, within budget, and meet the desired quality standards. They also manage the project team and communicate progress and status updates to stakeholders.

Scrum Master

A Scrum Master is the heart and soul of any Agile team. They're the ones who navigate the choppy waters of software development, keeping everyone on track and focused on what really matters - delivering value to the customer. Think of them as the captain of the Agile ship, but minus the pirate hat and parrot.

Scrum Masters are responsible for ensuring that the Scrum framework is followed by the team. They're there to facilitate communication, collaboration, and continuous improvement. They're like the ultimate cheerleader-coach hybrid, helping the team to self-organize and make the magic happen.

Now, let's talk tools. Scrum Masters have quite a few in their arsenal, so let me walk you through some of the highlights:

- **Scrum Board**: A physical or digital board that visualizes the team's work, from the backlog to the done column. It's like a roadmap, guiding the team through the twists and turns of a project.

- **Backlog**: The master list of everything the team needs to do. It's like a never-ending to-do list, but instead of "buy milk" and "call mom," it's full of user stories and tasks related to the project.

- **User Stories**: Bite-sized chunks of work that describe a feature from the perspective of an end-user. They're the building blocks of the Agile world, helping teams break down complex problems into manageable pieces.

- **Sprint Planning**: A crucial meeting where the team decides what work will be tackled in the upcoming sprint. It's like a huddle before the big game, setting the stage for a successful sprint.

- **Stand-up Meetings**: Quick, daily check-ins where team members share updates on their progress and discuss any roadblocks. It's like a morning pep talk, getting everyone on the same page and ready to tackle the day.

- **Sprint Review**: A meeting held at the end of each sprint where the team demonstrates what they've accomplished. It's like a show-and-tell for grown-ups, where everyone gets to bask in the glory of their hard work.

- **Retrospective**: A chance for the team to reflect on the sprint and identify areas for improvement. It's like group therapy, but with more sticky notes and less crying (hopefully).

So there you have it, folks! That's your crash course in Scrum Masters and their tools of the trade. Remember, the Agile world is all about flexibility, collaboration, and continuous learning, so buckle up and enjoy the ride.

RECAP: A Scrum Master is a facilitator and servant-leader responsible for ensuring that the Scrum framework is understood and implemented effectively by the development team. They guide the team through the agile process, remove obstacles, and promote collaboration and self-organization to achieve project goals.

Technical Writer

Let me tell you about the unsung heroes of the tech world, the technical writers. These talented folks are the ones who decipher the convoluted jargon and complex inner workings of tech products and translate them into language that mere mortals can understand. They are the grease that keeps the gears of understanding moving smoothly, ensuring that even your grandma can set up her new gadget without breaking a sweat.

Now, let's talk about the toolkit these maestros of simplification use to make magic happen. They're not the ones writing code or designing chips, but they've got their own arsenal of tools to help them create the kind of documentation that'll make you weep with gratitude.

First up, we've got word processors – you know, like Microsoft Word, Google Docs, or the oh-so-hip Markdown. These are the bread and butter of technical writing, where they craft their carefully worded instructions and explanations.

Next, we can't forget about graphic design software, like Adobe Illustrator or Canva, because sometimes, a picture really is worth a thousand words. These tools help them create diagrams, illustrations, and other visuals to clarify and support the text.

Screen capture tools like Snagit and video recording software such as Camtasia also make the cut, as they allow technical writers to show, not just tell, users how to navigate a software interface or troubleshoot a problem.

But wait, there's more! Technical writers also dabble in help authoring tools (HATs) like MadCap Flare or Adobe RoboHelp to create organized, searchable help documentation that users can access easily, without wanting to throw their devices out the window.

Now, let's not forget about the almighty version control systems like Git, which help technical writers track changes, collaborate with other writers, and make sure their work is always up-to-date and synced with the latest product updates.

So there you have it, a snapshot of the life and tools of a technical writer. They may not be the flashiest folks in the tech world, but they're the ones who make sure you can actually use and understand the shiny new gadgets and software you covet. And let's be honest, where would we be without them?

RECAP: A technical writer is a professional who communicates complex technical information in a clear and concise manner. They create various types of documentation, such as user manuals, instruction guides, and online help systems, to assist users in understanding and effectively using products, software, or processes.

UX/UI Designer

These creative minds are a crucial part of the tech world, responsible for blending aesthetics and functionality to craft seamless digital experiences. UX, or user experience, focuses on how users interact with products and services, while UI, or user interface, deals with the visual elements of those interactions. Essentially, they're the bridge between humans and technology, making sure we all can navigate our devices and apps without smashing our screens in frustration.

Now, let's talk about the tools these tech wizards wield. There are plenty of them, but some of the most popular include Sketch, Figma, and Adobe XD. These tools are critical for designing user interfaces, prototyping, and creating mockups. In addition, UX/UI designers rely on collaboration tools like InVision and Zeplin to share their ideas with the rest of the team.

Of course, they don't just whip out these tools and instantly create perfect designs. It's a process, people. They've got to carry out extensive user research, analyze data, and employ design thinking principles to craft solutions that address users' needs. You might even say they're a bit like detectives, tracking down problems and solving them with elegant, visually appealing designs.

So there you have it. UX/UI designers are the ones who make our digital lives less infuriating and more delightful, armed with a suite of tools that enable them to create sleek, user-friendly experiences. And let's be honest, we'd be lost without them.

RECAP: A UX/UI designer is responsible for creating the user experience (UX) and user interface (UI) of digital products, such as websites and mobile applications. They focus on designing intuitive and visually appealing interfaces that enhance user satisfaction and usability.

Security Engineer

A Security Engineer is that invaluable person who's responsible for designing, building, and maintaining the protective measures that shield an organization's digital infrastructure from cyber threats. It's their job to ensure that the bad guys don't get in and steal all the data, or worse, take down the entire system.

Now, let's talk about the tools these digital guardians use. Security Engineers have an impressive arsenal at their disposal, ranging from network monitoring tools to security frameworks and vulnerability scanners. They're like the tech world's Swiss Army knife, with a gadget for every situation.

A few examples of these tools include Wireshark, for sniffing out network traffic; Metasploit, for exploiting vulnerabilities; and Nmap, for mapping networks and identifying open ports. They also rely on security frameworks like the NIST Cybersecurity Framework or the ISO/IEC 27001 standard, which help guide their efforts to create a robust and compliant security system.

So, there you have it: Security Engineers are the digital superheroes that keep organizations safe in this ever-evolving cyber landscape. They leverage state-of-the-art tools and techniques to ensure that businesses can focus on what they do best, without fearing the cyber boogeyman.

RECAP: A Security Engineer is a professional responsible for designing, implementing, and maintaining the security measures and systems within an organization to protect against potential threats and vulnerabilities, ensuring the integrity and confidentiality of data and systems. They analyze security risks, develop security solutions, conduct security assessments, and provide recommendations to enhance overall security posture.

Machine Learning Engineer

Let me tell you about these fascinating creatures called Machine Learning Engineers. They're the tech world's newest superheroes, transforming industries and shaping the future with their digital sorcery. But don't worry, I've got the scoop on what they do and the tools they use, so sit back and enjoy.

First off, a Machine Learning Engineer is a delightful blend of a computer scientist and a statistician, with a pinch of domain expertise to boot. They spend their days (and, let's be honest, probably nights) developing algorithms and models that enable computers to learn from data. Their ultimate goal? To make predictions and decisions that would have humans saying, "Wow, that's some seriously intelligent AI!"

Now, as for the tools of their trade, these engineers have a veritable Swiss Army knife of programming languages and libraries at their disposal. Python is their go-to language, with its readability, flexibility, and extensive collection of libraries like TensorFlow, PyTorch, and scikit-learn. These libraries are the lifeblood of machine learning and help our valiant engineers create those magical algorithms.

But wait, there's more! They also dabble in other languages like R, Java, and Scala, as well as cloud platforms such as AWS, Google Cloud, and Azure. And let's not forget about data wrangling and visualization tools like Pandas, NumPy, and Matplotlib. Machine Learning Engineers are like modern-day alchemists, using these tools to turn data into digital gold.

In short, Machine Learning Engineers are the wizards behind the curtain of AI, concocting algorithms and models that make our world smarter and more efficient. And let me tell you, these engineers are transforming the world, one line of code at a time. So, if you ever meet one, be sure to tip your hat to their exceptional digital prowess.

RECAP: A Machine Learning Engineer is a professional responsible for designing, developing, and implementing machine learning models and systems. They work with large datasets, apply algorithms, and optimize models to create intelligent solutions for various domains such as healthcare, finance, and natural language processing.

Data Scientist

Let me tell you about this intriguing profession called "data scientist." It's like being Sherlock Holmes but with a whole lot more math and coding involved. You see, these data detectives are the cool, analytical minds who transform raw data into useful insights, helping businesses make smarter decisions and predict trends.

Now, let's get down to the nitty-gritty of the tools they use. Picture these wizards of the digital age with a wide array of gadgets in their utility belts. They've got programming languages like Python and R to manipulate data and create those oh-so-compelling visualizations. Then there's SQL for tapping into databases, and trust me, data scientists love their databases.

Machine learning? You betcha. These folks are all about algorithms that help their computers learn from data without explicit programming. Tools like TensorFlow, PyTorch, and scikit-learn are their go-to's for making machines smart and adaptive.

And don't even get me started on big data frameworks like Hadoop and Spark. They're like data scientists' secret weapons for managing and processing huge datasets. It's like they're building digital sandcastles with grains of data, except these sandcastles are extremely valuable and can impact entire industries.

But let's not forget about the cloud. Oh no, these data aficionados need their playgrounds like AWS, Google Cloud, and Microsoft Azure to store, process, and analyze data without breaking a sweat. They're like kids with an unlimited supply of LEGO bricks, and the cloud is their bottomless toy box.

So, there you have it: data scientists, the modern-day wizards who can make sense of the digital chaos we live in. They've got their coding wands and powerful tools, and they're out there shaping the future one byte at a time.

RECAP: A data scientist is a professional who uses their expertise in mathematics, statistics, and programming to analyze large and complex datasets, uncover patterns, and extract valuable insights that can be used to make informed business decisions or solve complex problems in various fields. They employ a combination of statistical analysis, machine learning techniques, and data visualization to derive actionable knowledge from data.

Infrastructure Engineer

Alright folks, let's dive into the world of infrastructure engineering, shall we? In the fast-paced tech landscape we live in today, infrastructure engineers are the backbone of the industry. These are the professionals who design, build, and maintain the hardware and software that keeps our digital world running. And I do mean RUNNING - seriously, these engineers are like the unsung heroes of the internet.

Infrastructure engineers work with an array of tools, and they're constantly adapting to new technologies to keep systems running smoothly. They're the kind of folks who never sit still, much like myself during an interview.

First up, we've got the big guns: cloud computing platforms like Amazon Web Services, Microsoft Azure, and Google Cloud Platform. These are the playgrounds where infrastructure engineers build and manage virtual servers, networks, and storage systems. They're also using automation tools like Terraform, Ansible, and Kubernetes to spin up infrastructure like they're flipping a light switch.

And they don't stop there. Monitoring and performance optimization are vital to keeping our systems in tip-top shape. That's where tools like Nagios, Grafana, and Prometheus come into play. They provide the crucial visibility needed to ensure that systems are running like a well-oiled machine.

Infrastructure engineers are also wizards when it comes to networking. They're deeply familiar with protocols like TCP/IP, DNS, and HTTP - without them, let's just say our online lives would be a lot less connected. And don't even get me started on cybersecurity - they're constantly fending off threats to keep our data safe and sound.

To sum it all up, infrastructure engineers are the architects of our digital world, using cutting-edge tools to build and maintain the complex systems that we all rely on every day. Their work is essential to the way we live and work, and frankly, they deserve a lot more credit than they often receive. So here's to the unsung heroes, the infrastructure engineers - we'd be lost without you.

RECAP: An Infrastructure Engineer is a professional responsible for designing, implementing, and maintaining the underlying systems and hardware that support the functioning of an organization's IT infrastructure. They focus on optimizing performance, scalability, and reliability to ensure the smooth operation of networks, servers, storage, and other critical components.

Site Reliability Engineer (SRE)

Well, buckle up, dear reader, because we're about to dive into the world of Site Reliability Engineering, or SRE for short. Picture this: it's the tech industry's answer to keeping your favorite digital services running smoothly, like a well-oiled machine. I mean, who doesn't want their apps and websites to work seamlessly all the time? That's where the superheroes called Site Reliability Engineers come in.

So, what do these SREs do, you ask? Their primary goal is to make sure that the software systems in a company are reliable, scalable, and efficient. They achieve this through a combination of software engineering and systems engineering practices. Think of them as the guardian angels of system performance and uptime, ensuring the companies can meet their Service Level Objectives (SLOs) and keep users like you and me happy.

But of course, no superhero is complete without their arsenal of gadgets and tools, right? SREs have their own suite of technological weapons to aid them in their quest for system stability. These tools can vary, but some of the most common ones are:

- Monitoring and observability tools like Prometheus[37], Grafana[38], or Datadog[39], which

---

[37] Prometheus, my friends, is an extraordinary creature in the realm of technology. Picture this: a revolutionary open-source monitoring and alerting toolkit that embodies the very essence of empowerment and enlightenment. Prometheus, much like the titan from Greek mythology who dared to steal fire from the gods, empowers us with the ability to uncover the hidden truths within our vast digital ecosystems.

In this digital age, where data reigns supreme, Prometheus emerges as a guardian of insights. It's a monitoring system that relentlessly scours through the intricacies of our applications, networks, and infrastructure, extracting valuable metrics and metadata. With an insatiable appetite for information, Prometheus paints a vivid picture of our systems' health, performance, and behavior.

But what truly sets Prometheus apart is its unwavering commitment to adaptability and extensibility. Like a chameleon, it effortlessly blends into any environment, embracing a wide array of integrations with popular software and services. Whether you're operating in the cloud, on-premises, or somewhere in between, Prometheus stands ready to capture the pulse of your digital domain.

Yet, Prometheus's allure goes beyond mere monitoring. It possesses an innate ability to forecast the future, thanks to its powerful alerting capabilities. Like an oracle of old, it can detect anomalies, predict imminent failures, and even warn us of potential catastrophes, allowing us to act swiftly and prevent digital disasters.

Prometheus is not just a tool, my friends. It's a force that empowers us to unlock the hidden potential of our systems, to illuminate the darkest corners of our digital realms. It's a testament to the triumph of human ingenuity and our unwavering pursuit of knowledge.

So let us embrace Prometheus, for it offers us the gift of insight and control in an increasingly complex and interconnected world.

help SREs keep a keen eye on their systems'

Let us harness its power to shape our digital destinies and conquer the challenges that lie ahead.

[38] Alright, folks, let's talk about Grafana. Now, this is one powerful tool that's been making waves in the world of data visualization and monitoring. If you're into tech or analytics, you better pay attention because Grafana is a game-changer.

So, what the heck is Grafana? Well, think of it as the Swiss Army knife for visualizing and analyzing data. It's an open-source platform that allows you to create stunning dashboards, charts, and graphs from a variety of data sources. Whether you're dealing with metrics, logs, or even real-time streaming data, Grafana's got your back.

But here's what really sets Grafana apart: it's all about the user experience, baby. This thing is so damn intuitive and user-friendly that even your grandma could whip up a killer dashboard in no time. Seriously, forget about spending hours fumbling with complicated tools or drowning in a sea of confusing code. Grafana takes simplicity to a whole new level.

And let's not forget the power of customization. With Grafana, you can tweak every little detail to fit your needs. From choosing the perfect color scheme to adding interactive elements and annotations, it's like having a personal data Picasso at your disposal.

But wait, there's more! Grafana doesn't just stop at visuals. It's a full-fledged monitoring platform that lets you set up alerts, track performance metrics, and dive deep into your data with its powerful query language. It's like having a data-driven crystal ball that keeps you one step ahead of the game.

So, my friends, whether you're a data nerd, an analytics aficionado, or just someone who loves beautiful visuals, Grafana is your ticket to data visualization heaven. It's revolutionizing the way we explore and understand data, and trust me, you don't want to be left behind.

health and performance.

Get your hands on Grafana, unleash your data's true potential, and take your analytics game to a whole new level. You won't be disappointed.

[39] Datadog is a formidable force in the realm of cloud monitoring and analytics. They possess an uncanny ability to tap into the pulsating veins of our digital infrastructure and extract invaluable insights. Think of them as the surgeons of the digital world, dissecting the intricate systems that power our businesses.

With their innovative platform, Datadog empowers organizations to gain comprehensive visibility into their entire tech stack. They monitor everything—from applications and servers to databases and networks. It's like having a high-definition surveillance system for your digital landscape, ensuring optimal performance, reliability, and security.

But what sets Datadog apart is their ability to transform raw data into actionable intelligence. They don't just bombard you with a deluge of information; they distill it into meaningful metrics and visualizations. It's as if they possess a sixth sense for unraveling the secrets hidden within the ones and zeros, helping businesses make informed decisions and unlock untapped potential.

Datadog's prowess extends beyond monitoring alone. They have forged alliances with major cloud providers, such as Amazon Web Services and Microsoft Azure, embedding their technology into the very fabric of our cloud-based infrastructure. This strategic move ensures seamless integration, scalability, and future-proofing for businesses operating in the digital age.

In a landscape where data reigns supreme, Datadog stands tall, armed with an arsenal of tools to conquer the challenges that lie ahead. They are the watchful guardians, the visionaries who illuminate the path forward, allowing businesses to navigate the turbulent seas of technology with confidence and precision.

So, my friends, behold the rise of Datadog—a true industry disruptor, a maestro conducting the symphony of data, and a

- Logging tools like Elasticsearch, Logstash, and Kibana (the ELK stack), which allow our heroes to track and analyze system logs and catch potential issues before they become full-blown crises.

- Incident management tools like PagerDuty or VictorOps, so when the going gets tough, our valiant SREs can spring into action and resolve issues with lightning speed.

- Configuration management and automation tools like Ansible, Chef, or Puppet, ensuring consistency and efficiency across systems.

- Version control systems like Git, keeping the code base organized and the SRE team in sync.

And that, my friends, is a whirlwind tour of what a Site Reliability Engineer is and the tools they use to keep the digital world running smoothly. In the age of information and rapid technological advances, SREs have their work cut out for them, and we've got their back as they face the challenges head-on. Until next time, stay curious, stay informed, and keep on enjoying those lightning-fast apps and websites, courtesy of your friendly neighborhood SRE.

---

partner for those seeking to unlock the transformative power of their digital domains.

RECAP: Site Reliability Engineering (SRE) is a discipline that combines software engineering and operations principles to ensure the reliable and efficient functioning of large-scale, complex software systems. SREs focus on designing, building, and maintaining systems that are scalable, highly available, and resilient, while also emphasizing automation, monitoring, and incident response to minimize downtime and improve overall system reliability.

Chapter Nine

Strategy Sessions

Alright, let's get down to business, and let's talk strategy. You see, my friends, the point of a strategy session, or a kickoff conversation, with a hiring manager before beginning a search for talent is like setting the stage for an epic blockbuster movie. I mean, who doesn't love a good story, right? And that's precisely what we're doing here—setting the stage for a compelling narrative that'll help us reel in the top talent.

First off, let's talk alignment. This is the "glue," the secret sauce that keeps everyone on the same page. In this initial huddle, the hiring manager and the recruiter need to align their expectations, goals, and objectives. Think of it as syncing your Apple devices—yeah, that level of harmony. If everyone's not on the same page, you're setting yourself up for a mess that even Marie Kondo couldn't tidy up.

Next up, we've got the job description. It's like crafting the perfect dating profile—you've got to sell yourself, the company, and the role to potential candidates. So, we've got to ensure that the hiring manager and recruiter are crystal clear about what skills, experience, and personality traits the ideal candidate should possess. Nobody wants to end up on a date with a dud, am I right?

Now, let's talk efficiency. Time is money, and we're all about getting the best bang for our buck. By having a clear understanding of the hiring manager's needs, the recruiter can streamline the search process and avoid wasting time on candidates who aren't the right fit. We're talking laser-like precision here, folks. It's like going to the grocery store with a well-thought-out list instead of wandering aimlessly through the aisles.

Lastly, communication is key. In this kickoff convo, the hiring manager and recruiter establish their communication preferences and touchpoints. It's like setting up a secret handshake—everyone needs to be in the loop to avoid missed opportunities or crossed wires. By fostering open communication, the hiring manager and recruiter become a dynamic duo, ready to conquer the world of talent acquisition.

So, there you have it. A strategy session or kickoff conversation with a hiring manager is the foundation for a successful talent search. It's the prologue to a gripping tale, the opening credits to a box-office hit. Without this crucial step, you're setting yourself up for a B-movie flop. And let's face it, nobody wants that.

What You Need To Get From a Kickoff Meeting

Alright, folks. Let's cut to the chase, shall we? We're talking about the good ol' intake session here. The starting point, the jumping-off spot, the ignition switch for the recruiter-hiring manager partnership. So, what crucial bits of information does a recruiter need to extract from a hiring manager in that all-important first meeting? Let's break it down:

- Numero uno: the role itself. You've got to get into the nitty-gritty. We're talking specifics – job title, responsibilities, expectations, and objectives. The recruiter needs the 411 on everything this position entails. It's essential intel, people.

- Secondly, the ideal candidate. The recruiter needs to pick the hiring manager's brain to form a composite sketch of their dream hire. Skills, qualifications, experience, soft skills, and cultural fit – these are the puzzle pieces that, when assembled, reveal the elusive candidate they're hunting for.

- Now, let's talk timeline. Time waits for no one, especially in the fast-paced world of business. The recruiter needs to know the hiring manager's expectations on when the role should be filled. We're talking urgency, deadline, and the potential consequences of not finding the right hire in the nick of time.

- Next up, the recruitment strategy. The recruiter and hiring manager need to collaborate, brainstorm, and concoct a plan of attack. That means discussing sourcing channels, advertising, interview processes, and selection criteria. It's about crafting the ultimate game plan to snag that top talent.

- Don't forget the budget, folks. The recruiter needs to be crystal clear on the salary range, benefits, and any potential negotiation wiggle room. No one wants to be blindsided by a last-minute budget bombshell, trust me.

- Finally, the company culture and work environment. The recruiter needs to understand the unique DNA of the organization, and that means diving deep into the company's values, mission, and work atmosphere. After all, the goal is to find someone who doesn't just fit the role, but fits the organization like a glove.

So, there you have it. The essential information a recruiter must gather during the intake session with a hiring manager. To sum it up, it's all about getting the facts, setting the expectations, and forming a united front in the quest for the perfect candidate.

Define The Hiring Plan

The blueprint, the master plan, the roadmap to success in recruiting. Why, you ask, is it so darn critical to have this plan locked and loaded before diving headfirst into the recruitment process?

First things first: time is money. No, seriously, it is. Every moment wasted on inefficient recruiting is another dollar bill down the drain. Having a solid hiring plan in place ensures everyone's on the same page, working toward the same goal, and not floundering around like a fish out of water. We need precision and efficiency, people.

Second, let's talk expectations. Without a hiring plan, you've got hiring managers and recruiters operating on a wing and a prayer. They're guessing, assuming, and, frankly, shooting in the dark. A well-thought-out plan aligns expectations, sets objectives, and ensures everyone knows their role in this high-stakes game of talent acquisition.

Now, competition. The job market is a battlefield, folks. Companies are duking it out for the best and brightest, and you better believe they've got their game faces on. A comprehensive hiring plan is your secret weapon, your competitive edge, your key to snatching up that top-tier talent before your rivals can say "you're hired."

Next up: the candidate experience. Let's not forget, the recruitment process is a two-way street. Candidates are evaluating your company just as much as you're evaluating them. A disorganized, haphazard approach is a one-way ticket to scaring off top talent. Having a hiring plan in place ensures a smooth, efficient, and professional candidate experience that leaves them wanting to sign on the dotted line.

Finally, the ultimate goal: finding the perfect fit. A hiring plan is like a finely-tuned compass guiding you toward the ideal candidate. It keeps your recruitment process on track, ensuring you're not swayed by distractions or tempted by shiny objects. It's about getting the right person in the right role at the right time.

So, there you have it. The reasons why determining a hiring plan before starting the recruiting process is absolutely critical.

Leveraging Data With Hiring Managers

Ah, data—the lifeblood of the modern business landscape. When it comes to collaborating with hiring managers, leveraging data is nothing short of a game changer. Allow me to elucidate why this matters and how it can transform your hiring process.

You see, in the age of information, gut feelings and intuition simply don't cut it anymore. Today's recruiters must navigate a complex and competitive talent market, and to do that, they need hard facts and cold, unadulterated data. Here's why it's crucial to harness the power of data when working with hiring managers:

- Objective decision-making: Data provides an unbiased, objective lens through which to assess candidates, enabling you and the hiring manager to make informed decisions based on evidence rather than subjective impressions. This not only leads to better hires but also reduces the risk of biased or unfair practices.

- Streamlined processes: By tracking key performance indicators (KPIs) and analyzing data from the hiring process, you can identify bottlenecks, inefficiencies, and areas for improvement. Armed with this knowledge, you can work with the hiring manager to optimize the process, saving both time and resources.

- Market insights: Data empowers you with invaluable insights into the talent market, such as salary benchmarks, demand for specific skills, and industry trends. This information can help you and the hiring manager craft compelling job offers and make strategic decisions that give your organization a competitive edge.

- Stronger relationships: By presenting hiring managers with concrete data, you can establish yourself as a credible and reliable partner. This not only strengthens your working relationship but also instills trust and confidence in your ability to deliver results.

- Continuous improvement: The power of data lies in its ability to drive continuous improvement. By regularly analyzing your hiring data, you can work with the hiring manager to refine your strategies, adapt to changing market conditions, and stay ahead of the curve.

In conclusion, leveraging data when working with hiring managers is akin to wielding a mighty sword in the battle for talent. It equips you with the tools to make objective decisions, streamline your processes, gain valuable market insights, build strong relationships, and drive continuous improvement.

Define The Interview Panel

We're about to dive into a topic that's absolutely vital when it comes to hiring – defining the hiring panel. Why, you ask?

Picture this: you're conducting an interview. You've got a lineup of rock star candidates and one coveted position. You're ready to evaluate these candidates and make your decision, right? Wrong! See, if you haven't defined your hiring panel, it's like trying to solve a complex puzzle without knowing what the final picture looks like.

The hiring panel serves as your team of experts. It's your all-star lineup of interviewers who will ask the questions and explore the different competencies required for the role. By clearly defining the panel, you're doing three crucial things:

1. Ensuring a well-rounded evaluation: Each panel member brings their own perspective and expertise to the table. The result? A comprehensive, in-depth assessment of the candidate. It's like assembling a team of superheroes, each with their own unique power, to save the day.

2. Streamlining the process: Let's face it, hiring can be chaotic. By assigning specific competencies and questions to each panel member, you're creating a smooth, organized interview process. No more haphazard, ad hoc questioning. No more stepping on each other's toes. It's a well-oiled machine.

3. Minimizing bias: We're all human, and that means we're susceptible to biases, whether we like to admit it or not. By having a diverse hiring panel with clearly defined roles and responsibilities, you're taking steps to mitigate those biases and make more objective, data-driven decisions.

So who's asking what questions? Who's exploring the different competencies? That's where the magic of the hiring panel comes in. Each panel member should be assigned specific areas of focus, based on their own expertise and knowledge of the role.

For example, you might have a technical expert diving into the candidate's coding skills, while an HR professional probes their soft skills and cultural fit. Meanwhile, a department head could focus on strategic thinking and problem-solving. It's a symphony of synchronized evaluation, and it's music to the ears of any successful hiring process.

In conclusion, defining the hiring panel is absolutely critical. It's the key to a well-rounded assessment, a streamlined process, and a more objective evaluation. So go forth, assemble your all-star team, and tackle that hiring challenge with confidence.

Diversity in Your Panel

Diversity in a panel interview is a cornerstone of a fair, effective, and forward-thinking hiring process. Let's take a look at why it's so crucial to have a diverse group of interviewers when trying to find the best candidate for a job:

- Comprehensive evaluation: A diverse panel brings together a variety of perspectives, experiences, and expertise. This ensures that the candidate is being assessed from multiple angles, leading to a more thorough and well-rounded evaluation. The more diverse the panel, the more likely they are to identify the candidate's strengths, weaknesses, and potential contributions to the organization.

- Minimizing bias: Every individual comes with their own set of unconscious biases, which can affect their judgment during an interview. A diverse hiring panel helps mitigate these biases by providing a range of viewpoints and backgrounds, leading to a more objective and fair decision-making process. This helps to minimize the impact of any single interviewer's bias on the final outcome.

- Improved decision-making: Research shows that diverse groups tend to make better decisions, as they consider a broader range of perspectives and are more likely to challenge assumptions. In the context of a panel interview, this translates to a more rigorous and thoughtful evaluation of each candidate, ultimately leading to a higher-quality hire.

- Enhanced employer brand: A diverse interview panel signals to candidates that the organization values diversity and inclusivity, which can be a significant selling point in today's competitive job market. Candidates are more likely to feel comfortable and engaged in the interview process if they see a representation of different backgrounds and experiences on the panel, which can lead to more positive impressions and outcomes.

In summary, having a diverse panel in an interview process is essential for ensuring a comprehensive evaluation, minimizing biases, making better decisions, and enhancing the organization's employer brand. Embracing diversity in the hiring process is not just an ethical responsibility; it's also a smart business move that can contribute to a company's overall success.

Best Practices To Create A Diverse Panel

Incorporating diversity into your hiring panel is an essential step in creating an equitable and effective recruitment process. To ensure a diverse hiring panel, consider implementing the following best practices:

- Commit to diversity: Make a clear and explicit commitment to fostering diversity within your organization. This should start at the leadership level and be communicated throughout the company. Establish diversity and inclusion goals, and include them in your company's overall strategy.

- Review panel composition: When assembling a hiring panel, aim for a diverse mix of interviewers in terms of gender, race, ethnicity, age, professional background, and experience. This will provide a broader range of perspectives and help to minimize biases in the hiring process.

- Provide training: Offer diversity and inclusion training to all employees involved in the hiring process. This should cover unconscious bias, cultural competence, and inclusive interviewing techniques. Regular training sessions will help to raise awareness and reinforce the importance of diversity in the hiring process.

- Standardize the interview process: Implement a structured interview format that ensures all candidates are assessed using the same criteria and questions. This helps to reduce the influence of biases and personal preferences and ensures a more objective evaluation of each candidate.

- Use diverse sourcing channels: To attract a diverse pool of candidates, use a variety of sourcing channels, including job boards, social media, professional networks, and industry events that cater to different demographics. Partnering with organizations that promote diversity in the workplace can also help you connect with underrepresented talent.

- Encourage diverse referrals: Encourage employees to refer diverse candidates from their networks. Offer incentives or recognition for successful referrals that contribute to your organization's diversity goals.

- Monitor and measure diversity: Track the diversity of your hiring panels, as well as the diversity of candidates at each stage of the hiring process. Analyze this data to identify trends and areas for improvement, and adjust your recruitment strategies accordingly.

- Collect feedback: Gather feedback from candidates about their experiences with the interview process, particularly regarding diversity and inclusion. This feedback can help you identify areas for improvement and ensure that your hiring process is both welcoming and inclusive.

- Communicate the value of diversity: Ensure that all employees understand the importance of diversity and inclusion in the workplace, and how it contributes to the success of the organization. This can help to create a culture that values and promotes diversity at all levels.

By implementing these best practices, you can work towards creating a diverse hiring panel and a more inclusive recruitment process. This will not only lead to better hiring decisions but also contribute to a more innovative, engaged, and successful workplace.

Questions For The Strategy Session

When meeting with a hiring manager about an engineering opening, a recruiter should aim to gather detailed information about the role, the team, and the company culture to effectively source and assess candidates. Here are some questions a recruiter can ask during the strategy session:

- What problem will this hire be responsible for solving?
- What's missing from the existing team?

- What are the key responsibilities and expectations of this engineering role?
- What are the specific technical skills and expertise required for this position? (e.g., programming languages, frameworks, tools, industry experience)
- Are there any certifications or educational qualifications that are essential or preferred for this role?
- What level of experience is needed for this position? (e.g., entry-level, mid-level, senior)
- What are the critical soft skills necessary for success in this role? (e.g., communication, teamwork, problem-solving, adaptability)
- Can you describe the engineering team's structure and dynamics? How will this new hire fit into the existing team?
- What is the team's working style? (e.g., agile, scrum, waterfall, pair programming)
- Are there any specific project management methodologies or tools the team uses that the candidate should be familiar with?
- What is the company culture like? How would you describe the ideal cultural fit for this role?
- What are the short-term and long-term goals for this role? How will the new hire contribute to the team's and company's objectives?

- What is the expected timeline for filling this position? Are there any deadlines or milestones that need to be considered?
- What is the salary range and benefits package for this role? Is there any flexibility in these aspects?
- What is the interview process for this position? Who will be involved, and what topics or assessments will be covered?
- Are there any unique challenges or requirements for this role that we should be aware of when sourcing candidates?
- How do you envision the onboarding process and ongoing professional development for the new hire?

By asking these targeted questions, the recruiter will be better equipped to understand the nuances of the engineering role and identify candidates who possess the right mix of technical skills, experience, and cultural fit for the company. This will ultimately lead to a more efficient and successful hiring process.

What Problem Will This Hire Be Responsible For Solving?

Ah, the quintessential question that cuts straight to the heart of the matter: "What problem will this hire be responsible for solving?" Let's take a moment to ponder the sheer gravity and brilliance of this query, shall we? So buckle up, and prepare to be enlightened.

You see, in the high-stakes game of talent acquisition, success is not just about finding someone who can merely fill a role, but rather someone who can tackle challenges head-on and propel the organization to new heights. And it all starts with this one, all-important question.

When a recruiter asks a hiring manager about the problem the new hire will be responsible for solving, they're essentially homing in on the value proposition of the position. This inquiry seeks to uncover the essence of the role, the raison d'être, if you will. The answer to this question is the North Star that guides the entire hiring process.

By understanding the specific problem or challenge, a recruiter can more effectively identify and assess candidates who possess the skills, experience, and temperament required to rise to the occasion. It's like a key that unlocks the door to a treasure trove of talent, just waiting to be discovered.

Furthermore, this question helps the recruiter to craft a compelling narrative around the role – a story that will resonate with potential candidates and pique their interest. After all, the most talented individuals are often drawn to opportunities that allow them to flex their problem-solving muscles and make a tangible impact.

In summary, the question "What problem will this hire be responsible for solving?" is a powerful tool in the recruiter's arsenal. It's the secret sauce that enables them to zero in on the true purpose of the role, identify the best candidates, and ultimately, ensure the success of the hiring process.

High Volume Tech Hiring Strategies

Ah, high volume hiring—where the rubber meets the road in the talent acquisition world. When the focus shifts to filling a multitude of roles at a breakneck pace, the hiring strategy must evolve to meet the demands of this high-stakes game. Let's talk strategy for hiring multiple Java Engineers as an example.

You see, my friends, when it comes to high volume hiring, the name of the game is efficiency. It's about finding the perfect balance between speed and quality, where you're able to identify top talent without sacrificing the rigor of the hiring process. Here's how you can adapt your strategy for hiring multiple Java Engineers in a high volume scenario:

- Standardize the process: Develop a consistent, structured interview process for all Java Engineer candidates. This ensures that each candidate is assessed using the same set of criteria, enabling you to make informed comparisons and streamline the decision-making process.

- Embrace technology: Leverage cutting-edge recruitment tools and platforms to automate repetitive tasks, such as screening resumes and scheduling interviews. Use skills assessment tools to quickly and effectively evaluate candidates' technical abilities, saving valuable time for both the hiring team and the candidates.

- Optimize job postings: Craft compelling, targeted job descriptions that speak directly to the Java Engineers you're seeking. Be specific about the technical skills and experience required, and highlight the unique value proposition of your organization to attract top talent.

- Cast a wide net: High volume hiring calls for a broad, proactive approach to sourcing. Utilize a variety of channels to reach Java Engineers, such as job boards, social media, professional networks, and industry events. The goal is to maximize your reach and increase the odds of finding the right candidates.

- Build a talent pipeline: Cultivate a reservoir of skilled Java Engineers who may not be the right fit for your current openings but could be perfect for future opportunities. By nurturing these relationships, you'll have a ready supply of top talent to tap into as the need arises.

- Collaborate with educational institutions: Forge partnerships with universities, coding boot camps, and other training programs that produce skilled Java Engineers. This will not only help you identify promising candidates but also contribute to the development of the talent pool in your industry.

- Measure and refine: Track key performance indicators (KPIs) to assess the effectiveness of your high volume hiring strategy. Identify areas for improvement and make data-driven adjustments to continually optimize your process.

In essence, high volume hiring demands an agile, focused approach that maximizes efficiency while maintaining the quality of your talent pool. By standardizing the process, embracing technology, optimizing job postings, casting a wide net, building a talent pipeline, collaborating with educational institutions, and measuring your success, you'll be well-equipped to conquer the challenge of hiring multiple Java Engineers.

Post Mortem

Ah, post mortems, the ultimate autopsy for the corporate talent search. Picture this: a hiring manager and their team, huddled together in a room, dissecting the lifeless remains of a candidate assessment process. What, dear friends, is the point of this seemingly macabre exercise? Allow me to illuminate your minds.

First and foremost, we have to recognize the value of data. Data, you see, is the new oil, the lifeblood that pumps through the veins of the modern business world. And just as any shrewd wildcatter would do, a post mortem session is all about drilling down to extract the most precious and valuable insights from that data.

By conducting a candidate debrief, the hiring manager and their team get to indulge in a luxurious feast of introspection, reflection, and learning. The main course? A deep dive into the factors that led to the selection (or non-selection) of a candidate. The side dish? A generous helping of lessons learned, served up with a delightful garnish of feedback and improvement.

Let's not forget that the hiring process is a high-stakes game, my friends. Every decision made in this labyrinthine maze of recruitment has a direct impact on the organization's performance, culture, and bottom line. A post mortem allows the team to evaluate and dissect each decision, like a master surgeon skillfully wielding a scalpel, to ensure that they emerge victorious in this relentless battle for talent.

And finally, the pièce de résistance: the continuous improvement of the hiring process itself. As any entrepreneur worth their salt knows, progress is a never-ending pursuit. A post mortem is the perfect opportunity to identify gaps, weaknesses, and inefficiencies in the hiring process, allowing the team to fine-tune their tactics and strategies in the ongoing war for talent.

In conclusion, the point of a post mortem – or candidate debrief session – is to extract those invaluable nuggets of information, to learn from past decisions, and to refine the hiring process. It's all about embracing the data, finding the signal amidst the noise, and ultimately, ensuring the continued success and growth of the organization.

What To Ask In The Debrief

Alright, so you're a recruiter looking to debrief with a hiring manager after interviewing a candidate. The key here is to gather valuable insights and assess whether the candidate fits the role and the company culture. Here are some crucial questions you should ask during the debrief:

- Overall impression: What was the hiring manager's first impression of the candidate? Did they come across as professional, enthusiastic, and a good fit for the team?

- Skills and qualifications: How well did the candidate demonstrate their skills and qualifications for the job? Did they provide concrete examples of their accomplishments and how they've applied their skills in previous roles?

- Cultural fit: How well does the candidate align with the company's values, culture, and work environment? Can the hiring manager envision them collaborating effectively with the team?

- Problem-solving and critical thinking: Were there any instances during the interview where the candidate showcased their problem-solving abilities or critical thinking skills? How did they handle tough questions or hypothetical situations?

- Communication and interpersonal skills: How effectively did the candidate communicate their ideas and experiences? Were they able to articulate their thoughts clearly and confidently? How were their interpersonal skills during the interview?

- Growth potential and ambition: Did the candidate express an interest in growing within the company? Did they seem ambitious and eager to take on new challenges?

- Concerns or red flags: Were there any concerns or red flags raised during the interview that the hiring manager would like to discuss further?

- Comparison to other candidates: How does this candidate compare to other potential candidates for the role? Do they stand out as the top choice, or are there other candidates who may be a better fit?

- Next steps: If the hiring manager feels positive about the candidate, could you discuss the next steps in the hiring process, such as reference checks, additional interviews, or extending an offer? If there are reservations, discuss whether it's worth proceeding with the candidate or if it's time to consider other options.

By asking these targeted questions during the debrief, you'll gain a comprehensive understanding of the candidate's strengths and weaknesses and help the hiring manager make a well-informed decision.

Silver Medalists & Multiple Finalists

Ah, the Silver Medalists—those who come achingly close to securing the job but ultimately fall just short of the finish line. So, what happens to these near-champions in the hiring process, and can we make a case for hiring multiple candidates?

You see, Silver Medalists are often exceptional candidates who possess a wealth of skills and experience. Their only "fault" is that they weren't quite as perfect a fit as the Gold Medalist. But let's not be hasty in discarding these valuable contenders. We're in a war for talent, my friends, and in this battle, the smart money is on making the most of every opportunity.

So, how can we capitalize on the Silver Medalists? First, consider maintaining a talent pipeline—a veritable reservoir of top-tier candidates that you can tap into when new opportunities arise. By keeping these Silver Medalists warm and engaged, you're ready to strike when the iron is hot, ensuring that you always have a steady stream of qualified candidates at your disposal.

Now, let's address the million-dollar question: Can a case be made for hiring multiple candidates? Absolutely! But, of course, it's all about the circumstances. If your organization has multiple roles to fill or anticipates a surge in demand, these Silver Medalists could be your secret weapon. By bringing them on board, you're not only maximizing your return on investment in the hiring process but also arming yourself with a formidable team of high-caliber professionals.

However, one must exercise caution in pursuing this strategy. The key is to ensure that there's a genuine need and a well-defined role for each candidate. After all, haphazardly adding resources without a clear plan can lead to a bloated, inefficient workforce—a scenario that no organization wants to find itself in.

In conclusion, Silver Medalists should not be overlooked in the hiring process. By maintaining a talent pipeline and considering the potential to hire multiple candidates when appropriate, organizations can optimize their recruitment efforts and build a workforce poised for success.

Chapter Ten

Next Level

Technology recruiting is a relentless quest for the elusive unicorns of the talent market. Let's explore how to elevate your recruiting efforts by asking the right screening questions, networking in the right groups, and harnessing the almighty power of Boolean search to find the "unfindable." Let's break it down:

- **Applicable technologies:** The technologies associated with a particular engineering job aren't just buzzwords; they're the lifeblood of the role. They are the tools that engineers use to sculpt the digital landscape, and they're constantly evolving. To find the right candidate, you need to understand these technologies as intimately as possible. This isn't just about separating the wheat from the chaff, it's about identifying the very best stalk of wheat in the entire field.

- **Screening questions:** The art of asking the right questions is a skill that separates the amateur recruiters from the true masters of their craft. To uncover the gems in the rough, you must delve deep into the candidate's experience and technical prowess. Craft targeted, incisive questions that probe their expertise in specific languages, frameworks, tools, and methodologies. Inquire about their problem-solving abilities, collaboration skills, and capacity to adapt in a dynamic environment. By asking the right screening questions, you'll separate the wheat from the chaff, bringing you one step closer to the coveted prize.

- **Networking in the right groups:** In the ever-evolving landscape of technology, the most valuable connections are often forged in the trenches of online forums, discussion groups, and social media platforms. Seek out these hallowed digital grounds where technology professionals congregate and engage in spirited discourse. Join groups on LinkedIn, follow influential voices on Twitter, and immerse yourself in the vibrant communities on GitHub, Stack Overflow, and Reddit. By networking in the right groups, you'll expand your reach, gain insider knowledge, and tap into a veritable goldmine of potential candidates.

- **Boolean search:** Ah, the mighty Boolean search—a potent tool that allows you to pierce the veil of obscurity and uncover the hidden gems lurking in the digital shadows. With the strategic use of AND, OR, and NOT operators, along with quotation marks, parentheses, and asterisks, you can craft powerful search queries that hone in on the specific skills, qualifications, and experience you seek. Use Boolean search to scour the depths of LinkedIn, Google, and other search engines, deftly navigating the vast sea of information to find the "unfindable."

Taking your technology recruiting efforts to the next level is a matter of asking the right screening questions, networking in the right groups, and mastering the art of Boolean search. By wielding these tools with skill and finesse, you'll conquer the challenges of the talent market and emerge victorious in your quest for the finest technology professionals. We'll tackle this triad in a unique way, reviewing the roles that we enumerated in previous sections.

Front-end Developer

A front-end developer is a skilled professional who designs, develops, and implements user interfaces for web and mobile applications, ensuring seamless user experiences. They utilize programming languages and technologies such as HTML, CSS, and JavaScript to bring designs to life and optimize performance across various devices and platforms.

Applicable Technologies

The common technology stack for a front-end developer generally consists of a combination of languages, libraries, and frameworks that enable the creation of visually appealing and interactive web applications. Here's a breakdown of the key components of a typical front-end technology stack:

- **HTML (HyperText Markup Language)**: HTML is the backbone of any web page, providing the basic structure and content. It is essential for defining elements like headings, paragraphs, lists, tables, and forms.

- **CSS (Cascading Style Sheets)**: CSS is responsible for the visual appearance and styling of a web page, including layout, colors, fonts, and other design elements. It allows developers to apply styles consistently across multiple pages and ensure that websites look good on different devices and screen sizes.

- **JavaScript**: JavaScript is the primary programming language for front-end development, enabling interactivity and dynamic content on web pages. It allows developers to manipulate HTML and CSS elements, handle user input, and create animations and transitions.

In addition to these core languages, front-end developers often utilize various libraries and frameworks to streamline their work and enhance functionality:

- **jQuery**: jQuery is a widely used JavaScript library that simplifies tasks like DOM manipulation, event handling, and animation, making it easier to work with JavaScript.

- **React**: React is a popular JavaScript library developed by Facebook, designed for building user interfaces with reusable components. It enables developers to create complex, high-performance applications with a more manageable codebase.

- **Angular**: Angular is a powerful front-end framework developed by Google, suitable for building complex, large-scale web applications. It uses a declarative approach to building user interfaces, and supports features like two-way data binding, dependency injection, and modular architecture.

- **Vue.js**: Vue.js is a lightweight, flexible, and easy-to-learn JavaScript framework for building user interfaces. It is known for its simplicity, clear documentation, and adaptability, making it a popular choice for both small and large projects.

- **CSS Preprocessors** (e.g., Sass[40], LESS[41]): CSS preprocessors extend the capabilities of CSS,

---

[40] What's Sass?

Now, when it comes to web development, we all know that CSS (Cascading Style Sheets) is the language responsible for styling our websites, giving them that eye-catching appeal. But here's the thing: CSS can be a bit, well, tedious and repetitive. That's where Sass swoops in, like a superhero of efficiency and elegance.

Sass, short for Syntactically Awesome Style Sheets, is a CSS preprocessor that takes the power of CSS and enhances it with a range of incredible features. Imagine Sass as a magical translator that understands a more human-friendly language and converts it into CSS that browsers can understand.

Now, why should we care? Well, my friends, Sass brings productivity gains and sanity to the world of front-end developers. With Sass, you can write cleaner, more modular, and reusable code. It introduces variables, mixins, functions, and nesting capabilities, allowing developers to create CSS stylesheets that are easier to maintain and scale. Think of it as injecting efficiency and organization into your style sheets, making them more powerful and flexible.

Sass empowers developers to establish consistent design patterns, reduce code duplication, and effortlessly manage complex styling requirements. It facilitates the creation of style guides and component libraries, promoting consistency and collaboration across projects. With Sass, you can make your code more concise and expressive, freeing up time to focus on higher-level design and functionality.

In the ever-evolving landscape of web development, Sass has emerged as a game-changer, streamlining workflows and elevating the quality of CSS development. Its relevance is not to be underestimated, as it continues to be embraced by industry professionals and serves as a valuable tool for enhancing productivity and maintaining codebases.

So, my friends, embrace the power of Sass and let it revolutionize the way you approach CSS. Harness its capabilities, unlock your creative potential, and create remarkable web experiences that captivate users and elevate your digital presence.

41 What's LESS?

LESS, my friends, is a game-changer in the realm of CSS preprocessors. It's like taking the best parts of CSS and injecting them with a dose of efficiency and awesomeness. You see, writing CSS can be a laborious task, full of repetitive code and limited functionality. But fear not, for LESS swoops in to save the day!

This magical tool extends CSS with dynamic features, making your stylesheets more powerful and flexible. It introduces variables, mixins, functions, and nesting, giving you the ability to create reusable code snippets, define constants, and manipulate styles like never before. It's like having a secret weapon up your sleeve, empowering you to write cleaner, more maintainable CSS code.

Now, why should you care about LESS? Well, my friends, it's all about productivity and scalability. With LESS, you can organize your stylesheets more efficiently, reduce redundancy, and make updates a breeze. Need to change a color scheme throughout your entire website? No problem! Just update the variable, and watch the magic happen across all your stylesheets.

But wait, there's more! LESS also integrates seamlessly with your existing CSS workflow. You can compile LESS code into standard CSS, ensuring compatibility with all browsers. Plus, it plays nicely with popular build tools like Grunt and Gulp, automating the compilation process and saving you precious time and effort.

rules, mixins, and other advanced features that make it easier to manage and maintain stylesheets.

- **Version Control Systems** (e.g., Git[42]): Version control systems are essential for managing code

---

So, my dear comrades in the world of web development, embrace the power of LESS! Unlock the potential of CSS preprocessors and join the ranks of the efficient, the savvy, and the future-minded. With LESS, you'll elevate your CSS game to new heights and leave your competition in the dust.

[42] What is Git?

Alright, folks, let's dive into the world of version control and the game-changer known as Git. Strap in, because this is one of those technological innovations that's making waves across industries.

Git, my friends, is the rockstar of version control systems. It's a distributed version control system that allows developers to track changes in their codebase over time. Think of it as a superhero's tool belt, enabling collaboration, efficiency, and transparency in software development.

In the realm of version control, Git reigns supreme. It allows multiple developers to work on the same project simultaneously, seamlessly merging their changes. No more convoluted email threads or overwritten code nightmares. Git takes care of it all, ensuring that everyone's contributions are preserved and conflicts are resolved intelligently.

What sets Git apart is its distributed nature. It means that every developer has a local copy of the entire code repository, allowing them to work offline and independently. Gone are the days of reliance on a central server for every little task. Git empowers developers to explore, experiment, and iterate at lightning speed.

and collaborating with other developers. Git is the most widely used version control system, allowing developers to track changes, create branches, and merge code seamlessly.

- **Build Tools and Task Runners** (e.g., Webpack[43], Grunt[44], Gulp[45]): Build tools and

But wait, there's more! Git brings sanity to version control with its branching and merging capabilities. Developers can create branches to work on specific features or fixes without disturbing the main codebase. And when it's time to bring it all together, Git's merging prowess shines bright, ensuring a seamless integration of changes.

Now, Git isn't just for the coding elite; it's for all of us who value efficiency and collaboration. From small startups to giant enterprises, Git has revolutionized how teams work together, enhancing productivity and accelerating innovation.

So, my friends, embrace Git and its powers. With Git, version control is no longer a headache but a symphony of collaboration, creativity, and control. It's time to unlock the true potential of your code and soar to new heights.

Git on, my fellow innovators. Git on.

[43] Tell me more about Webpack. Well, think of it as the ultimate bundler, the maestro of module bundling in the web development symphony.

Webpack takes your JavaScript code, along with all its dependencies, and bundles them together into a single, optimized file. It's like packing up all the components of a complex machine into a neat, efficient package. This bundling process not only improves performance by reducing the number of requests needed to load your application, but it also enables you to leverage cutting-edge JavaScript features, like ES6 modules, without worrying about browser compatibility.

task runners help automate repetitive tasks, such

But webpack doesn't stop there. It's not just about bundling; it's about transforming and optimizing your code too. With its powerful loaders and plugins, webpack can handle all sorts of tasks, from transpiling and minifying your JavaScript and CSS to optimizing images and even injecting required assets into your HTML. It's like having a Swiss Army knife for web development, saving you time and effort.

Furthermore, webpack embraces the concept of code splitting, allowing you to divide your application into smaller chunks that can be loaded on-demand. This means faster initial page loads and improved user experience. It's all about delivering the right code at the right time, optimizing performance in ways that make your competitors green with envy.

In summary, webpack is the superhero of web development tools. It bundles, optimizes, and transforms your code, while also providing incredible flexibility and performance enhancements. It's like having a genius assistant that takes care of the heavy lifting, allowing you to focus on crafting exceptional web experiences. So, embrace webpack and unlock a world of possibilities in your web development endeavors.

[44] I am Grunt... no really, what is Grunt?

Grunt, much like the name suggests, is a workhorse—a hardworking, no-nonsense tool designed to simplify repetitive tasks in web development. It takes those laborious, monotonous chores that developers once had to endure and swiftly handles them, sparing precious time and sanity.

Picture this: You're a developer, knee-deep in lines of code, battling a horde of files to concatenate, minify, and optimize. Enter Grunt, galloping to your rescue. With its mighty configuration files and an arsenal of plugins, Grunt allows you to automate these mind-numbing tasks effortlessly. Concatenating and minifying CSS and JavaScript files? Piece of cake. Optimizing images? Done in a blink of an eye.

as minification, compilation, and concatenation,

But Grunt isn't just about brute force; it's a versatile creature. Need to compile Sass or Less files into CSS? Grunt's got your back. Want to run unit tests, linters, or even deploy your project to a remote server? Fear not, for Grunt can handle it all.

Its true beauty lies in its extensibility. With an abundance of community-developed plugins, Grunt can adapt to your specific needs, making it a powerful ally in your development journey. Whether you're building a simple website or tackling a complex web application, Grunt is there, snorting and stomping through the challenges.

So, my friends, embrace the power of Grunt. Let it carry the burden of repetitive tasks, freeing you to focus on the artistry of code. Harness the mighty beast and unleash its potential to conquer the digital realm. For in the realm of web development, Grunt reigns supreme, bringing efficiency and automation to the brave warriors of code.

Ride on, dear developers. Ride on with Grunt by your side!

[45] Gulp, my friends, is a task runner. It's like having your very own assistant handling the repetitive and mundane tasks that eat away at your precious time. With Gulp, you can automate a plethora of development tasks, from bundling and minifying your JavaScript and CSS files to optimizing images and even refreshing your browser automatically as you make changes. Yes, you heard that right - it's all about making your life easier, more efficient, and dare I say, more enjoyable.

Imagine this: You're knee-deep in code, trying to optimize your website's performance. Instead of tediously minifying each CSS and JavaScript file by hand, Gulp swoops in like a superhero and does it all for you with just a few lines of code. It's like having a magic wand that eliminates the tedium and gets you back to doing what you love - creating remarkable digital experiences.

And Gulp doesn't stop there. It has an extensive ecosystem of plugins that you can leverage to supercharge your development

improving development workflow and optimizing the final output for production.

This is by no means an exhaustive list, but it provides a solid foundation for understanding the common technology stack used by front-end developers. It's important to note that different projects and teams may have preferences for specific tools and frameworks, depending on their requirements and expertise.

Screening Questions

A recruiter should ask a front-end developer a mix of technical and behavioral questions[46] to assess their skills,

---

process. Need to compile Sass into CSS? Gulp has you covered. Want to automatically prefix your CSS for cross-browser compatibility? Gulp will take care of that too. The possibilities are as vast as your imagination.

But here's the best part, my friends: Gulp is built on Node.js, a platform that powers some of the most innovative and scalable applications out there. This means you're tapping into a world of cutting-edge technology, backed by a vibrant community of developers who are constantly pushing the boundaries of what's possible.

So, if you're ready to level up your development game and reclaim your time, Gulp is the tool for you. Embrace the power of automation, and let Gulp be your trusty sidekick in the realm of web development.

Stay innovative, my friends, and may your code flow as smoothly as a glass of fine single malt scotch. Cheers!

[46] What's a Behavioral Question? Well, let me tell you about

experience, and compatibility with the team. Here are ten suggested questions:

- Can you describe your experience with HTML, CSS, and JavaScript, and how you've used these technologies in your previous projects?
- How do you approach responsive web design? Can you share an example of a project where you implemented responsive design techniques?
- Which JavaScript frameworks or libraries are you most comfortable working with, such as

behavioral interview questions, dear listener. Picture yourself in the hot seat, being grilled by a potential employer who's trying to determine if you're the perfect fit for their company. A behavioral interview question is designed to help them do just that.

These types of questions are rooted in the belief that your past behavior is the best predictor of your future performance. So instead of asking you to simply list your skills or speculate about hypothetical situations, they delve into your actual experiences. And boy, do they expect you to come prepared with stories that illustrate how you've handled various scenarios.

So, imagine they ask you something like, "Tell me about a time when you had to navigate a difficult team dynamic." They're not looking for you to sugarcoat it or give them a cookie-cutter answer. They want to hear about a real experience that demonstrates your problem-solving abilities, communication skills, and emotional intelligence.

In other words, they're trying to see if you can walk the walk, not just talk the talk. It's like a sneak peek into how you might handle challenges at their company. So, the next time you find yourself in an interview, be prepared to strut your stuff with some well-crafted anecdotes that showcase your brilliant, problem-solving abilities.

React, Angular, or Vue.js? Can you discuss a project where you used one of these frameworks or libraries?

- Can you explain the concept of the Document Object Model (DOM)? How do you manipulate the DOM using JavaScript?
- How do you ensure web accessibility in your projects? Can you provide an example of how you've implemented accessibility best practices in a previous project?
- What tools and techniques do you use to optimize website performance, such as minimizing file sizes, reducing HTTP requests, or caching resources?
- Can you discuss your experience with version control systems like Git? How do you use them to collaborate with other developers in a team setting?
- How do you handle browser compatibility issues? Can you give an example of a challenge you faced in this area and how you resolved it?
- Can you talk about a challenging front-end project you've worked on? What obstacles did you encounter, and how did you overcome them?
- How do you stay up-to-date with the latest front-end development trends and best practices? What resources do you use to continue learning and improving your skills?

Networking Groups

Well, my friend, it appears that you're on the prowl for some exquisite networking opportunities to mingle with the front-end developer elite. Fear not, for I shall illuminate your path to greatness with a smattering of both online and IRL congregations that'll have you rubbing elbows with the coding glitterati in no time.

First, let's dive into the wondrous world of online communities. I present to you:

- **Stack Overflow**: Ah, the crown jewel of the developer's domain. A place where your insatiable thirst for knowledge can be quenched, and your brilliant insights shared with eager minds.

- **GitHub**: Where the cool kids of code hang out. Contribute to open-source projects, strut your code-stylings, and mingle with the crème de la crème of the developer world.

- **Reddit**: Venture into the subreddits such as r/frontend, r/webdev, or r/javascript. You'll find a treasure trove of wisdom and camaraderie amongst these digital denizens.

- **Frontend Masters**: This online learning platform is a veritable buffet of knowledge, offering the chance to connect with experts and fellow developers as you sharpen your skills.

Now, let us transition to the realm of IRL associations, where the intoxicating aroma of coffee fuels the creative synapses of front-end maestros:

- **Meetup.com**: This platform is a smorgasbord of local gatherings and events tailored to your interests. Seek out front-end development or coding meetups in your area, and prepare to be immersed in a sea of like-minded individuals.

- **Hackathons**: The gladiatorial arenas of the coding world. Test your mettle in these epic coding battles and forge alliances with fellow warriors along the way.

- **Conferences**: The star-studded galas of the front-end scene. Events like JSConf, CSSConf, and ReactConf are where the luminaries of the industry gather to share knowledge and network.

- **Local coding bootcamps and workshops**: Enroll in these intensive, hands-on courses to not only level up your skills but also to mingle with fellow aspiring developers.

So, my friend, gird yourself with the knowledge I have bestowed upon you, and embark on your journey to conquer the front-end universe. Connect, collaborate, and ascend to your rightful place among the coding elite. Godspeed!

Boolean Search

Looking inside of LinkedIn:
"front-end developer" AND (HTML OR CSS OR JavaScript)

Using a site search to X-Ray LinkedIn:
site:linkedin.com/in ("web developer" OR "frontend engineer") (React OR Vue OR Angular)

Using a site search to X-Ray Github:
site:github.com/* "UI developer" ("responsive design" OR Bootstrap OR "Material-UI")

Using a filetype command to uncover resumes:
filetype:pdf resume ("user interface" OR "user experience" OR UX OR UI) developer JavaScript

Back-end Developer

A back-end engineer is responsible for designing, developing, and maintaining the server-side components of web applications, ensuring seamless data processing and storage. They focus on optimizing system performance and functionality, laying the foundation for a robust and scalable digital architecture.

Applicable Technologies

The technology stack for a back-end developer can vary widely depending on the organization, the specific project, and the developer's own preferences. However, some common technologies and tools that are frequently used in back-end development include:

- **Programming languages**: Back-end developers often work with languages like Python, Java, PHP, Ruby, C#, Go, and Node.js (JavaScript). These languages are used for server-side scripting and building the core logic of an application.

- **Web frameworks**: Web frameworks provide a structure and set of tools for building web applications. Common web frameworks for back-end development include Django and Flask (Python), Ruby on Rails (Ruby), Express.js (Node.js), Laravel (PHP), and Spring Boot (Java).

- **Databases**: Back-end developers need to work with databases to store, retrieve, and manage data. Common database management systems include relational databases like MySQL, PostgreSQL, and Microsoft SQL Server, as well as NoSQL databases like MongoDB, Cassandra, and Redis.

- **API design and development**: Back-end developers often create APIs (Application Programming Interfaces) to enable communication between the server-side and client-side of an application. Tools and technologies for API development include RESTful APIs, GraphQL, and tools like Postman, Swagger, and Insomnia for API testing and documentation.

- **Web servers**: Web servers handle client requests and serve web content. Common web servers include Apache, Nginx, and Microsoft's Internet Information Services (IIS).

- **Version control systems**: Version control systems help developers collaborate and manage changes to their code. Git is the most widely used version control system, and platforms like GitHub, GitLab, and Bitbucket provide web-based repositories for Git projects.

- **Containerization and virtualization**: Tools like Docker and Kubernetes are used to create, deploy, and manage application containers, making it easier to develop, test, and deploy applications across different environments. Virtualization tools like VirtualBox and VMware are also useful for creating and managing virtual machines to run applications in isolated environments.

- **Continuous integration and continuous deployment (CI/CD)**: CI/CD tools help automate the process of building, testing, and deploying applications. Popular CI/CD tools include Jenkins, GitLab CI/CD, Travis CI, and CircleCI.

- **Cloud platforms**: Back-end developers may work with cloud platforms like Amazon Web Services (AWS), Google Cloud Platform (GCP), or Microsoft Azure for deploying and managing applications, databases, and other services.

This list is not exhaustive, as back-end developers may work with a wide variety of tools and technologies. The specific stack used will depend on factors such as the project requirements, industry, and company preferences.

Screening Questions

A recruiter can ask a variety of questions to assess a back-end developer's technical skills, problem-solving abilities, and experience working in a team. Here are ten sample questions:

- Can you briefly explain your experience with back-end development and the programming languages you are proficient in?
- How do you ensure the security of a web application? Can you provide examples of best practices to prevent common security vulnerabilities?
- Can you explain the differences between SQL and NoSQL databases? When would you choose one over the other?
- What is RESTful API design, and why is it important for back-end developers? Can you describe a project where you implemented RESTful APIs?
- Describe your experience with version control systems, such as Git. How do you handle merge conflicts, and what strategies do you use to avoid them?
- Can you explain the concept of horizontal and vertical scaling in a distributed system? What factors should be considered when deciding between the two?
- How do you approach performance optimization in your projects? Can you provide an example of a performance issue you faced and how you resolved it?
- What tools or frameworks do you use for testing and debugging back-end code? Can you discuss

the importance of automated testing in the development process?
- Can you describe a challenging problem you faced during a past project and how you collaborated with your team to solve it? What was the outcome?
- How do you stay up-to-date with the latest trends and technologies in back-end development? What resources do you use for continuous learning?

Networking Groups

You want to know where to find the masters of the code universe, those back-end engineers who hang out at the intersections of Java, Python, and Ruby? Let's cut to the chase.

First, as we orbit the virtual universe:

- **Reddit** - It's like New York City. There's a neighborhood for everyone. Subreddits like r/java, r/python, and r/ruby can help you drill down to specifics.

- **LinkedIn Groups** - Still one of the most underappreciated social networks. Groups like Java Developers, Python Developers Network, and Ruby on Rails Developers are gold mines.

- **Slack Communities** - These are the hip, new office water coolers. Check out communities like the Python Community Slack, Java programmers on Javarelated, and Rails on Ruby on Rails Link.

Now, let's disembark the digital vessel and venture into the real world:

- **Conferences** - These are the big leagues. PyCon, RubyConf, and Oracle's JavaOne are like the Super Bowl for their respective languages. These are places to learn, network, and party with your fellow code warriors.

- **Tech Hubs and Co-working Spaces** - These are the modern-day monasteries, where the monks of code come to transcribe the digital scriptures. Check out the events and networking opportunities that they offer.

- **Professional Associations** - For the serious players. IEEE Computer Society, Association for Computing Machinery, and others often have specialized groups focused on specific languages.

Boolean Search

Looking inside of LinkedIn:

"Back-end engineer" AND (java OR j2ee OR "java enterprise") AND (mysql OR nosql)

Using a site search to X-Ray LinkedIn:
site:linkedin.com/in ("back-end developer" OR "back end engineer") ("node.js" OR "express.js") (mongodb OR dynamodb)

Using a site search to X-Ray Github:
site:github.com/* ("back-end developer" OR "back end engineer") (ieee OR "apache foundation")

Using a filetype command to uncover resumes:
filetype:pdf resume (("back-end" OR "back end") (developer OR engineer)) (grails OR rails) (ruby OR groovy)

Full-stack Developer

A full-stack developer is a professional who is capable of handling all the work of databases, servers, systems engineering, and clients. They are involved in a project from start to end i.e., from the planning stage to the finished product.

Full-stack development involves two key areas:

- **Front-End Development**: This involves developing the interface that users interact with. This includes everything you see in the browser, including forms and layouts, user interaction, design, and more. Front-end developers usually work with technologies like HTML, CSS, and

JavaScript, along with libraries or frameworks like React, Angular, or Vue.js.

- **Back-End Development**: This involves the server-side of applications, ensuring that data or services requested by the front end are delivered effectively. It includes creating, maintaining, and testing databases, servers, APIs, and handling security and data management issues. Back-end developers usually work with programming languages like Python, Ruby, Java, PHP, or .NET, as well as database technologies like SQL, PostgreSQL, MySQL, or MongoDB.

In essence, a full-stack developer has a broad knowledge base and is able to work on and understand all layers of software development. They are often key assets in small teams or startups where a wide range of skills is needed. However, it's important to note that while a full-stack developer can work across multiple layers, they may not necessarily have the same depth of expertise in all areas as a specialist would.

Applicable Technologies

A full-stack developer needs to be proficient in various software technologies across the front-end (client-side), the back-end (server-side), as well as in handling databases and other infrastructure concerns. Here are examples of a few popular tech stacks that a full-stack developer may use:

Front-End:

- **HTML/CSS**: The foundation of any web application. HTML is used for the structure, and CSS is used for styling.

- **JavaScript**: A critical programming language for front-end development. It allows for the creation of interactive and dynamic web pages.

- **Frameworks and Libraries**: These include Angular, React, Vue.js for JavaScript and Bootstrap for CSS. They provide pre-written code to help speed up development.

- **Preprocessors**: These include Sass for CSS and TypeScript for JavaScript. They extend the features of the base language.

Back-End:

- **Programming Languages**: These include JavaScript (Node.js), Python, Ruby, Java, PHP, and C#. The choice often depends on the requirements of the project or the team's familiarity.

- **Frameworks**: These include Express.js for Node.js, Django or Flask for Python, Rails for Ruby, Spring for Java, Laravel for PHP, and .NET for C#.

- **Database Systems**: SQL-based databases like PostgreSQL, MySQL, or MSSQL, and NoSQL databases like MongoDB or Cassandra.

- **Server Technologies**: Technologies like Nginx, Apache, Microsoft IIS.

DevOps/Infrastructure:

- **Containerization Tools**: Docker, Kubernetes are commonly used for creating and managing containers.

- **Cloud Providers**: AWS, Google Cloud, Azure are commonly used for hosting applications and databases, and also provide a suite of related services.

- **Continuous Integration/Continuous Deployment (CI/CD)**: Tools like Jenkins, GitLab CI, or GitHub Actions are used for automating the deployment process.

Version Control System:

- **Git**: Most developers use Git for version control, along with platforms like GitHub, GitLab, or Bitbucket for code storage and collaboration.

Testing tools:

- Unit Testing: Tools like Jest, Mocha, Jasmine, or unittest.
- End-to-End Testing: Tools like Selenium, Puppeteer, or Cypress.

Screening Questions

There are any number of questions that a recruiter can ask a full-stack developer; a recruiter can ask a variety of questions to assess a full-stack developer's technical skills, problem-solving abilities, and experience working in a team. Here are a few:

- Can you describe your current (or most recent) role and your responsibilities there?
- Can you tell me about the most complex project you've worked on? What was your role in that project?
- How do you keep your technology skills current?
- What languages are you most comfortable coding in?

- Can you describe your experience with front-end technologies like HTML/CSS/JavaScript and any particular libraries or frameworks you've used, like React, Angular, or Vue.js?
- What back-end technologies do you have experience with? This could include languages like Python, Java, or Ruby and frameworks like Django, Spring, or Rails.
- Could you describe your experience with databases? Do you have a preference for SQL or NoSQL databases? What specific systems have you used (e.g., MySQL, PostgreSQL, MongoDB)?
- How comfortable are you with cloud-based services (like AWS, Google Cloud, Azure)?
- What version control systems have you used (like Git, Mercurial)?
- Can you describe a time you encountered a difficult bug or issue in your code? How did you go about diagnosing and fixing it?
- How do you approach problem-solving when you're given a task with an open-ended solution?
- Can you describe your experience working in a team? What was your role, and how did you collaborate with others?
- Have you ever had to explain a technical problem or concept to a non-technical colleague or stakeholder? How did you approach this?

- What kind of work environment do you thrive in?

Networking Groups

Hey, there you go. In the realm of tech, being part of a tribe, a collective group of minds, can be a catalyst for your growth, your innovation, and your advancement. And yes, we're talking about networking. I'm not talking about sipping terrible cocktails at some Holiday Inn. I'm talking about connecting in the digital world and at conferences where ideas are exchanged at the speed of light.

Let's dive into the specifics. If you're looking for a full-stack engineer, consider the following groups:

- **GitHub**: Okay, it might seem obvious, but if you're not on GitHub, you're missing out. It's the world's largest community of developers to discover, share, and build better software.

- **Stack Overflow**: Another no-brainer. Stack Overflow isn't just a platform for solving your bug issues. It's a community. Dig deeper and you'll find networks of engineers sharing knowledge and experience.

- **Meetup**: This platform has tech-specific groups where you can connect with like-minded individuals. Just search "Full Stack Developers" and voila.

- **Google Developer Groups**: Google has done a stellar job building communities around the globe. They often organize conferences, hackathons, and coding bootcamps.

- **Full Stack Reddit**: Subreddits can be surprisingly helpful. r/webdev and r/learnprogramming are some you should check out.

But let's get more granular. You want Cloud Engineers? DevOps Engineers? Strap in:

- **AWS User Groups**: Find local AWS user groups in your city. The networking at these groups is a goldmine for cloud engineers.

- **Google Cloud Community**: Just as Amazon does with AWS, Google has its own community of cloud engineers. You'll find plenty of resources and connections here.

- **Azure DevOps User Group**: For DevOps, Microsoft's Azure DevOps User Group is an excellent resource.

- **DevOps Subreddit (r/devops)**: Reddit's r/devops is another hotspot for DevOps professionals to share, learn, and connect.

- **LinkedIn Groups**: LinkedIn isn't just for self-promotion. Join groups like 'Cloud Computing, Cybersecurity, & SaaS Community' or 'Global DevOps' to get insights and establish connections.

For IRL meetups and associations, consider these:

- **AWS Summits**: Attend these to learn about new technologies and connect with cloud engineers in person.

- **Google Cloud Next**: Google's annual conference for developers and businesses on Google Cloud.

- **DevOps Days**: A worldwide series of technical conferences covering topics of software development, IT infrastructure, and the intersection between them.

In summary, the web is full of communities and groups for full-stack, cloud, and DevOps engineers. But remember, networking is a two-way street. Don't just take, give. Share your knowledge, offer help, and build relationships based on trust and mutual respect. These platforms are just the beginning, your curiosity is the real catalyst.

And yes, the cocktails at most conferences are still terrible, but who knows? You might meet your next co-founder or discover the missing piece to your cloud architecture puzzle while downing that third margarita. And that's the beauty of it.

Boolean Search

Looking inside of LinkedIn:
"Full Stack Engineer" AND (JavaScript OR Python OR Ruby) AND ("Node.js" OR Django OR Rails) AND (React OR "Vue.js" OR Angular) AND sql

Using a site search to X-Ray LinkedIn:
site:linkedin.com/in ("Full Stack Developer" OR "Software Engineer") (HTML OR CSS OR JavaScript) ("Front-end" "Back-end") (REST OR GraphQL)

Using a site search to X-Ray Github:
site:github.com/* ("Full Stack Engineer" OR "Full-stack Developer") AWS (MySQL OR PostgreSQL) ("Version Control" OR Git) Agile

Using a filetype command to uncover resumes:

filetype:pdf resume ("Software Engineer" OR "Web Developer") (Python OR JavaScript OR Java) (Django OR "Express.js" OR "Spring Boot") "Full-stack"

Remember to adjust these search strings based on the specific requirements for your full-stack engineer role.

DevOps Engineer

A DevOps engineer is a professional who works with software developers, system operators (SysOps), and other production IT staff to oversee code releases and deployments. The role of a DevOps engineer is to bridge the gap between development and operations teams, fostering a culture of collaboration and shared responsibility.

DevOps is a combination of two terms, "Development" and "Operations." It's a practice that aims at merging software development (Dev) and software operation (Ops). The primary goal of DevOps is to shorten the product system development life cycle while also delivering features, fixes, and updates frequently in close alignment with business objectives.

A DevOps engineer may be involved in tasks such as:

- **Configuration Management**: Automation of the configuration of servers using tools like Puppet, Chef, Ansible, or SaltStack.

- **Infrastructure as Code (IaC)**: Writing scripts to automate infrastructure deployment using tools like AWS CloudFormation, Google Cloud Deployment Manager, or Terraform.

- **CI/CD Pipeline Management**: Building, setting up, maintaining, and improving Continuous Integration/Continuous Deployment pipelines. Tools used for this purpose can include Jenkins, Travis CI, CircleCI, GitLab, or GitHub Actions.

- **Containerization and Orchestration**: Managing and deploying applications in containers using tools like Docker and orchestrating them with Kubernetes.

- **Monitoring and Logging**: Implementing monitoring and logging solutions for application and infrastructure health. Tools for this can include Grafana, Prometheus, ELK Stack (Elasticsearch, Logstash, Kibana), or Splunk.

- **Cloud Services**: Managing and working with cloud resources in platforms like AWS, Google Cloud Platform (GCP), or Microsoft Azure.

- **Security Operations**: Ensuring the security and compliance of the delivered code and infrastructure, a practice often referred to as DevSecOps.

The exact role of a DevOps engineer can vary from organization to organization, as it can be tailored to fit the specific needs of the company or the project at hand. Some organizations don't even have a specific DevOps role, but rather a DevOps culture where the development and operations teams share DevOps responsibilities.

Applicable Technologies

A DevOps engineer should have a strong understanding of a broad range of technologies. Some of the most important include:

- Version Control Systems (VCS): Git is the most commonly used version control system, and it's critical for DevOps engineers to understand how to version code and configuration, handle branches, merges, and pull requests.

- Continuous Integration/Continuous Deployment (CI/CD): Tools such as Jenkins, GitLab CI/CD, Travis CI, CircleCI, and GitHub Actions are used to automate the testing and deployment of applications. Understanding of these tools and the principles of CI/CD is essential.

- Infrastructure as Code (IaC): DevOps engineers often use tools like Terraform, AWS CloudFormation, or Google Cloud Deployment Manager to automate the provisioning of infrastructure.

- Configuration Management: Tools like Ansible, Puppet, Chef, or SaltStack are used to manage and configure software and systems.

- Containerization Technologies: Docker is the primary technology used for creating and managing containers, which are lightweight, standalone, executable software packages that include everything needed to run a piece of software.

- Container Orchestration: Kubernetes is the leading technology used for managing and orchestrating containers at scale. Other options include Docker Swarm and Apache Mesos.

- Cloud Platforms: Many DevOps roles require proficiency in major cloud platforms such as Amazon Web Services (AWS), Microsoft Azure, or Google Cloud Platform (GCP). Understanding how to deploy, manage, and scale applications in these environments is critical.

- Scripting Languages: DevOps engineers often need to write scripts to automate tasks. This requires proficiency in at least one scripting language, such as Python, Ruby, Bash, or Perl.

- Monitoring and Logging Tools: Tools like Splunk, Elasticsearch/Logstash/Kibana (ELK stack), Prometheus, Grafana, or Datadog are used for monitoring infrastructure and applications and collecting and analyzing logs.

- Security Tools and Practices: Knowledge of security best practices is essential in DevOps to ensure that the infrastructure and applications are secure. This might involve using tools like Chef Inspec, Gauntlt, or OWASP Zap, or practices like integrating security checks into CI/CD pipelines (DevSecOps).

- Networking and System Administration: Understanding of networking concepts (like DNS, TCP/IP, HTTP, network protocols) and system administration (in Linux or Windows) is also essential for a DevOps engineer.

These are just some of the many technologies that a DevOps engineer might need to be proficient in. The specific requirements will vary depending on the role and the organization.

Screening Questions

Here are several questions you might ask in an interview with a potential DevOps engineer:

- What is the DevOps methodology, and how does it benefit an organization?
- Can you explain the difference between Continuous Integration, Continuous Delivery, and Continuous Deployment?
- What are the advantages and disadvantages of mutable and immutable infrastructure?
- Describe how you've used Infrastructure as Code (IaC) in a previous role.
- Tell me about a time when you had to design a scalable, fault-tolerant system. What tools did you use, and what were the considerations you had to take into account?
- What is a version control system? Can you explain how you've used Git (or another version control system) in a previous project?
- How have you used Docker or other containerization technologies in your previous projects?
- Explain what container orchestration is and describe a situation where you used Kubernetes or another orchestration tool.

- Can you describe your experience with cloud platforms like AWS, GCP, or Azure? How have you used them in your projects?
- How do you monitor the health and performance of an application and infrastructure? What tools have you used to do this?
- Tell me about a challenging situation you encountered in a previous DevOps role, and how you resolved it.
- Explain what a CI/CD pipeline is and how you would set one up.
- What scripting languages are you proficient in, and how have you used them in your previous work?
- What is the role of testing in DevOps?
- Can you describe a situation where you implemented a security measure in a DevOps context?

These questions not only test the candidate's theoretical knowledge but also their hands-on experience. Always remember to ask follow-up questions to gain a deeper understanding of their thought process and problem-solving skills.

Networking Groups

Alright, let's rip the Band-Aid off and do this. DevOps engineers, those paragons of digital wizardry, live and breathe in an ecosystem teeming with opportunities for networking, collaboration, and growth. They strut their stuff in various realms, digital and physical, populated by legions of their own kind, reveling in the common currency of ideas, hacks, and late-night, caffeine-fueled rants about Kubernetes.

First off, DevOps. Online. The top-tier platform. You know it, I know it, everyone and their grandmother's Roomba knows it: GitHub. GitHub is like the Studio 54 of DevOps, only without the white suits and coke. It's the mecca of coding, where the huddled masses yearning to SSH freely mingle, share code, and collaborate on projects. It's like LinkedIn for people who actually do stuff. Not on it yet? Well, pull up your big boy or big girl pants, because you're missing out.

Next up is the enigmatic, addictive, and sometimes just straight-up bizarre world of Reddit. A DevOps engineer without a Reddit account is like a hipster without a beard – possible, but highly suspicious. /r/devops and /r/sysadmin are the main hubs for those looking to network, learn, and just generally bathe in the cool, refreshing waters of DevOps culture.

LinkedIn is your spot for a more professional, polished interface. Keep an eye out for groups like DevOps

Professionals. It's less 'hacker's paradise' and more 'white-collar tech talk', but it's invaluable for its trove of career advice and job listings.

But we're not just living in the Matrix here.

Real-life, flesh-and-blood interaction still matters, even if you spend most of your life behind a terminal. Groups like the DevOps Days are your ticket to meat-space networking. These cats host global conferences with self-organizing communities. The events are a veritable Coachella of DevOps, packed with talks, workshops, and presumably more Red Bull than is medically advisable.

Meetups are another surefire bet, like The DevOps Exchange, which holds regular meetings across the globe. This ain't your momma's book club - expect hardcore tech talk, presentations, and a chance to rub shoulders with the people behind the avatars.

If you're willing to throw down some coin, consider getting involved with a professional organization like the DevOps Institute. They've got courses, certifications, and a network that stretches to the moon and back.

So whether you're a certified DevOps badass or just an aspirational noob, there's a spot for you somewhere in this beautiful, chaotic world of code and collaboration.

So get out there, start networking, and remember – the command line is mightier than the sword.

Boolean Search

Looking inside of LinkedIn:
"DevOps Engineer" AND ("CI/CD" OR "continuous integration" OR "continuous delivery") AND ("AWS" OR "Azure" OR "Google Cloud")

Using a site search to X-Ray LinkedIn:
site:linkedin.com/in "DevOps Engineer" Python (automation OR scripting) (ansible OR chef OR puppet)

Using a site search to X-Ray Github:
site:github.com/* (DevOps OR "Cloud Engineer") (terraform OR CloudFormation) (monitoring OR Prometheus OR Grafana OR Datadog)

Using a filetype command to uncover resumes:
filetype:pdf resume (DevOps OR "System Engineer") (containerization OR "virtualization") Linux ("Red Hat" OR Ubuntu OR CentOS)

Quality Assurance (QA) Engineer

A Quality Assurance (QA) Engineer is a professional who ensures that the final product observes the company's quality standards. In essence, they are responsible for the implementation of inspection activities, detection and resolution of problems, and the delivery of satisfactory outcomes.

Here are some of their responsibilities:

- Develop and Implement Quality Assurance Procedures: QA Engineers are often responsible for developing procedures for testing product quality. These procedures provide the framework for the QA process and ensure that it is effectively implemented.

- Test Product Functionality and Output: QA Engineers conduct tests to ensure that products function as expected and deliver the desired output. This involves testing the product under various conditions and scenarios.

- Identify Quality Issues and Implement Solutions: They work to identify any issues with product quality, and once these issues have been identified, they develop and implement solutions to these problems.

- Monitor Efforts to Resolve Product Issues: QA Engineers monitor efforts to resolve product issues to ensure that solutions are implemented and that product quality is maintained.

- Report on Product Quality: They also provide reports on product quality to key stakeholders. These reports provide information on the status of product quality and any issues that need to be addressed.

- Collaborate with Other Teams: QA Engineers often work closely with other teams, including development and product management, to ensure that quality is maintained throughout the product lifecycle. This collaboration allows for the early detection and resolution of quality issues.

In order to perform their roles effectively, QA Engineers need to have strong technical skills, a keen attention to detail, good problem-solving abilities, and excellent communication skills. They often have a background in engineering or a related field and have extensive knowledge of quality assurance methodologies and standards.

Applicable Technologies

Quality Assurance (QA) Engineers work with a range of technologies and tools depending on the specifics of their role and the nature of the project. They often need to be familiar with a variety of software testing tools (for functional testing, regression testing, performance testing, etc.), bug tracking tools, and sometimes even software development and automation tools.

Here are some examples:

- Software Testing Tools: There are many tools available for various types of testing, such as Selenium, Appium, JUnit, TestNG, Postman, and SoapUI. These tools are used for different kinds of tests like functional, performance, API testing, etc.

- Test Management Tools: QA Engineers often use test management tools to organize and manage the testing process. Examples include Zephyr, qTest, and TestRail.

- Bug Tracking/Project Management Tools: Tools such as Jira, Bugzilla, Mantis, and Trello are often used to track defects and manage project tasks.

- Automation Tools: Automation is a big part of modern QA, and QA Engineers may use tools like Selenium, TestComplete, Katalon Studio, or Appium to automate repetitive tests.

- Performance Testing Tools: Tools like Apache JMeter, LoadRunner, Gatling are used to perform load and performance testing.

- Continuous Integration/Continuous Deployment Tools: Tools such as Jenkins, Bamboo, or CircleCI help in integrating the development and testing environments for seamless delivery.

- Version Control Systems: Knowledge of systems like Git is also essential for tracking changes in source code during software development.

- Databases/SQL: QA Engineers often need to interact with databases to verify data, so knowledge of SQL and familiarity with databases (like MySQL, PostgreSQL, Oracle, etc.) is often required.

- Virtualization and Containerization Tools: Tools like Docker and technologies like virtual machines can be used to create controlled and consistent testing environments.

- Cloud Platforms: Knowledge of cloud platforms like AWS, Azure, Google Cloud can be useful for testing applications in cloud environments.

Remember, the exact set of tools a QA Engineer will need to use can vary widely based on their specific role and the nature of the projects they're working on.

Screening Questions

Here are some potential interview questions that a recruiter may ask a Quality Assurance (QA) Engineer:

- Tell us about your experience with automation testing. What tools have you used?
- Can you describe the process you follow for creating test cases?
- Can you discuss a time when you found a significant defect in a product? How did you find it, and how did you handle it?
- How have you used SQL in your previous positions? Can you provide an example of a complex query you had to write?
- What role do you think QA plays in software development?
- What is your approach to regression testing, and how do you decide which test cases to include in a regression suite?
- What types of testing are important for ensuring the quality of software, and why?
- Can you explain the concept of a "test pyramid"? How does it guide your work as a QA engineer?
- Describe a situation where you had to deal with difficult developers or stakeholders regarding a defect or issue you found.

- What tools have you used to manage defects? How did they help you manage your workflow?
- What experience do you have with performance and load testing?
- Tell me about a time you had to learn a new tool or technology to improve the testing process at your previous job.
- How do you determine the severity and priority of a defect?
- What are the key things you would consider when reviewing requirements and design documents from a QA perspective?
- How have you incorporated Agile or Scrum methodologies in your QA process?

These questions aim to gauge the candidate's technical knowledge, problem-solving skills, and understanding of the QA process, as well as their communication skills and ability to handle issues and work as part of a team. The specific questions asked may vary based on the job's requirements and the company's needs.

Networking Groups

Young Jedi, be prepared to thrust your sabers of knowledge and skills into the fray of quality assurance. Let's cut through the haze of the universe, and find those golden gatherings where QA Engineers unite, both in the flesh and in the pixels.

- American Software Testing Qualifications Board (ASTQB) Software Testing Conference: Huddle up, team. This is the Super Bowl of software testing. ASTQB is the who's who, the VIP list of the QA world. You want to be there, brushing shoulders with the best, if you're someone who's really serious about software quality.

- Quality Assurance Institute (QAI) Quest Conference: This isn't just an event. No, no, it's a pilgrimage of sorts, a journey into the heart of quality assurance. Get ready for days jam-packed with workshops, classes, and speeches, all designed to keep you at the top of your game.

- Atlassian Summit: The world of QA doesn't spin without tools like Jira, and who's behind that? Atlassian. Their summit is a vibrant collection of discussions, workshops, and plenty of networking opportunities. Get a taste of the future, and maybe a cocktail or two.

- StarEAST / StarWEST Conference: These are where the Jedi Masters of software testing gather, share their wisdom, and welcome the young Padawans eager to learn. One on the East Coast, one on the West, like the twin suns of Tatooine. Catch them if you can.

- Ministry of Testing: This is not your granddad's ministry, it's a global network, a community of QA fanatics. They host meetups, workshops, and even full-blown conferences both in real life and in the Matrix. Connect with them and find your QA tribe.

- TestBash: Virtual, baby, but with real impact. A global software testing conference that's gone digital. It's like the Netflix of QA - you can binge-watch those quality talks on your own time, no plane ticket needed.

And remember, the digital realm is ripe with countless webinars, forums, online meetups, and social media groups. LinkedIn, Reddit, Stack Overflow, they're all bursting with communities where QA enthusiasts like you converge. As I always say, in this age of connectivity, you don't need a visa to network.

Now go out there, make your mark, and remember: networking isn't just about getting, it's about giving. Be ready to share your expertise, your insight, your charisma. Give generously, and you'll find the world opens up in return.

Boolean Search

Looking inside of LinkedIn:
("QA Engineer" OR *"Quality Assurance Engineer") AND ("software testing"* OR *"test scripts")*

Using a site search to X-Ray LinkedIn:
site:linkedin.com/in ("QA Engineer" OR "QA tester") (Jira OR Bugzilla) "mobile applications"

Using a site search to X-Ray Github:
site:github.com/ "QA Engineer" "performance testing" (LoadRunner OR JMeter)*

Using a filetype command to uncover resumes:
filetype:pdf resume "QA Engineer" "security testing" (OWASP OR "penetration testing")

Test Automation Engineer

A Test Automation Engineer is a professional who specializes in designing, developing, and implementing automated testing solutions for software applications. Their primary responsibility is to create and maintain automated test scripts and frameworks that can efficiently and accurately test software functionality, performance, and reliability.

Test Automation Engineers work closely with software developers, quality assurance (QA) analysts, and other stakeholders in the software development process. They collaborate to define test requirements, identify test scenarios, and develop test cases. Test Automation Engineers use various tools, technologies, and programming languages to create automated test scripts that simulate user interactions, validate software functionality, and compare actual results with expected outcomes.

The key objectives of a Test Automation Engineer include:

- **Efficiency and Accuracy**: Automating repetitive and time-consuming test cases improves testing efficiency and accuracy, reducing the effort required for manual testing.

- **Test Coverage**: Test Automation Engineers aim to cover a wide range of test scenarios and edge cases to ensure comprehensive test coverage.

- **Regression Testing**: Automated tests are crucial for performing regression testing, which involves retesting previously tested functionalities to ensure that new changes or updates haven't introduced any defects.

- **Continuous Integration and Continuous Delivery (CI/CD)**: Test Automation Engineers integrate automated tests into CI/CD pipelines to enable continuous testing and faster software delivery cycles.

To excel in this role, Test Automation Engineers need a strong understanding of software development processes, testing methodologies, and programming concepts. They should have expertise in test automation frameworks, scripting languages (such as Python, Java, or JavaScript), version control systems, and test management tools. Additionally, knowledge of software testing best practices and the ability to analyze test results and identify defects are essential skills for a Test Automation Engineer.

Applicable Technologies

Well, if we're going to get down to the brass tacks of test automation engineering, we first need to understand that it's like the backstage crew in a theater production. You know, the invisible hands that keep the show running seamlessly. But instead of actors and props, they're juggling software applications and test scripts. And instead of audience applause, they get the satisfaction of bug-free, quality software.

Now, let's talk about the array of tools and technologies that are the secret weapons in a test automation engineer's arsenal. Firstly, they use what's called 'test automation frameworks.' These are sets of guidelines or rules used for creating and designing test cases – a kind of blueprint, if you like. There are several types of these, including Linear Scripting, Modular Testing, Data-Driven Testing, Keyword-Driven Testing, and Hybrid Testing Framework. The choice of framework depends on the application under test, project requirements, and team expertise.

Now, if you're not familiar with these, let me give you the CliffsNotes version. A testing framework is a bit like the "director" in our backstage crew analogy. It gives the general flow and structure of how the testing process is going to go down.

Software programming languages are another must-have in the toolbox. Java, Python, C# – these are the scriptwriters for our theater crew. They're vital because they help create the test scripts that'll simulate user behavior. Java, for instance, is a popular choice due to its platform independence and extensive open-source libraries. Python, on the other hand, is loved for its simplicity and readability, perfect for rapid test development.

Automation tools are the bread and butter of a test automation engineer's toolkit. These tools are like the stagehands that do the actual work. Selenium, Appium, TestComplete, Postman, JMeter – these names might not mean much to you, but to a test automation engineer, they're the heroes of the show. They help create, manage, execute and report on automated tests.

Now, some of these tools like Selenium are for web-based applications while others like Appium are for mobile app testing. Then you have tools like JMeter for performance testing and Postman for API testing. It's a smorgasbord of choices, but the right selection can make or break the quality of the end product.

And let's not forget version control systems like Git. They are used to track and manage changes to code, enabling multiple team members to work on the same codebase without stepping on each other's toes. Think of it as the script supervisor, ensuring all changes are accounted for, and no one's deviating from the script.

Lastly, they use continuous integration/continuous delivery (CI/CD) tools like Jenkins, Bamboo, or CircleCI. These tools are like the showrunners, making sure that the whole production (or in this case, the development and delivery process) runs smoothly from start to finish.

So, in summary, test automation engineering is a complex job, requiring a mastery of a range of tools, technologies, and techniques. But when done right, it ensures that the software you use every day works as smoothly as a well-rehearsed Broadway production.

Screening Questions

Here are 15 questions that a recruiter might ask a Test Automation Engineer during the hiring process:

- Can you explain your experience with test automation frameworks and tools?
- How do you approach test case design and test coverage when automating tests?

- What programming languages and scripting languages are you proficient in for test automation?
- Have you worked with continuous integration and continuous delivery (CI/CD) pipelines? If so, which tools have you used?
- Can you describe your experience in creating and maintaining automated test scripts?
- How do you handle data-driven testing and parameterization in your automation scripts?
- Have you implemented or used any BDD (Behavior-Driven Development) or TDD (Test-Driven Development) frameworks in your automation projects?
- What strategies do you employ for handling dynamic elements or UI changes in test automation?
- Can you provide an example of a complex test scenario you automated and the challenges you faced?
- How do you ensure the reliability and stability of your automated tests?
- Have you integrated your automated tests with any defect tracking or test management tools?
- How do you collaborate with developers and QA analysts to improve the effectiveness of automated testing?

- Can you discuss your experience with performance testing and how you incorporate it into your automation efforts?
- Have you utilized any cloud-based testing platforms or services for test automation?
- How do you stay updated with the latest trends and advancements in test automation?

These questions are designed to assess the candidate's technical skills, problem-solving abilities, experience with relevant tools and frameworks, collaboration and communication skills, and their overall approach to test automation.

Networking Groups

So, you're looking to rub shoulders with the Illuminati of Test Automation Engineering, the wizards behind the curtain of software reliability? Well, let me tell you, you're in for a treat because these guys and gals don't hide in the shadows. No, no, they're the rockstars of the tech industry, ensuring your latest hotshot app doesn't collapse like a house of cards. They're out there, in the real world and the virtual realm, sharing trade secrets and cutting-edge tools like they're at a Silicon Valley garage sale.

First off, they hit the real world, the so-called "IRL." They make a beeline for events like the Selenium Conference, which is the Burning Man for folks who geek out on automated testing frameworks. Then there's STAR Conferences, a Mardi Gras of sorts for Software Testing Analysis & Review. Don't miss out on the QA or the Highway conference. And if you think the name is cheeky, wait till you meet the innovative minds at the event.

And let's not forget TestBash. It's not some frat party, mind you, but an international meetup where the gods of the software testing pantheon gather.

In the virtual realm, these wizards aren't just playing Minecraft or Fortnite. They're dialed into webinars and virtual events like Automation Guild Conference, offering an onslaught of insights from the comfort of their own command centers (read: living rooms). And QAI's Quest Conference, which sounds like a World of Warcraft campaign, but in reality, is a globe-spanning quality engine meetup in the cloud.

Finally, they're also regulars at the online Test Automation Days, a festival of sharing the best practices and tools. It's the Coachella of automation testing - all from the comfort of your Herman Miller (or if you're still bootstrapping, your IKEA chair).

So, whether you're an extrovert who enjoys the bustle of a packed convention center, or an introvert who prefers soaking up knowledge in your pajamas, there's a networking event for you. Remember, in the world of test automation engineering, the only bug you should fear is the one you haven't found yet.

Boolean Search

Looking inside of LinkedIn:
"Test Automation Engineer" AND (Selenium OR Appium OR JMeter) AND (Java OR Python OR JavaScript)

Using a site search to X-Ray LinkedIn:
site:linkedin.com/in ("Automated Testing" OR "Test Automation") Cucumber "CI/CD" Jenkins

Using a site search to X-Ray Github:
site:github.com/* "Test Automation Engineer" "Mobile Testing" (Appium OR Espresso OR XCUITest)

Using a filetype command to uncover resumes:
filetype:pdf resume "Test Automation Engineer" Cloud (AWS OR "Google Cloud" OR Azure) (Terraform OR Ansible)

Mobile Developer

A mobile developer is a software developer who specializes in creating applications specifically for mobile devices, such as smartphones and tablets. They are responsible for designing, coding, testing, and maintaining mobile applications across different platforms, such as iOS (iPhone and iPad) or Android.

Mobile developers typically have expertise in programming languages such as Swift or Objective-C for iOS development, and Java or Kotlin for Android development. They work with integrated development environments (IDEs) and software development kits (SDKs) provided by the respective platforms to build and optimize mobile applications.

Their role involves understanding user requirements, designing the app's user interface (UI), implementing features and functionality, and ensuring the application's performance, usability, and security. Mobile developers also need to keep up with the latest trends and technologies in mobile development to create innovative and engaging applications.

In addition to technical skills, mobile developers often collaborate with designers, product managers, and quality assurance teams to ensure that the mobile app meets the desired specifications and user experience. They may also be involved in app store submission processes and provide post-launch support and updates.

Overall, mobile developers play a crucial role in the booming mobile app industry, enabling users to access a wide range of applications on their mobile devices for various purposes, such as communication, entertainment, productivity, and more.

Applicable Technologies

Sure, let's dive into the intriguing world of mobile development. Imagine, if you will, a digital loom. The mobile developers, those tech wizards, they're the weavers. They weave together codes, frameworks, and APIs like they're creating a beautiful digital tapestry.

The tools, oh they're fascinating and extensive, from programming languages like Swift and Objective-C for our iOS artists, and Java and Kotlin for the Android aficionados. iOS developers exclusively use Xcode, Apple's own integrated development environment, complete with tools, compilers, and frameworks. On the flip side, Android developers might cozy up to Android Studio, Google's official platform.

Let's talk a bit about those languages, shall we? Swift, Apple's own baby, is the star of the show for iOS. It's modern, it's safe, and it's relatively easy to read and maintain. For those clinging to the echoes of the past, Objective-C is still around, but Swift is the clear favorite here.

Over at the Android camp, Java was the king. It's robust, it's flexible, but hey, it's also a little bit verbose, which makes it time-consuming to write and debug. And then, in walked Kotlin, all shiny and new, and stole the show. It's interoperable with Java, but much more concise, null-safe, and offers a lot of modern features that developers just love.

But the world of mobile development is not just languages and IDEs, oh no. The platforms offer sophisticated SDKs (Software Development Kits) with a range of libraries and tools for things like network access, database management, graphics, and so much more. You've also got the UI frameworks: UIKit and SwiftUI for iOS, Android's own framework, and Jetpack Compose.

Now, there's also a space for developers who don't want to pick a side, who want to straddle that iOS-Android divide. They use cross-platform technologies like React Native, Flutter, Xamarin. These let you write code once and deploy it on multiple platforms. That's all very kumbaya, but bear in mind, they do come with their own trade-offs.

One more thing to throw into the mix is the importance of knowing your APIs (Application Programming Interfaces) which are like the bridges for your apps to interact with the OS and other apps. There are system APIs, but also third-party APIs for everything from payments to social media integrations.

And remember, this is a landscape that's ever-changing, always evolving. These developers, they're not just coding machines, they're innovative thinkers, problem solvers, staying on top of the latest trends, the hottest technologies, to ensure their apps are smooth, fast, and user-friendly. They're the behind-the-scenes rockstars of the mobile world.

So yes, mobile development is as diverse and nuanced as a tapestry, with a myriad of choices and possibilities. It's an ongoing symphony of creative problem-solving, coding wizardry, and technology choices that differ in the iOS and Android camps.

Screening Questions

While the specific questions asked by a recruiter may vary depending on the company and job requirements, here are 15 common questions that a recruiter may ask a Mobile Developer during the hiring process:

- Can you provide an overview of your experience as a Mobile Developer?
- What programming languages and frameworks have you worked with in mobile development?
- Have you developed applications for both iOS and Android platforms?
- Can you describe your experience with mobile app architecture and design patterns?
- How familiar are you with mobile UI/UX principles and best practices?
- Have you integrated third-party APIs and libraries into mobile applications? If so, can you provide examples?

- What tools and technologies do you use for mobile app development, testing, and debugging?
- Can you discuss your experience with version control systems like Git?
- Have you worked on projects that involved mobile app security and data protection?
- Are you familiar with the process of publishing mobile applications to app stores?
- Can you describe a challenging mobile development project you worked on and how you overcame obstacles?
- How do you ensure mobile app performance and optimize for different device specifications?
- Have you worked in a team environment and collaborated with designers, backend developers, or QA testers?
- Can you provide examples of mobile apps you have developed, and what was your role in those projects?
- How do you stay up-to-date with the latest trends and advancements in mobile development?

These questions help the recruiter assess the candidate's technical skills, experience, familiarity with industry practices, ability to work in a team, and their passion for staying updated in the field of mobile development.

Networking Groups

Well, here's the thing. As a mobile developer, your daily life might oscillate between sips of coffee and staring at Xcode or Android Studio. But, life is not just about zeros and ones, my friend. There's a wild world out there, even for coders and especially for mobile developers. And, as I've said before, you don't want to be the smartest person in the room. You want to network with people who can challenge your thoughts, inspire you, and offer new opportunities.

So, where does one find this promised land? Listen up, here's the scoop:

For the "IRL" (In Real Life) scene:

- Apple Worldwide Developers Conference (WWDC): The Disneyland for iOS developers. WWDC is the 'The Met Gala' of mobile development – it's where the coolest of the cool are hanging out, learning about Apple's latest developments and sharing insights.

- Google I/O: The Burning Man for Android developers. It's big, it's Google, and it's pivotal. Every major Android developer should attend at least once.

- TechCrunch Disrupt: Picture this, you're sipping on your drink, and the guy next to you just sold his startup for a billion. That's Disrupt for you. It's a fantastic place for tech networking, not just mobile developers.

Now, in the virtual realm:

- Stack Overflow: A lot of you might say, "Brian, that's not networking, that's solving problems." But hey, who said networking can't solve problems? It's one of the best platforms to share knowledge and connect with developers around the world.

- GitHub: Engage in projects, contribute, collaborate, and build a strong profile. GitHub is LinkedIn for developers - but with more street cred.

- Online Meetups and Hackathons: Events on sites like Eventbrite or Meetup.com provide fantastic opportunities. These events might be smaller, but they can pack a punch in terms of connections and learning.

Remember, in today's world, it's all about networks and nodes. The more you connect, the higher your value. So, get out there, either in the physical or digital world, and start networking!

Boolean Search

Looking inside of LinkedIn:
("mobile engineer" OR "software engineer") AND (Swift OR Kotlin) AND (iOS OR Android)

Using a site search to X-Ray LinkedIn:
site:linkedin.com/in ("mobile developer" OR "application developer") AND ("React Native" OR Flutter)

Using a site search to X-Ray Github:
site:github.com/* ("Android developer" OR "iOS Developer") (Unity OR "Unreal Engine")

Using a filetype command to uncover resumes:
filetype:pdf resume ("mobile developer" OR "app developer") (Xcode OR "Android Studio")

Data Engineer

A data engineer is a professional responsible for designing, developing, and maintaining the systems and infrastructure that enable the collection, storage, processing, and analysis of large volumes of data. They play a crucial role in managing the entire data lifecycle, from data ingestion to data transformation and storage, and finally to data delivery for analysis and decision-making.

The primary focus of a data engineer is to ensure that data is properly collected, stored, and made accessible to data scientists, analysts, and other stakeholders. They work closely with data scientists and data analysts to understand their requirements and build data pipelines and systems that facilitate the extraction, transformation, and loading (ETL) of data from various sources.

Data engineers are proficient in programming languages like Python, Java, or Scala, and they use tools and technologies such as Apache Hadoop, Apache Spark, SQL databases, data warehousing solutions, and cloud platforms like Amazon Web Services (AWS) or Google Cloud Platform (GCP). They also possess knowledge of data modeling, data integration techniques, and data quality management.

Key responsibilities of a data engineer may include:

- **Data ingestion**: Designing and implementing processes to extract data from various sources such as databases, APIs, log files, or streaming platforms.

- **Data storage**: Building and maintaining data storage systems, including data warehouses, data lakes, or NoSQL databases, to ensure efficient and reliable data storage.

- **Data transformation**: Developing ETL processes to clean, transform, and enrich data, ensuring its quality and compatibility with downstream analysis and reporting.

- **Data pipeline development**: Creating scalable and efficient data pipelines that automate the flow of data from source systems to target systems, considering data integrity, security, and performance.

- **Data infrastructure management**: Overseeing the setup, configuration, and optimization of data infrastructure components such as clusters, servers, and databases.

- **Data governance and security**: Implementing data governance policies and ensuring compliance with data protection regulations. Managing access controls and data security measures.

- **Collaboration with stakeholders**: Collaborating with data scientists, data analysts, and other team members to understand their data requirements and deliver reliable and high-quality data solutions.

In summary, a data engineer is responsible for building and maintaining the data infrastructure and pipelines necessary to support data-driven processes within an organization, enabling efficient data analysis and decision-making.

Applicable Technologies

Well, kiddos, if you're looking to dive into the labyrinthine, mind-boggling realm of data engineering, you're in for a real treat. The life of a data engineer, my friends, is a never-ending joyride through a carnival of technologies.

First and foremost, let's talk databases. A data engineer's world practically orbits around them. The old reliables like Oracle, MySQL, and PostgreSQL are your bread and butter. Then you have your NoSQLs – think MongoDB, Cassandra, or CouchDB. This isn't a game of either/or; data engineers need to juggle both, because in this circus, the more skills you have, the longer you stay on the high wire.

Now, for handling big data, you're going to need some heavy machinery. That's where Hadoop and Spark saunter onto the stage. The Hadoop ecosystem is a bit like the Justice League of data tools – Hive, Pig, and HBase all have their own superpowers. And Spark? Well, that's like your Superman – it's fast, it's powerful, and when it teams up with the rest, it's practically unstoppable.

Data warehousing solutions like Redshift, BigQuery, and Snowflake are another big act in this show. With the amount of data that organizations are dealing with these days, these technologies are as necessary as a net under a trapeze artist.

ETL – Extract, Transform, Load. It's the sleight-of-hand trick every data engineer needs to master. It's about pulling data from one place, changing it so it makes sense, and putting it somewhere else. Tools like Informatica, Talend, and good old Python scripts can come into play here.

Now, if you're going to tame the wild beast of real-time data, then you'll need something like Kafka or Kinesis. These are for handling the gushing firehose of data that organizations are constantly trying to gulp down.

Lastly, we've got cloud computing platforms – AWS, Google Cloud, Azure. These platforms are like the circus tents, housing all the fantastic, gravity-defying acts that a data engineer performs.

And, let's not forget about data visualization tools like Tableau, PowerBI, and Qlikview. They're like the grand finale of the circus show, the dazzling spectacle that makes everyone's jaw drop.

All these technologies, they're not just tools – they're the rings of fire that data engineers must jump through, the tightropes they must walk, the cannons they must shoot themselves out of. Data engineering, folks, it's not a job. It's a performance, and these technologies are the stage.

Screening Questions

During a phone screen, a recruiter for a Data Engineer position may ask a range of questions to assess the candidate's skills, experience, and fit for the role. Here are 15 interview questions that a recruiter may ask a Data Engineer:

- Can you provide an overview of your experience as a Data Engineer and the projects you have worked on?
- What programming languages and technologies do you typically use for data engineering tasks?
- Have you worked with large-scale data processing frameworks like Hadoop or Spark? Can you describe your experience with them?
- How do you ensure data quality and integrity in your data engineering projects?
- Can you explain the steps involved in the data pipeline from data ingestion to data storage and analysis?
- Have you worked with any ETL (Extract, Transform, Load) tools or frameworks? If so, which ones?

- Can you discuss your experience with data modeling and database design principles?
- How do you handle data integration and data transformation tasks in your projects?
- Have you worked on real-time data processing or streaming data projects? If yes, what technologies have you used?
- Can you explain your experience with cloud-based data platforms like AWS, Azure, or Google Cloud?
- How do you approach performance optimization and scalability in data engineering projects?
- Have you worked with any workflow management tools or schedulers for data processing? Which ones?
- Can you describe a challenging data engineering project you have worked on and how you tackled it?
- What measures do you take to ensure data security and privacy in your projects?
- How do you stay updated with the latest advancements and trends in the field of data engineering?

These questions help the recruiter gauge the candidate's technical skills, experience with relevant technologies, understanding of data engineering processes, ability to handle complex projects, and their dedication to continuous learning in the field of data engineering.

Networking Groups

In the real world, that's IRL for those of you born post 2000, Data Engineers are like wolves, moving in packs, sharing insights, and chasing the technological gazelles of Big Data. These wolves can be found prowling the concrete jungles of conventions like Strata Data & AI Conference, where like-minded data enthusiasts are sucking up knowledge faster than a Dyson in a dust bunny convention. There's also the Kafka Summit, the holy grail for real-time data engineers.

But the big daddy of all conventions, the Super Bowl, World Series, and Champions League Final all wrapped up into one for Data Engineers, is AWS re:Invent. This Vegas-based spectacle is the data equivalent of Burning Man, where thousands of engineers, developers, and data scientists gather around the fire of Amazon's latest releases and updates, with their eyes glistening like kids on Christmas morning.

But, hey, not everyone can jet off to Vegas or New York, especially in this Covid-riddled era where a simple cough can clear out a room faster than yelling "Fire!" So, we've got virtual gigs too. Online webinars, workshops, and meetups are the norm now. I mean, who doesn't love learning about Hadoop clusters while in their sweatpants, right?

ODSC (Open Data Science Conference) does a fantastic job at virtual conferences, with hundreds of speakers, and thousands of attendees. It's like a big data Woodstock, but without the mud and questionable substances. Then there's Databricks, the Picasso of Apache Spark, offering online tech talks, perfect for those wanting to fine-tune their Spark skills.

And let's not forget about the good old-fashioned webinars from Cloudera, Google Cloud, and other data-focused companies that provide enough information to make your brain feel like it's in a CrossFit session.

Whether in-person or virtual, the goal here is to learn, network, and push the envelope of what's possible in the data realm. So, pick your poison, pack your enthusiasm, and for God's sake, don't forget to hydrate. Data is a marathon, not a sprint.

Boolean Search

Looking inside of LinkedIn:
"Data Engineer" AND (Python OR Java OR Scala) AND ETL

Using a site search to X-Ray LinkedIn:
site:linkedin.com/in "Data Engineer" NoSQL (Cassandra OR MongoDB OR "HBase")

Using a site search to X-Ray Github:
site:github.com/ "Data Engineer" AWS (Redshift OR EMR OR Glue)*

Using a filetype command to uncover resumes:
filetype:pdf resume ("Data Engineer" OR "ETL Developer") Snowflake "Data Modeling"

Cloud Engineer

A Cloud Engineer is a professional who specializes in designing, implementing, and managing cloud infrastructure and services. They are responsible for leveraging cloud technologies to build and maintain scalable, reliable, and secure computing environments for businesses and organizations.

Cloud Engineers work with various cloud platforms, such as Amazon Web Services (AWS), Microsoft Azure, Google Cloud Platform (GCP), and others, depending on the specific requirements of their organization. They have a deep understanding of cloud architecture, infrastructure as code (IaC), virtualization, and networking principles.

The primary responsibilities of a Cloud Engineer may include:

- **Cloud Infrastructure Design**: They design cloud-based architectures and solutions to meet specific business needs, taking into consideration factors like scalability, high availability, security, and cost optimization.

- **Implementation and Deployment**: Cloud Engineers are involved in deploying and configuring cloud resources, such as virtual machines, storage, databases, and networking components. They use automation and infrastructure as code tools to streamline the provisioning process.

- **Security and Compliance**: They implement security measures to protect cloud environments, including access controls, encryption, and monitoring. Cloud Engineers also ensure compliance with relevant industry standards and regulations.

- **Performance Optimization**: They optimize cloud infrastructure for performance, making sure that applications and services run efficiently and meet the desired performance metrics.

- **Troubleshooting and Support**: Cloud Engineers diagnose and resolve issues related to cloud services, infrastructure, and applications. They provide technical support to internal teams or customers, ensuring smooth operation of cloud-based systems.

- **Cost Management**: They monitor cloud resource usage and work towards cost optimization by implementing cost-effective solutions, rightsizing resources, and leveraging pricing models offered by cloud providers.

Cloud Engineers need to stay updated with the latest cloud technologies and trends, as the cloud computing landscape is continuously evolving. They often collaborate with other IT professionals, such as software developers, system administrators, and data engineers, to ensure the successful implementation and integration of cloud-based solutions within an organization.

Applicable Technologies

Absolutely, here's how a Cloud Engineer operates—now, imagine I'm saying this in my usual 'take no prisoners' tone.

First things first, let's get one thing straight: Cloud Engineers are not just glorified IT folks. No, they are the backbone of every tech company's infrastructure. Whether you're a nimble startup or a lumbering tech behemoth like Google or Amazon, the Cloud is where your data lives, and these engineers are the masters of that domain.

So, what do these wizards use? Their toolkits would make any tech enthusiast swoon.

Number one, and you better believe it's a big one, they use cloud service platforms like Amazon Web Services (AWS), Google Cloud Platform (GCP), or Microsoft Azure. These platforms are like the grand ballrooms where the magic happens. They provide all the building blocks—from computing power and storage to advanced analytics tools and machine learning capabilities—that a Cloud Engineer uses to build and maintain a company's cloud infrastructure.

Next up, we've got programming languages. Like any good engineer, these cloud gurus need to know how to code. They usually have a solid grasp of languages like Python, Java, or Go, and they're probably dabbling in a few others on the side.

Then we've got container technologies like Docker and Kubernetes. If cloud platforms are grand ballrooms, containers are the movable walls that let you change the room layout. They package software into standardized units for development, shipment, and deployment—a must-have in the age of microservices architecture.

Let's not forget Infrastructure as Code (IaC) tools. They write, you heard it right, CODE, to automate the provisioning and management of their infrastructure. Tools like Terraform or CloudFormation are their best friends.

And for managing operations? They've got DevOps tools like Jenkins for continuous integration and continuous delivery, and Ansible for IT automation. Cloud Engineers also rely on monitoring and logging tools like Prometheus or Elasticsearch to keep an eye on everything and ensure smooth sailing.

Finally, we can't skip security. With all the data breaches and cyberattacks we've seen recently, you bet your bottom dollar that these engineers are proficient in security tools and principles.

So that's what a Cloud Engineer's toolbox looks like. It's a hard job, but hey, somebody's got to do it. In our ever-increasingly digital world, these are the unsung heroes that make sure everything keeps humming along. You may not think about them when you're binge-watching your favorite show on Netflix or uploading your cat pictures on Instagram, but they're there, working behind the scenes, making the magic happen.

Screening Questions

When conducting a phone screen for a Cloud Engineer position, the recruiter may ask a variety of questions to assess the candidate's technical skills, experience, and fit for the role. Here are 15 interview questions that a recruiter may ask a Cloud Engineer:

- Can you provide an overview of your experience as a Cloud Engineer and the cloud platforms you have worked with?

- What cloud services and technologies are you most familiar with?
- Have you worked on cloud migration projects? If so, can you describe your role and the challenges you faced?
- How do you ensure the security and compliance of cloud-based systems and applications?
- Can you explain the concept of scalability in cloud computing and how you have implemented it in your previous projects?
- Have you worked with infrastructure-as-code tools like Terraform or CloudFormation? Can you provide examples of how you have used them?
- How do you handle monitoring and troubleshooting of cloud-based systems? Are there any specific tools or methodologies you prefer?
- Have you worked with containerization technologies like Docker and orchestration tools like Kubernetes? If so, can you discuss your experience?
- Can you explain the concept of high availability and fault tolerance in cloud architectures? How have you implemented these concepts in your projects?
- Have you worked on serverless computing platforms like AWS Lambda or Azure

Functions? Can you share your experience with them?

- How do you ensure cost optimization in cloud environments? Are there any strategies or tools you have used?
- Have you participated in the design and implementation of cloud-based disaster recovery plans? Can you provide an example?
- Can you discuss your experience with cloud automation and configuration management tools like Ansible or Chef?
- How do you handle data backup and restoration in cloud environments? What strategies or tools do you use?
- Can you provide an example of a complex cloud project you have worked on and explain your role and the outcome?

These questions cover various aspects of cloud engineering, including cloud platforms, infrastructure management, security, scalability, monitoring, automation, and disaster recovery. The recruiter aims to evaluate the candidate's depth of knowledge, problem-solving abilities, hands-on experience, and familiarity with industry best practices.

Networking Groups

Oh boy, you're diving into the world of cloud engineering, aren't you? If you're ready to ride the techno tsunami, you'd better keep your floaties on because I'm about to hit you with the top networking events that Cloud Engineers typically cannonball into.

First off, we can't ignore the absolute monster in the room - the AWS re:Invent conference. Think of it as the Super Bowl of cloud computing, but with less padding and more Jeff Bezos. It's the who's who of the cloud universe, with everyone from the evangelists, coders in their hoodies, to the Fortune 500 CTOs soaking up the knowledge. The sweet, sweet knowledge.

Next up, there's Google Cloud Next. Don't let the friendly colors and playful logo fool you; this isn't kid stuff. It's another titan of cloud technology, where attendees don't just walk, they glide on cutting-edge insights, best practices, and all things Google Cloud. Got Kubernetes on your mind? This is your Disneyland, my friend.

Microsoft Azure also has its fan club meeting - Microsoft Ignite. If you're one of the Azure disciples, get ready to set your mind on fire with sessions on Azure, .NET, and other Microsoft tech. These are not your mom's PowerPoint presentations.

But hey, let's not forget about the smaller but equally important gatherings. The Serverlessconf is a prime example - a hub for the serverless crowd, who are reshaping the cloud landscape without even provisioning servers. Fancy that.

In the virtual world, the pandemic has made the 'Zoom Shirt' a fashion staple. KubeCon + CloudNativeCon is a standout. It's a hotspot for open-source, cloud-native aficionados. Then there's the Cloud Computing Expo, the SaaStr Annual, the Cloud Foundry Summit, all offering a buffet of online sessions to savor from the discomfort of your ergonomic home office chair.

And don't forget the meetups - smaller, more intimate gatherings on platforms like Meetup.com. Think of it as speed dating for professionals, without the awkwardness and with a lot more Docker discussions.

Remember, networking isn't just about attending these events. It's about engaging, putting yourself out there, and asking questions. In the cloud world, there's no such thing as a dumb question. Well, maybe "Is the cloud actually made of water vapor?" might raise a few eyebrows. Get out there, meet your tribe, and let the knowledge osmosis begin.

Boolean Search

Looking inside of LinkedIn:
("Cloud Engineer" OR "Cloud Specialist") AND (Python OR Java OR Go)

Using a site search to X-Ray LinkedIn:
site:linkedin.com/in Cloud (Engineer OR Specialist OR Architect) (Certified OR Certification)

Using a site search to X-Ray Github:
site:github.com/* *"Cloud Engineer" (Serverless* OR *"Microservices Architecture")*

Using a filetype command to uncover resumes:
filetype:pdf resume ("Cloud Engineer" OR "Cloud Specialist") ("Big Data" OR Hadoop OR Spark)

Technical Architect

A Technical Architect is a professional who plays a crucial role in the design and implementation of complex technology solutions within an organization. They are responsible for creating the overall technical strategy and ensuring that it aligns with the organization's business goals and objectives.

The main responsibilities of a Technical Architect include:

- **Solution Design**: Technical Architects analyze business requirements and translate them into technical solutions. They design the architecture of systems, applications, or software, considering factors such as scalability, security, performance, and integration with existing systems.

- **Technology Evaluation**: They research and evaluate different technologies, frameworks, and tools to determine their suitability for a given project. They stay updated with the latest industry trends and emerging technologies to make informed decisions.

- **Collaboration**: Technical Architects work closely with various stakeholders, including business leaders, project managers, developers, and system administrators. They collaborate to understand the requirements, provide technical guidance, and ensure the successful execution of projects.

- **System Integration**: They oversee the integration of different systems and components, ensuring seamless communication and data flow between them. This involves designing interfaces, defining data exchange formats, and implementing integration patterns.

- **Performance Optimization**: Technical Architects identify potential bottlenecks and performance issues within a system and propose optimizations to improve efficiency. They conduct performance testing and analysis to validate the effectiveness of their recommendations.

- **Security and Compliance**: They incorporate security measures into the architecture, ensuring that the system meets industry standards and regulatory requirements. They assess risks, develop security strategies, and implement appropriate controls to protect sensitive data and prevent unauthorized access.

- **Technical Leadership**: Technical Architects provide technical leadership and guidance to development teams. They mentor and coach developers, help them troubleshoot technical challenges, and promote best practices and coding standards.

Overall, a Technical Architect combines their technical expertise, domain knowledge, and business acumen to design and deliver robust and scalable technology solutions. They bridge the gap between business requirements and technical implementation, ensuring that the resulting systems meet the organization's needs while adhering to industry standards and best practices.

Applicable Technologies

Strap in because we're about to dive into the day-to-day grind of a Technical Architect, in a language that even a technophobe could understand. If you think this is some desk job, well, you couldn't be more wrong. It's like being an orchestra conductor, but instead of violins and flutes, you're wrangling databases, software, and cloud services, and if that sounds like some kind of sci-fi symphony, you're not wrong.

First, there's the alphabet soup of languages: your Java, Python, C++, JavaScript, SQL, and so on. These aren't quaint ways of saying 'hello' in different tongues; they're the bedrock of everything digital. They're like the sheet music for our architect.

Then, there's data. Databases, to be exact. Think SQL Server, Oracle, or MySQL. Without these data guardians, the infrastructure would be a shambles, like a conductor losing his sheet music mid-performance.

Thirdly, architects need a way to manage all their "instruments". So they use technologies like Docker and Kubernetes for containerization, or serverless architecture when it comes to cloud services. You might have heard of AWS, Google Cloud, Azure? These are like the grand theaters where the music plays.

Networking technologies are also paramount - no orchestra can function without proper communication. So things like TCP/IP, HTTP, VPNs, firewalls, and routers become the nerve center, ensuring that every piece of our symphony works in harmony.

Security tools are another cornerstone - our architect has to play bodyguard, too. Tools like intrusion detection systems, firewalls, and encryption protocols ensure that no uninvited guests crash our beautiful performance.

Then there's a bunch of software and tools for building and designing systems, such as UML, BPMN, and CASE tools. They're like the architect's baton, guiding every aspect of the performance to create a perfect harmony.

Lastly, don't forget the project management tools - our architect isn't just a conductor, they're also a planner. Jira, Trello, and Asana are often their go-to. These keep everything on track, like a good stage manager.

So, let's not underestimate our dear Technical Architect, okay? They're the unsung heroes, making sense of a tech cacophony and turning it into a symphony. It's not some nerdy job locked in a server room. It's conducting the orchestra of our digital age, and let me tell you, that's no small feat.

Screening Questions

When conducting a phone screen for a Technical Architect position, recruiters often ask a combination of technical, problem-solving, and behavioral questions to assess the candidate's expertise and suitability for the role. Here are 15 interview questions that a recruiter may ask a Technical Architect:

- Can you provide an overview of your experience as a Technical Architect and the types of projects you have worked on?

- What is your approach to designing scalable and robust software architectures?
- Can you explain the difference between monolithic and microservices architectures? When would you choose one over the other?
- How do you ensure that a software architecture is secure and complies with industry standards and best practices?
- Have you implemented cloud-based architectures? If so, can you describe your experience with cloud platforms and services?
- Can you discuss a complex technical problem you encountered in your previous projects and how you resolved it?
- How do you assess the performance and scalability of a software architecture? What tools or techniques do you use?
- Can you explain the concept of service-oriented architecture (SOA) and its benefits in software development?
- How do you handle architectural trade-offs, such as balancing performance and maintainability or flexibility and security?
- Have you worked with distributed systems and handled challenges related to data consistency and synchronization?
- Can you describe your experience with integrating third-party systems or APIs into a software architecture?

- How do you collaborate with development teams, stakeholders, and business users to gather requirements and define architectural solutions?
- Can you discuss your experience with software development methodologies, such as Agile or DevOps?
- How do you stay updated with the latest technologies, trends, and advancements in the field of software architecture?
- Can you provide examples of successful software architectures you have designed and implemented, and their impact on the projects?

These questions help recruiters evaluate a Technical Architect's technical knowledge, problem-solving skills, ability to design scalable and secure architectures, collaboration capabilities, and their approach to keeping up with industry trends.

Networking Groups

Ah, here we are, talking about the crossroads of physical and digital, old school handshakes and modern, mind-bending virtual realities. Exciting, isn't it? Let's break it down.

In real life, the romantic charm of traditional networking is still alive and kicking. Conferences like the O'Reilly Software Architecture Conference are a hotbed of architects looking to test their mental mettle against the best in the business. TechEd by Microsoft, AWS re:Invent, Google Cloud Next, Oracle OpenWorld – these are the equivalent of what you might call the "Ivy League" of networking events for the creme de la creme of the tech architect universe. The conversation here is like a championship boxing match, each participant jabbing and weaving with insights and counterpoints.

Then we move to the realm of the virtual, where one might argue that networking has taken on a whole new level. The International Conference on Software Architecture (ICSA), for instance, has gone online, which is no surprise in a world where an architect's lifeblood is digital. Webinars, podcasts, Slack groups – your Tech Architect may as well be in a 24/7 networking event.

And let's not forget platforms like GitHub – a digital agora where tech architects can network through collaboration. And they've got a gazillion meetup groups, right from Silicon Valley to Bangalore, to swap war stories and pro-tips.

The catch here is that networking isn't just about throwing business cards at each other anymore, virtual or otherwise. It's about building relationships, sharing knowledge, solving problems, and yes, having a few laughs along the way. After all, what's the point of being at the top of your game if you can't enjoy the view?

So whether it's a swanky conference in Vegas or a heated debate on a Reddit thread, the savvy Technical Architect knows the game is always on. They're connecting, influencing, and leading - in a world where the only constant is change, and the only language is innovation. And whether it's IRL or virtual, they're lapping up every opportunity to be a part of this exhilarating ride. Isn't it beautiful?

Boolean Search

Looking inside of LinkedIn:
("Technical Architect" OR "Software Architect") AND mobile AND (Android OR iOS)

Using a site search to X-Ray LinkedIn:
site:linkedin.com/in "Technical Architect" eCommerce (Magento OR Shopify)

Using a site search to X-Ray Github:
site:github.com/* "Technical Architect" (DevOps OR "CI/CD")

Using a filetype command to uncover resumes:
filetype:pdf resume "Technical Architect" ("solution design" OR "system integration")

Project Manager

A project manager is a professional responsible for planning, organizing, and overseeing the successful completion of a project. They are typically employed in various industries and organizations, including construction, engineering, IT, software development, marketing, and many others.

The primary role of a project manager is to ensure that projects are completed within the defined scope, budget, and timeline, while meeting the desired objectives and quality standards. They work closely with stakeholders, team members, and resources to coordinate and execute project tasks effectively.

Here are some key responsibilities of a project manager:

- **Project Planning**: Defining project objectives, scope, deliverables, and timeline. Creating a comprehensive project plan that outlines tasks, milestones, and resource allocation.

- **Team Management**: Building and leading a project team, assigning roles and responsibilities, and facilitating effective communication and collaboration among team members.

- **Risk Management**: Identifying potential risks and developing strategies to mitigate them. Monitoring risks throughout the project lifecycle and taking appropriate actions to minimize their impact.

- **Budgeting and Cost Control**: Estimating project costs, developing budgets, and tracking expenditures. Ensuring that the project remains within the approved budget and implementing cost-saving measures when necessary.

- **Stakeholder Management:** Engaging with project stakeholders, including clients, sponsors, and other key individuals or groups. Keeping them informed about project progress, addressing concerns, and managing their expectations.

- **Progress Monitoring**: Tracking project activities, milestones, and deliverables. Regularly assessing project progress, identifying deviations from the plan, and implementing corrective actions to keep the project on track.

- **Quality Assurance**: Establishing quality standards and ensuring that project outputs meet the specified requirements. Conducting quality reviews and implementing quality control measures throughout the project.

- **Communication and Reporting**: Facilitating effective communication among project stakeholders, both internal and external. Providing regular project status updates, preparing progress reports, and presenting findings to relevant parties.

Project managers need a combination of technical and interpersonal skills to excel in their role. They must have strong leadership abilities, excellent communication and negotiation skills, problem-solving capabilities, and the ability to manage and motivate a diverse team.

It's important to note that the specific duties and requirements of a project manager may vary depending on the industry, organization, and the nature of the project they are working on.

Applicable Technologies

Well, I can assure you, whoever's reading this, the role of a Project Manager isn't for the faint of heart. It requires a sharp wit, a keen eye, and some tech chops to match. I mean, if you can't keep up with the pace of today's tech, honey, you're better off arranging tea parties.

Let's start with the staples, shall we?

First off, we've got Project Management software, the digital holy grail of any Project Manager. And no, I'm not talking about the outdated MS Project, though it had its heyday, sure. Today, it's all about apps like Asana, Trello, JIRA, or Microsoft Teams. These are powerful tools that help keep everyone in line, in the loop, and, hopefully, on schedule. Just like running a good tech firm, it's all about the execution, darling.

Then there's productivity software. Google Workspace (formerly G Suite) or Office 365, these are as crucial to your daily life as air and water - maybe more so. Spreadsheets, documents, presentations, you name it. You're gonna be swimming in them. And if you don't know your way around these tools, let's just say, you'll be sinking instead of swimming.

Next up, Communication platforms. Slack, Zoom, Microsoft Teams, WebEx, what have you. You think you can run a project with a string and tin cans? Think again.

To manage resources and finances, they use ERP systems like SAP or Oracle. Some people say ERP stands for "Enterprise Resource Planning", but after seeing so many implementations, I can assure you, to some it really means "Expensive, Really Painful".

And, listen up, if you're handling tech projects, you need to know about version control systems like Git, or Continuous Integration/Continuous Deployment (CI/CD) tools like Jenkins, Travis CI, and others. Don't get me started on container technologies like Docker and orchestration tools like Kubernetes. Believe me, in the world of tech project management, you'll be as lost as a kitten in a dog show without these.

Last, but not least, data. Project Managers need business intelligence tools, think Tableau, PowerBI, to glean insights from project data. You can't fly blind in the tech world and expect to land safely, right? Right.

So, to wrap this up, being a Project Manager in the tech industry is like being a maestro conducting a symphony. Only your orchestra members are all kinds of tech platforms and tools, and your audience is... well, everybody else in the company eagerly waiting for you to hit the right notes. It's a tough gig, but someone's got to do it.

Screening Questions

During a phone screen interview, a recruiter may ask the following 15 questions to assess a Project Manager's qualifications and suitability for the role:

- Can you provide an overview of your experience as a Project Manager?
- What project management methodologies or frameworks have you used in previous roles?
- How do you approach project planning and setting project milestones?
- Can you describe a challenging project you managed and how you ensured its successful completion?
- What strategies do you employ to manage project risks and mitigate potential issues?

- How do you prioritize tasks and allocate resources to meet project deadlines?
- Can you discuss your experience in managing project budgets and controlling project costs?
- Have you worked in cross-functional teams? If so, how do you foster collaboration and ensure effective communication among team members?
- How do you handle project scope changes or client requests for additional features during the project lifecycle?
- Can you describe a situation where you had to resolve conflicts or manage difficult team members?
- Have you implemented any project management tools or software? If so, which ones have you used?
- How do you measure project success and ensure that project deliverables meet client expectations?
- Can you provide an example of a project where you had to adapt to unexpected changes or setbacks?
- How do you ensure effective stakeholder management and keep project stakeholders informed and engaged?
- Can you discuss your experience in leading and motivating project teams to achieve project goals?

These questions help the recruiter gauge the candidate's experience in project management, their ability to handle project challenges and conflicts, their communication and leadership skills, as well as their proficiency in using project management methodologies and tools.

Networking Groups

In the whirlwind, disruptive age we're living in, staying connected and up-to-date with industry trends is more crucial than ever. That's true whether you're a Jedi-master coder or a project manager who's more agile than a Russian gymnast.

In Real Life (IRL) events – remember those, the pre-COVID times when we actually pressed the flesh and slapped backs, instead of just staring into Zoom windows? The old-school, face-to-face networking opportunities that are high-impact – ranging from industry-specific project management conferences like the Project Management Institute's Global Conference, where the brightest minds in PM gather to pontificate on subjects like risk mitigation and waterfall vs agile. You can also consider events such as the Gartner Program & Portfolio Management Summit, and regional Agile conferences. These events are like Burning Man for PMs – minus the dust and eccentric outfits.

However, as we've seen in this post-pandemic world, the metaverse doesn't disappoint. Virtual events have taken the center stage - from PMI's Virtual Experience Series to webinars hosted by leading software vendors like Atlassian and Microsoft. Tech behemoths like Google and IBM also host webinars on project management topics, shedding light on the nexus between cutting-edge tech and project management.

For a broader scope, you might want to attend events like TechCrunch Disrupt or the Collision Conference, both of which attract a melange of project managers, tech nerds, startups, and VCs. These events give a holistic, bird's-eye view of the landscape, like looking at Earth from a Virgin Galactic flight.

Remember, networking isn't just about collecting business cards or LinkedIn connections. It's about starting and fostering relationships. It's about kindling connections that could spark the next billion-dollar idea, or, at the very least, give you some insight to make your next project less of a dumpster fire. So, get out there – or stay in, if it's a virtual event – and start mingling. You're only as good as your network.

Boolean Search

Looking inside of LinkedIn:
"Senior Project Manager" AND "Six Sigma"

Using a site search to X-Ray LinkedIn:

site:linkedin.com/in *("Project Manager" OR PM) "PMP Certification"*

Using a site search to X-Ray Github:
site:github.com/* *"("Project Manager" OR "Project Coordinator") ITIL*

Using a filetype command to uncover resumes:
filetype:pdf resume "Project Manager" (Healthcare OR Medical) PMP

Scrum Master

A Scrum Master is a key role in the Scrum framework, which is an agile project management methodology. The Scrum Master is responsible for ensuring that the Scrum team adheres to the principles and practices of Scrum and helps facilitate the team's progress towards its goals.

Here are some key responsibilities of a Scrum Master:

- **Facilitating Scrum processes**: The Scrum Master guides the team in understanding and implementing Scrum practices. They ensure that Scrum ceremonies, such as daily stand-up meetings, sprint planning, sprint reviews, and retrospectives, are conducted effectively.

- **Removing obstacles**: The Scrum Master identifies and removes any obstacles or impediments that may hinder the team's progress. They work to create an environment where the team can work smoothly without unnecessary disruptions.

- **Coaching and mentoring**: The Scrum Master provides guidance, coaching, and mentoring to the team members, Product Owner, and stakeholders on the Scrum framework, agile principles, and best practices. They help the team improve its self-organization and cross-functionality.

- **Promoting collaboration**: The Scrum Master fosters a collaborative and self-organizing culture within the team. They encourage effective communication, cooperation, and transparency among team members, as well as with stakeholders.

- **Monitoring progress**: The Scrum Master keeps track of the team's progress during the sprint and ensures that the work is aligned with the sprint goals and the overall project objectives. They may use tools like burndown charts to visualize the team's progress and identify any potential issues.

- **Facilitating continuous improvement**: The Scrum Master promotes a culture of continuous improvement by facilitating sprint retrospectives. They help the team reflect on its practices, identify areas for improvement, and implement changes in subsequent sprints.

It's important to note that the Scrum Master is not a traditional project manager or team lead. Instead, they serve as a servant-leader, working alongside the team to enable their success and help them maximize their potential within the Scrum framework.

Applicable Technologies

Let's talk tech, Scrum Master style. For those who aren't tech literate, a Scrum Master is the heart of the Agile Scrum methodology. They're not your classic boss-figure, they're more like shepherds, guiding the team through the hurdles of a project, ensuring things are done smoothly and efficiently. Now, what kind of tools do they use to do this job? Let's dive in.

First off, we've got Project Management Tools. JIRA, Trello, Asana - these are the Scrum Master's bread and butter. Agile is all about adaptability, visibility and swift iteration, and these tools make it happen. They provide a platform for task management, tracking progress, and reporting, with features that align with Scrum and Agile principles. Plus, they offer transparency to stakeholders, so there's no mystery about what the team is doing.

Communication tools are next on the list. Slack, Microsoft Teams, Zoom - these aren't just for work-from-home folks, they're critical to any Scrum Master's toolkit. The Scrum Master's role involves a lot of communication, from daily stand-ups to sprint retrospectives, and they need to ensure that all team members are on the same page. With these tools, they can streamline communication, keep everyone updated, and create a space for discussion, irrespective of geography.

Then, there's Version Control Systems like Git or Mercurial. This might not be the Scrum Master's go-to, but they need a solid understanding of it. It's about keeping track of all the changes to the project, making sure every version is catalogued properly, and ensuring multiple developers can work without stepping on each other's toes.

Finally, we can't forget about Continuous Integration/Continuous Delivery (CI/CD) tools like Jenkins, Travis CI, or CircleCI. A Scrum Master might not be neck-deep in these, but they definitely need to be familiar with them. Why? These tools automate the process of software delivery - from integration, testing, to deployment. In other words, they help maintain the quality and reliability of the software, which aligns with the ultimate goal of the Scrum Master - delivering value to the customer.

All in all, these aren't just tools, they're weapons in the arsenal of the Scrum Master, helping them foster an environment of collaboration, transparency, and efficiency. And it's not just about knowing what these tools do - it's about understanding how they contribute to the Agile philosophy. How they drive productivity and efficiency. Because that's what being a Scrum Master is all about.

So, keep innovating, keep iterating, and as always, keep it Agile.

Screening Questions

When conducting a phone screen interview for a Scrum Master role, recruiters often aim to assess the candidate's knowledge and experience in Agile methodologies, Scrum practices, and their ability to facilitate effective team collaboration. Here are 15 interview questions that a recruiter may ask a Scrum Master:

- Can you explain the role of a Scrum Master and how it differs from other project management roles?
- What is your experience with Agile methodologies, specifically Scrum?
- How do you ensure that the Scrum team follows the Scrum framework and adheres to Agile principles?

- Can you describe a situation where you facilitated a successful Agile transformation within an organization?
- How do you handle conflicts within the Scrum team or between the team and stakeholders?
- Can you provide examples of metrics or key performance indicators (KPIs) you have used to track the progress of Agile projects?
- How do you ensure effective communication and collaboration among team members and stakeholders?
- Can you explain the concept of user stories and how they are used in Agile development?
- How do you handle changes or scope creep during a Sprint or Agile project?
- Can you describe a situation where you faced challenges in implementing Scrum practices and how you resolved them?
- How do you facilitate Sprint planning, daily stand-ups, Sprint reviews, and retrospectives?
- What techniques do you use to identify and remove obstacles or impediments that may hinder the team's progress?
- How do you ensure the Scrum team maintains a sustainable pace and avoids burnout?
- Can you provide an example of how you have promoted continuous improvement within an Agile team?

- How do you measure the success and effectiveness of a Scrum team?

These questions help recruiters evaluate a Scrum Master's knowledge of Agile principles, their ability to guide and support teams, and their experience in handling various aspects of Scrum and Agile project management. Additionally, recruiters may inquire about specific scenarios or challenges to gauge the candidate's problem-solving skills and adaptability in real-world situations.

Networking Groups

Whew! We're living in an era of immense connectivity, the flux of digital and real-world exchanges that spin the globe faster than a hyperloop on steroids. Yes, you guessed it right, we're talking about networking events for the Scrum Masters, the Agile alchemists of our era.

- Scrum Gathering: These are hosted by Scrum Alliance, one of the world's leading certification bodies for Scrum and Agile professionals. They're big, they're brash, they're bold – just like everything else in this zany, hyper-connected world of ours. Scrum professionals huddle together here, swarming the conference halls like bees to a honey pot. They've got workshops, keynotes, networking sessions. The works.

- Agile Conferences: These aren't just for Scrum Masters, but they're so stuffed to the gills with valuable information and networking opportunities that any Scrum Master would be foolish not to gate crash. Or rather, click crash, since many of these events have taken to the virtual realm like ducks to water in the era of Zoom and Teams.

- Meetups and Local Agile Groups: The internet is a sprawling behemoth of connection and community, and websites like meetup.com are cashing in on that. But it's not all bad for us end users. Scrum Masters can use these platforms to find local Agile groups, virtual or otherwise, and network like their careers depend on it. Because guess what? They do.

- LinkedIn and other Social Media Events: If you're a Scrum Master and you're not on LinkedIn, well, let me tell you something: you're falling behind faster than a brick in freefall. Social media platforms are like the cocktail parties of the virtual world – you've got to show up, and you've got to work the room. LinkedIn Learning sessions, webinars, live Q&A's – they're all ripe for the picking.

- Corporate Events: If your company is worth its salt – and let's face it, you wouldn't be working there if it wasn't – it's going to host regular corporate events, training sessions, and team-building activities. These are gold mines for networking. Rub virtual elbows with project managers, product owners, and developers. Who knows? It might just pave the way for your next big career move.

In short, my friend, the world is your oyster, and Scrum Masters are the pearls. So, go on, get out there. Network, connect, and conquer. And remember: in the era of the virtual, your reach is only as limited as your WiFi signal. So, make sure you've got a good one!

Boolean Search

Looking inside of LinkedIn:
"Scrum Master" AND ("JIRA" OR "Confluence")

Using a site search to X-Ray LinkedIn:
site:linkedin.com/in ("Scrum Master" OR "Agile Coach") ("Scrum Alliance" OR "Scrum.org")

Using a site search to X-Ray Github:
site:github.com/* ("Scrum Master" OR "Agile Project Manager") "Product Owner" -("Product Manager")

Using a filetype command to uncover resumes:
filetype:pdf resume "Scrum Master" ("Sprint Planning" OR "Backlog Grooming") (Retrospective OR "Sprint Review") ("Servant Leader" OR Facilitator)

Technical Writer

A technical writer is a professional who specializes in creating documentation and written content that explains complex technical concepts, procedures, and instructions in a clear and concise manner. Their primary goal is to communicate technical information to a specific audience effectively. Technical writers are commonly employed in industries such as software development, engineering, manufacturing, pharmaceuticals, telecommunications, and information technology.

The role of a technical writer involves researching, gathering, and organizing information from subject matter experts, engineers, developers, or other technical professionals. They then transform this information into user-friendly documentation, such as user manuals, technical guides, online help systems, FAQs, tutorials, and other forms of instructional materials.

Technical writers play a crucial role in bridging the gap between technical experts and end-users or consumers. They need to possess strong writing skills, a good understanding of technology and technical concepts, and the ability to adapt their writing style to suit the target audience. They often collaborate with cross-functional teams, including engineers, product managers, designers, and customer support personnel, to gather information and ensure the accuracy and clarity of the content they produce.

In addition to creating written documentation, technical writers may also be involved in editing, proofreading, and reviewing technical content, as well as maintaining a consistent style and tone across various materials. They may work with specialized authoring tools, content management systems, and graphics software to enhance the visual appeal and usability of their documentation.

Overall, technical writers play a vital role in making complex technical information accessible and comprehensible to users, helping them effectively use products, services, or systems and troubleshoot issues.

Applicable Technologies

If you're a technical writer, you're not just twiddling your thumbs all day. You're wrestling with a handful of software tools and technologies that you need to help translate the nerdy language of engineers into something that even your technophobic grandmother could understand.

First off, there's the holy trinity of Microsoft Office: Word, Excel, PowerPoint. Those are a given. They're like the knives in a chef's kitchen. You're writing, tabulating, and presenting all day, every day. This is the stuff that you need to organize your thoughts, your data, and then present it in a way that doesn't put people to sleep.

And then you've got your Adobe suite: Acrobat, Photoshop, Illustrator. These are your special spices. You're manipulating PDFs, you're tweaking images, you're creating diagrams. Because let's be honest, we're all just big kids who want pictures in our books. And it's not enough to just slap a picture on a page. It has to be pretty. It has to be informative. And it has to be done right.

Now, let's dive into the nerdier tools. Because guess what? Technical writers have to get their hands dirty too. There's GitHub, because you're constantly working with developers, and they love their code repositories. So, you need to know how to navigate around there, submit changes, and so on. And then there's XML authoring tools like FrameMaker, because you're not just writing. You're structuring. You're formatting. You're making it so that a thousand-page manual doesn't read like a Russian novel.

And then there's the whole world of content management systems, or CMS for short. This is where things like Joomla!, WordPress, or Confluence come into play. Because once you've created all this content, you need to manage it. You need to organize it, tag it, and make it searchable.

Then we're talking about project management tools like Jira or Trello. Because trust me, you're not just managing words. You're managing deadlines, tasks, and teams. And if you're not on top of that, your whole project can go south real fast.

And last but not least, you have to be comfortable with various video conferencing and communication tools, like Zoom or Slack. Because guess what? Not every meeting is going to be face-to-face, especially in this day and age.

So there you have it. That's the toolbox. The toys of a technical writer. And if you're not comfortable with them, then you better start learning, because this is the reality of the job. It's not just words on a page. It's technology. And if you're going to survive in this world, you have to keep up.

Screening Questions

During a phone screen for a Technical Writer position, a recruiter may ask a variety of questions to assess the candidate's skills, experience, and fit for the role. Here are 15 potential interview questions for a Technical Writer:

- Can you provide an overview of your experience as a Technical Writer and the types of documentation you have created?

- What tools and software do you use for creating and managing technical documentation?
- How do you approach gathering information and conducting research for creating technical documentation?
- Can you discuss your experience working with subject matter experts (SMEs) and other stakeholders to gather information?
- How do you ensure that technical documentation is accurate, clear, and easily understandable for the intended audience?
- Have you worked with style guides and documentation standards? If so, which ones?
- Can you provide an example of a complex technical concept or process you had to explain in your documentation and how you approached it?
- Have you collaborated with development teams or engineers to understand technical concepts and translate them into user-friendly documentation?
- Can you discuss your experience with version control systems for documentation, such as Git?
- How do you handle documentation updates and revisions to ensure consistency and accuracy?
- Can you describe a situation where you had to meet tight deadlines for delivering technical documentation?

- Have you worked on projects that involved multiple documentation deliverables, such as user manuals, API documentation, or release notes?
- Are you familiar with any specific tools or methodologies for creating interactive or multimedia documentation?
- How do you approach localizing and translating technical documentation for an international audience?
- Can you share examples of your technical writing portfolio or samples of documentation you have created?

These questions help the recruiter assess the candidate's technical writing skills, experience with documentation tools and processes, ability to work with subject matter experts, attention to detail, and their understanding of audience needs. Additionally, they provide insights into the candidate's ability to meet deadlines, work in a team, and adapt to different types of documentation projects.

Networking Groups

Okay, so let's get this straight. As a technical writer, you're a hybrid creature, part techno-wizard, part prose aficionado, part translator of coder-speak. You're on the frontline of an ever-evolving landscape of bleeding-edge technology and riveting rhetoric. It's a tough gig, but someone's got to do it.

Now, if you're looking to get your geek on and mingle with fellow wordsmiths who've traded in Shakespeare for Java and Python, you're in luck. The ecosystem is rife with both IRL and virtual networking events for technical writers. It's like the Coachella of code, the Burning Man of blockchains, the Sundance of software.

In the physical realm, you've got the **Society for Technical Communication Summit**, the Coachella for tech writers, where industry professionals gather for insightful sessions, workshops, and, of course, networking. You're not only brushing elbows with other technical writers but also the very people who use the docs you're crafting.

And then there's the **Write the Docs Conference**—think of it as your Glastonbury, with stages full of experts and tents full of knowledge. It's more than just a conference; it's a community of people passionate about documentation and their roles in it.

In the digital realm, you've got the **tcworld Conference**. Think of this as your virtual South by Southwest (SXSW), a confluence of minds and talent in the industry, where you can learn, network, and engage without ever leaving your home office (or couch, no judgment).

Write the Docs Meetups are another goldmine, the virtual equivalent of popping into a local pub for a pint with the crew. It's a relaxed space to discuss your challenges and wins, and share advice and tools of the trade.

Finally, there's the **Technical Communication UK (TCUK) Conference.** This event, available both in-person and online, is like the technical writing Oscars—professionals from across the UK and beyond gather to share knowledge, learn new skills, and network.

And remember, networking isn't just a game of collecting business cards or LinkedIn connections. It's about growing your knowledge, enhancing your skills, and leveraging the power of your community to supercharge your work. So get out there and connect! After all, you're writing the manual for the future.

Boolean Search

Looking inside of LinkedIn:
"Technical Writer" AND (SaaS OR Cloud)

Using a site search to X-Ray LinkedIn:
site:linkedin.com/in ("Technical Writer" OR "Documentation Specialist") (Medical OR Healthcare)

Using a site search to X-Ray Github:
site:github.com/* "Technical Writer" (Fintech OR Blockchain OR Cryptocurrency)

Using a filetype command to uncover resumes:

filetype:pdf resume "Technical Writer" (Engineering OR "Software Development")

UX/UI Designer

A UX/UI designer is a professional who works on designing the user experience (UX) and user interface (UI) of a digital product, such as a website or an application. They play a crucial role in the development process because they are responsible for ensuring that the product is not only aesthetically pleasing but also easy and intuitive to use.

Here's a little more detail about each aspect:

- **User Experience (UX) Design**: UX design is all about enhancing user satisfaction and designing the complete user journey through a product. UX designers analyze and understand how users feel about a system, looking at such things as ease of use, perception of the value of the system, utility, and efficiency in performing tasks. They might construct personas, perform user research, design wireframes and prototypes, and perform user testing to validate and improve the design.

- **User Interface (UI) Design**: UI design is about the look and feel, the presentation and interactivity of a product. UI designers are in charge of designing each screen or page with which a user interacts, taking care of the product's graphical layout such as button designs, color schemes, font choices, and any other visuals that the user might interact with. The UI design part of the process is about translating the brand's strengths and visual assets to a product's interface to best enhance the user's experience.

In many teams and companies, these roles are separate, with UX designers focusing on the user journey and research, and UI designers focusing on the aesthetic and interactive design. However, in smaller teams or companies, these roles might be combined into one, hence the term "UX/UI designer". The designer will work on both aspects of the product design, from understanding the user and planning the user journey to deciding the look and feel of the product.

Applicable Technologies

Alright, let's dive right into the digital battlefield where pixels and user satisfaction skirmish day in, day out. We're talking about the world of UI and UX design, the under-the-hood tinkering that keeps your apps looking slick, your websites user-friendly, and your overall digital experience a smooth cruise, rather than a bumpy off-road journey.

Let's start with the soldiers in this battlefield, the technologies UI and UX designers use. Adobe XD, Sketch, Figma - you may have heard these names, and yes, they are important. They're software programs for creating and prototyping design, as indispensable to a designer as a sword is to a knight. You'd use them to make wireframes, mockups, and interactive prototypes, basically the blueprints of any digital product.

But wait, there's more. We're in 2023, not in the stone age, so naturally, we have more advanced weapons in our armory. We've got InVision for improved design collaboration, and Balsamiq for low fidelity wireframing, making it easier to create and refine the basic structure of your app or site. For UI, there's also the need to know front-end languages like HTML, CSS, and JavaScript. They're the bricks and mortar of the internet, transforming those lovely designs into functional webpages.

Moving to UX, it's not just about making pretty pictures. It involves understanding the users, their needs, their pain points, and then refining the design to provide a solution. Tools like UserZoom or UsabilityHub can be used for conducting user research and testing. There's also an increasing trend of using AI and analytics tools, because let's face it, numbers can speak louder than words.

Now, let's clear up some confusion: UI and UX are not the same thing, despite what your technologically-challenged uncle might say at Thanksgiving. UI, or User Interface, is about the look and layout. It's what you see, touch, or click on an app or website. It's the colors, the buttons, the images, the typography – it's all the elements that make your digital product look as beautiful as a Monet painting.

On the other hand, UX, or User Experience, is, as the name suggests, all about the experience. It's how a user feels when interacting with your digital product. It's about creating a seamless, efficient, and enjoyable journey from point A to point B. A good UX designer doesn't just make something that looks good – they create something that feels good to use.

In essence, UI makes interfaces beautiful, UX makes them work beautifully. And together, they bring us digital experiences that are not just functional, but also delightful. Because let's face it, in today's digital age, we don't just need things that work, we need things that work for us. So, let's give a virtual applause to all the UI and UX designers out there, working their magic to keep our digital world spinning smoothly.

Screening Questions

UI Designer Interview Questions

Here are 15 interview questions that a recruiter conducting a phone screen might ask a UI Designer:

- Can you provide an overview of your experience as a UI Designer?
- What design tools and software do you use to create user interfaces?
- Can you explain your design process and how you approach creating user-centered designs?
- Have you worked on projects that involved responsive design and designing for multiple devices?
- How do you incorporate user research and usability testing into your design process?
- Can you discuss your experience with creating wireframes, prototypes, and mockups?
- Have you collaborated with developers and other stakeholders to ensure successful implementation of your designs?
- Can you provide examples of projects where you solved a complex design challenge and explain your approach?
- How do you stay up-to-date with the latest UI design trends, tools, and best practices?

- Can you describe a time when you received feedback on your design and how you incorporated it into your work?
- Have you worked on projects that required creating a design system or style guide?
- Can you discuss your experience with designing for accessibility and ensuring inclusive user experiences?
- How do you balance creativity and aesthetics with usability and user experience principles in your designs?
- Have you collaborated with UX designers or conducted user interviews to gather insights for your designs?
- Can you provide a portfolio or examples of your previous UI design work and walk me through the thought process behind a specific project?

These questions aim to assess the candidate's experience, technical skills, design process, ability to collaborate with stakeholders, knowledge of design principles and trends, and their passion for continuous learning and improvement in UI design.

UX Designer Interview Questions

When conducting a phone screen for a UX Designer, recruiters often focus on assessing the candidate's skills, experience, and approach to user experience design.

Here are 15 interview questions that a recruiter may ask a UX Designer:

- Can you provide an overview of your experience as a UX Designer?
- What design process or methodologies do you follow when approaching a new project?
- Can you describe a project where you conducted user research and how it influenced your design decisions?
- How do you ensure that user interfaces are intuitive and user-friendly?
- Have you worked on projects that required collaboration with cross-functional teams? How did you contribute to the team's success?
- Can you provide examples of wireframing or prototyping tools you have used in your previous work?
- How do you incorporate user feedback into your design iterations?
- Can you describe a time when you had to balance user needs and business goals in your design work?
- How do you approach creating user personas and user journey maps?
- Can you discuss your experience with conducting usability testing and how it impacted your design decisions?

- How do you keep up-to-date with the latest trends and best practices in UX design?
- Can you provide examples of a project where you had to solve a particularly challenging design problem?
- What techniques do you use to prioritize features or design decisions in a project with tight deadlines?
- How do you approach designing for accessibility and inclusivity in your work?
- Can you discuss a project where you had to iterate on your design based on user analytics or data?

These questions help the recruiter gauge the candidate's knowledge of UX design principles, their experience with user research and testing, collaboration skills, ability to balance user needs and business goals, and their overall approach to the design process.

Networking Groups

Alright, my friend, here's the deal. UX/UI Designers, they're a savvy bunch, they're not just pushing pixels and making things look pretty, they're shaping how we interact with the digital world. So, it's no surprise they're rubbing shoulders at some of the most innovative and thought-provoking events out there.

In-person or "IRL" as the kids say, you're gonna find them at the big ones like **SXSW Interactive** in Austin - a melting pot of tech, design, and innovation. It's where the cool kids hang out, brushing up on the latest trends, and probably sipping some sort of overpriced artisanal coffee. Then there's **Adobe MAX**, put on by the gods of design software themselves. Think about it, it's like Christmas came early for these creatives.

Out in San Francisco, you've got the **Designers + Geeks meetups** - casual, yet insightful. Across the pond in the UK, there's **UX London** - a veritable 'Who's Who' of UX/UI design. These events are your hot tickets, the Ivy League of networking opportunities, the mingling equivalent of a Tesla Roadster - sleek, innovative, and just a touch exclusive.

In the virtual world, or as I like to call it, 'The Metaverse's less flashy cousin', there's a boatload of opportunities too. How about the **Nielsen Norman Group's UX Conference**? They've gone all-digital, baby, bringing together some of the best minds in the UX/UI sphere. It's like getting a masterclass from the UX/UI gurus themselves.

Then you've got the virtual versions of the big players - Adobe MAX and SXSW have impressive online offerings, taking their world-class content into the virtual realm. There's also **Smashing Conference**, an absolute must for web designers and developers.

And don't forget about webinars, online meetups, and virtual round tables - LinkedIn and even Twitter Spaces are buzzing with these. In the age of remote work, these digital events are the golden keys to the kingdom, the Harvard of the internet, where screen-to-screen schmoozing is king.

Bottom line: whether you're a UX/UI virtuoso or just dipping your toes in the water, these events are your springboard to greatness. Your network is your net worth, after all. Now go forth and mingle!

Boolean Search

Looking inside of LinkedIn:
"UX Designer" AND (Photoshop OR Illustrator OR Sketch)

Using a site search to X-Ray LinkedIn:
site:linkedin.com/in "UI Designer" Figma -("Graphic Designer")

Using a site search to X-Ray Github:
site:github.com/* "UI/UX Designer" (SaaS OR "e-commerce" OR eCommerce)

Using a filetype command to uncover resumes:
filetype:pdf resume "User Interface Designer" HTML CSS

Security Engineer

A Security Engineer is an IT professional who specializes in designing and implementing systems to enhance the security of an organization's computer networks and systems. They are responsible for protecting sensitive data from threats like cyber attacks, hacking attempts, and unauthorized access.

Here are some of the common responsibilities of a Security Engineer:

- **Designing security systems**: They create new ways to solve existing production security issues and work on Security Information and Event Management (SIEM) systems which provide real-time analysis of security alerts generated by applications and network hardware.

- **Implementing protection measures**: Security engineers install and use software, such as firewalls and data encryption programs, to protect an organization's sensitive information. They might also use penetration testing tools to identify vulnerabilities that can be exploited.

- **Monitoring for security breaches**: Regular audits of systems and software are performed to detect intrusions or anomalies. In case of a breach, they are responsible for identifying the source and managing the situation effectively.

- **Creating security policies**: They establish protocols for use in case of a breach and devise plans for disaster recovery. They also develop policies that dictate how employees should use security measures and educate staff on these protocols.

- **Staying updated**: It's important for Security Engineers to keep abreast of the latest news and trends in cybersecurity to ensure their organization's security measures are updated accordingly. This might involve continuous learning and attending relevant industry events or training sessions.

The exact duties of a Security Engineer can vary depending on the specific needs and size of the organization they work for. In smaller companies, a Security Engineer may be a generalist handling a wide variety of tasks, while in larger corporations, they might specialize in a particular area of security.

Applicable Technologies

In the fast-paced, ever-evolving world of tech, if you're not sharp as a tack and on your toes, you'll be left in the dust. That's particularly true for Security Engineers - the unsung heroes of the tech realm who work relentlessly to safeguard our digital lives.

So, what's their secret sauce? Tools and technologies, baby. And not just a few, but an ever-growing, mind-boggling array.

For starters, they're big on firewalls and intrusion detection systems. It's like having a rottweiler at the gate of your palatial estate, always ready to fend off unwanted visitors. They set up, maintain, and relentlessly tweak these systems to ensure nothing gets past them.

Then there's encryption technologies. You know, it's like whispering secrets in code. Without the right key, it's all gibberish to the unintended listener. AES, RSA, DES, you name it. These Security Engineers are fluent in this secret language.

They also use Security Information and Event Management (SIEM) systems. These are like the spies of the digital world, collecting intel and reporting back. They collect log and event data and combine that with actual intelligence to identify potential security threats. Think of it as the CIA of cybersecurity.

Don't forget about antivirus software, anti-spyware, and anti-malware tools. These guys are like the digital version of an immune system, always on the hunt for foreign entities trying to wreak havoc.

Then there's the world of Identity and Access Management (IAM) systems, enabling the right individual to access the right resources at the right times for the right reasons. It's like a super-efficient, supremely meticulous bouncer at a nightclub.

Of course, I can't leave out the plethora of testing tools they use. Tools for vulnerability scanning, penetration testing, and security audits. It's all about poking and prodding their own systems before someone else does. Like a game of 'catch me if you can,' where they are both the cop and the robber.

And lastly, they're always nose-deep in programming and scripting languages like Python, Java, or JavaScript. These languages are like their Swiss army knives, enabling them to create, customize, and deploy various security solutions.

That's your primer on the tech arsenal of a Security Engineer. Remember, it's an ongoing tech arms race. It's not just about the tools you have, but how you use them. Staying ahead of the game is everything. As they say in Silicon Valley, "move fast and break things." But in this case, "move fast and protect things."

Screening Questions

During a phone screen for a Security Engineer position, a recruiter may ask a variety of questions to assess the candidate's knowledge, experience, and suitability for the role. Here are 15 sample interview questions a recruiter may ask a Security Engineer:

- Can you provide an overview of your experience as a Security Engineer and the specific areas you have worked on?
- What are some common security vulnerabilities and threats you have encountered and how did you mitigate them?
- How familiar are you with security frameworks and standards such as OWASP, NIST, or ISO 27001?
- Can you explain the concept of defense in depth and how it applies to securing systems?
- Have you conducted security assessments or penetration testing? If so, can you describe your approach and tools used?
- What security monitoring and incident response tools or systems have you worked with?
- How do you stay up-to-date with the latest security trends, vulnerabilities, and best practices?
- Can you discuss your experience with securing cloud-based environments, such as AWS, Azure, or GCP?
- Have you implemented secure coding practices and worked with developers to address security concerns?
- Can you explain the process you follow to conduct a security risk assessment?

- How do you approach designing and implementing access controls and authentication mechanisms?
- Can you discuss your experience with network security, including firewalls, IDS/IPS, and VPNs?
- Have you worked on incident response plans or participated in security incident investigations?
- Can you describe your experience with data privacy regulations, such as GDPR or CCPA?
- How do you collaborate with cross-functional teams and communicate security concerns to non-technical stakeholders?

These questions aim to gauge the candidate's knowledge of security principles, experience with security assessments and incident response, familiarity with industry frameworks and regulations, and ability to work in a team and communicate effectively. The recruiter may also ask additional questions based on the specific requirements of the position and the organization's security needs.

Networking Groups

So, you're looking for a Security Engineer. Looking for the best and brightest events to rub virtual elbows with these digital gatekeepers, huh?

Let's break it down in a truth-bomb sandwich.

In Real Life (IRL) events:

- **Black Hat USA**: This is the Super Bowl, the Cannes, the Davos of cybersecurity. It's like a nerd Burning Man but with more practical applications. An amalgamation of the smartest minds in the industry, Black Hat is a forum for the latest threats and defenses in the infosec world. You'll leave this Vegas-hosted event with your brain buzzing.

- **RSA Conference**: Another tentpole event. It's got the heft of Black Hat but with a San Francisco vibe. That means a bit more corporate, a bit more polished, but still a hotbed for innovative ideas and critical insights.

- **DEF CON**: Think of this as the Woodstock of hacker conferences. It's less corporate, more hands-on, and, like, totally in Vegas, man. From Capture The Flag to Hacker Jeopardy, this event isn't just about learning; it's about doing.

Virtual Networking Events:

- **SANS Webcasts**: These webcasts are like the MasterClass of cybersecurity. They provide a steady stream of fresh content from the best in the business. Tune in, learn something new, connect with other attendees, and update your arsenal.

- **Cybersecurity & Cloud Expo Virtual**: Here we're talking about the Netflix binge-watch equivalent for security professionals. High-quality, on-demand content focusing on cybersecurity, cloud, and other critical tech sectors.

- **BrightTALK Webinars**: This is the LinkedIn of the webinar world. It's all about networking, sharing, and gaining insights in a virtual, professional setting.

To win in this space, it's not just about attending the right events, but engaging, connecting, and applying what you learn. You need to understand that in this digital era, information is the currency, and protecting it is the business. Attend, learn, and network.

Boolean Search

Looking inside of LinkedIn:
"Security Engineer" AND "CISSP"

Using a site search to X-Ray LinkedIn:
site:linkedin.com/in ("Security Engineer" OR "Cybersecurity Analyst") "intrusion detection"

Using a site search to X-Ray Github:

site:github.com/* "Security Engineer" "cloud security" (AWS OR Azure OR GCP))

Using a filetype command to uncover resumes:
filetype:pdf resume "Security Engineer" "ethical hacking" CEH

Machine Learning Engineer

A Machine Learning Engineer is a professional who designs, develops, and implements machine learning models into applications or systems. They work in the intersection of computer science and statistics to create models that can process and learn from large amounts of data, typically to achieve specific tasks or make predictions.

Their primary responsibilities often include:

- **Understanding and translating business requirements**: Before starting on any project, it's important for machine learning engineers to understand what the company needs. This can include everything from predicting customer churn to automating content moderation.

- **Data collection and preprocessing**: Machine learning models require large amounts of data. Machine learning engineers need to identify relevant data, collect it, and preprocess it to make it suitable for training models. Preprocessing can involve cleaning the data, handling missing values, normalizing features, and more.

- **Feature engineering and selection**: This involves identifying the most relevant information (or "features") in the dataset that will be used to train the machine learning model. It also includes creating new features from existing data which can help improve model performance.

- **Model development and training**: Machine learning engineers build and train models using different algorithms and techniques (like neural networks, decision trees, etc.). This process also involves adjusting the parameters of these algorithms to improve the accuracy of the models.

- **Evaluation and optimization**: Once a model is built, it needs to be tested and evaluated to ensure it works as expected. This process may involve tweaking the model or the features used based on the performance of the model.

- **Deployment and maintenance**: After a model is trained and tested, machine learning engineers deploy it to a production environment. After deployment, they monitor the model to ensure it's working as expected, and update it as necessary when new data becomes available or when the performance degrades.

- **Staying updated**: The field of machine learning is rapidly evolving, so machine learning engineers need to stay up-to-date on the latest research, tools, and techniques.

To accomplish these tasks, Machine Learning Engineers need a solid foundation in computer science, mathematics, and statistics. They also need to be proficient in several programming languages (most commonly Python, and sometimes R or Java), and tools such as TensorFlow, PyTorch, or other machine learning libraries. Familiarity with data processing tools (like SQL) and cloud platforms (like AWS or Google Cloud) is often required as well.

Applicable Technologies

We can't talk about the everyday tech arsenal of a machine learning engineer without starting with Python. Now, it's not just that Python is to a machine learning engineer what a Swiss Army knife is to a camper, it's the tool of choice for a variety of reasons. Python is a programmer's nirvana with its simple syntax, great readability, and robust collection of libraries purpose-built for machine learning, like NumPy for numerical computations, Pandas for data manipulation, or Matplotlib for data visualization. In essence, Python is the duct tape that binds the machine learning universe together.

Now, let's move onto the big guns of the machine learning world: TensorFlow and PyTorch. The first is an open-source library developed by Google Brain, and the second is a brainchild of Facebook's AI Research lab. They're akin to the Coke and Pepsi of the machine learning world. Both are frameworks used for creating, training, and deploying machine learning models, but each has its own devotees. TensorFlow is often lauded for its robust capabilities and scalability, whereas PyTorch is praised for its simplicity and ease of use.

Another tool in the kit is Scikit-learn, an open-source Python library that, let me tell you, is just about as versatile as a well-seasoned Broadway actor. From regression, clustering, and classification to model selection and pre-processing, Scikit-learn has got it covered.

A machine learning engineer also needs to be well-versed in SQL, the language of databases. Why? Because much of machine learning involves working with huge volumes of data, and SQL is the tool par excellence for managing and manipulating this data.

In addition to these, there are cloud platforms like AWS, Google Cloud, and Microsoft Azure. If machine learning is a rocket, then cloud platforms are the launchpads. They provide the necessary infrastructure to build, train, and deploy machine learning models at scale, and they are just as integral to the machine learning process as the algorithms themselves.

So that's the 101 on the tech tools of the trade for machine learning engineers. It's a dazzling array, each one with its own strengths and quirks, but when used together, they form the backbone of any machine learning endeavor. Just remember, tools are only as good as the folks who wield them. All the Python in the world won't do you any good if you don't know how to leverage it. And that, my friends, is why machine learning engineers are the superheroes they are.

Screening Questions

When conducting a phone screen for a Machine Learning Engineer position, recruiters may ask a variety of questions to assess the candidate's technical knowledge and experience. Here are 15 potential interview questions:

- Can you explain the difference between supervised and unsupervised learning?
- What evaluation metrics would you use to assess the performance of a classification model?
- Have you worked with any deep learning frameworks like TensorFlow or PyTorch? Can you describe your experience with them?

- How do you handle imbalanced datasets in machine learning?
- Can you explain the concept of overfitting and how you would address it in a machine learning model?
- What is regularization, and why is it important in machine learning?
- Can you describe the bias-variance tradeoff in machine learning?
- Have you implemented any feature selection or dimensionality reduction techniques? If so, which ones and why?
- How do you handle missing data in a machine learning dataset?
- Have you worked with any natural language processing (NLP) tasks or models? If yes, can you provide an example?
- Can you explain the process of training a convolutional neural network (CNN)?
- Have you used any clustering algorithms? Can you provide an example of a clustering task you worked on?
- Can you discuss a machine learning project you worked on that involved handling large-scale datasets or big data?
- How do you approach model deployment and monitoring in a production environment?

- Can you describe any experience you have with hyperparameter tuning and optimization techniques?

These questions cover various aspects of machine learning, including fundamentals, algorithms, evaluation, data preprocessing, model deployment, and practical experience. They help the recruiter gauge the candidate's understanding of machine learning concepts, their familiarity with popular frameworks and techniques, and their ability to apply machine learning in real-world scenarios.

Networking Groups

Alright, let's break this down. You're looking for aMachine Learning (ML) engineer. They've got the big brains. They"re in the command line cooking up algorithms like a Michelin-star chef. But even the best ML maestros need to get out there, to pound the pavement, mix it up, and join the teeming throng of fellow data fanatics.

After all, networks aren't just for computers, right?

In the flesh, you've got a whole buffet of options. There's the classics like **NeurIPS**, which stands for **Neural Information Processing Systems**. They've been going strong since the '80s and are the big show for anyone who's serious about machine learning. It's like the Coachella of ML – if Coachella was full of TensorFlow devotees discussing bias-variance tradeoff.

Then there's **ICML** - the **International Conference on Machine Learning**. Another golden oldie, it's a global meet-up for ML luminaries. It's more international than an airport departure lounge and just as buzzy.

On the domestic front, don't overlook **O'Reilly's Artificial Intelligence Conference**. It's got a wide focus, covering everything from ML to AI ethics. It's a great way to keep your finger on the pulse, and hey, you might even bump into me there.

In the virtual world, you're spoiled for choice. There's the **Kaggle Days Meetups** – think of it as the internet's local ML club. It's a great way to meet like-minded souls who live and breathe machine learning. Also, consider tuning into ML webinars and live streams from top universities like Stanford or MIT, because, let's face it, that's where the magic happens.

The legendary **Coursera, edX, and Udacity** often host interactive online events, which is a great chance to pick up some new skills and connect with other ML enthusiasts without changing out of your pajamas.

Remember, in the ML world, just like high school, the cool kids are the ones who share. Open-source is your best friend and **GitHub** is your playground. Check out virtual hackathons, you'll find them happening on platforms like **Devpost**. They're a fantastic way to flex your ML muscles and collaborate with others.

So, get out there, start networking. Yes, even if you're introverted. Remember, the next big idea in machine learning might come from a chance encounter at one of these events. And if you don't show up, the only algorithm you'll be dealing with is FOMO.

Boolean Search

Looking inside of LinkedIn:
"Machine Learning Engineer" AND (Python OR R) AND (TensorFlow OR PyTorch)

Using a site search to X-Ray LinkedIn:
site:linkedin.com/in ("Machine Learning" OR AI) ("Software Engineer" OR Developer) (Scikit-Learn OR Keras)

Using a site search to X-Ray Github:
site:github.com/* "Machine Learning" (Python OR R) AWS

Using a filetype command to uncover resumes:
filetype:pdf resume "Machine Learning Engineer" (SAS OR SQL OR MATLAB)

Data Scientist

A data scientist is a professional role responsible for collecting, analyzing, and interpreting large, complex datasets in order to develop data-driven solutions for business challenges. This role involves the use of various techniques from statistics, machine learning, and data mining, along with knowledge of programming languages such as Python, R, or SQL.

Here are some responsibilities of a data scientist:

- **Data Analysis**: Data scientists sift through large amounts of data to provide insights and information that can be used to make decisions.

- **Predictive Modeling and Algorithms**: They use machine learning algorithms to create predictive models. These models can predict future outcomes based on historical data.

- **Data Visualization**: Data scientists often need to present their findings in a way that's easily understood by others. This includes creating charts, graphs, and other visual representations of data.

- **Problem-solving**: They are tasked with addressing business-related problems by using data analysis and interpretation.

- **Communication**: A critical part of their job involves communicating complex data in a clear, understandable manner so that others can make informed decisions.

- **Data Cleaning and Preparation**: Often, data isn't ready for analysis straight away and needs to be cleaned and prepared. This can involve dealing with missing data, eliminating irrelevant data, or transforming data so it's ready for analysis.

- **Stay Updated**: Data Science is a rapidly evolving field. Hence, data scientists need to stay up-to-date with the latest techniques, tools, and trends.

Data scientists require a strong foundation in mathematics, statistics, and programming. They also need expertise in data wrangling, machine learning, and data visualization tools. As data science is often applied in a business context, domain knowledge and good communication skills are also important.

Applicable Technologies

Alright, let's get down to brass tacks here and unpack the world of data science. As a data scientist, your toolbox isn't exactly what you'd find in a hardware store. No hammers, saws or screwdrivers here. Instead, you're dealing with technologies as esoteric and complex as they are powerful.

So, what's in the data scientist's toolkit? I'm glad you asked.

First off, Python. It's not a snake, but it might as well be, because it's wrapped around pretty much everything in data science. Python has a myriad of libraries like pandas for data manipulation, matplotlib for data visualization, and scikit-learn for machine learning. It's become the lingua franca of data science due to its simplicity and power.

R is another key player in the data science sphere. Some prefer it for statistical analysis and graphic models. You know, crunching the numbers and making them look pretty.

Then there's SQL, or "sequel" if you're into the whole brevity thing. It's the standard for managing and querying data in databases. If data's in a database, SQL's your ticket in.

In the modern age, the quantity of data being handled is often monstrous - we're talking big data. So, enter technologies like Hadoop and Apache Spark. Hadoop lets you store and process big data across computer clusters, while Spark does similar things, only faster.

You've also got cloud platforms like AWS, Google Cloud, and Microsoft Azure. These platforms offer powerful tools for storing, processing, and analyzing massive amounts of data. They're like a godsend for data scientists, with services for everything from machine learning to data warehousing.

But what's a data scientist doing with all these tools? Well, they're building machine learning models, of course. And for this, they might use libraries like TensorFlow or PyTorch. And let's not forget Keras, which acts as a user-friendly interface for the former.

Now, don't even get me started on the importance of good visualization. Tools like Tableau, PowerBI, and even humble Excel are paramount in presenting data in a digestible way.

Lastly, let's talk about Jupyter Notebooks, the data scientist's sketchbook. It lets them write code, run it, and see the results all in the same place. It's like a digital playground for experimenting with data.

So there you have it, the data scientist's toolbox. It's not exactly a walk in the park, but with the right skills and these tools, a data scientist can extract knowledge from data that can quite literally change the world.

Screening Questions

When conducting a phone screen for a Data Scientist position, recruiters typically ask a combination of technical and behavioral questions to assess the candidate's skills, knowledge, and fit for the role. Here are 15 interview questions a recruiter might ask a Data Scientist:

- Can you provide an overview of your experience as a Data Scientist and the projects you have worked on?
- What programming languages and statistical tools are you proficient in?
- Can you explain the steps involved in the data science project lifecycle?
- How do you approach data cleaning and preprocessing tasks?
- Can you describe a machine learning algorithm you have used in a project and explain how it works?
- Have you worked with both structured and unstructured data? How did you handle the challenges associated with each?
- Can you discuss a complex data analysis or modeling problem you solved and explain your approach and results?
- How do you determine the most appropriate statistical or machine learning techniques for a given problem?
- Have you worked with large datasets or big data technologies? If so, what tools or frameworks did you use?
- Can you explain the process of feature selection and how you determine which features are most relevant?

- How do you evaluate the performance of a machine learning model? What metrics do you consider?
- Have you deployed machine learning models in a production environment? If so, can you describe the process?
- Can you discuss a time when you faced challenges or obstacles during a data science project and how you overcame them?
- How do you stay updated with the latest trends and advancements in the field of data science?
- Can you provide examples of how you have effectively communicated complex technical concepts to non-technical stakeholders?

These questions help the recruiter assess the candidate's technical proficiency in data science, problem-solving abilities, knowledge of relevant tools and techniques, experience with real-world projects, and their ability to communicate effectively.

Networking Groups

Okay, let's do this with a bit of flair.

IRL (In Real Life) Networking Events:

- **Strata Data & AI Conferences**: This is the Coachella of data science – a massive gathering of big-brains converging to share ideas, shake hands, and probably drink overpriced coffee. It's like LinkedIn, but with faces and actual personalities.

- **KDD (Knowledge Discovery and Data Mining)**: It's the Olympics for data scientists. Serious, hardcore stuff happens here. You'll have more algorithms thrown at you than you can shake a stick at.

- **The Data Science Salon**: This one is a bit like a sophisticated cocktail party. It's a smaller, more focused gathering where industry-specific discussions take place. Grab a martini, and let's talk about how AI is going to render us all jobless, shall we?

Virtual Networking Events:

- **ODSC (Open Data Science Conference) Virtual Events**: ODSC is like the Burning Man of data science, except it's online and everyone's sober (hopefully). Still, it's a great place to learn about the latest in AI, machine learning, and predictive analytics.

- **Data Science GO Virtual**: This event is like a TED Talk for data scientists. Insightful, inspiring, and conveniently accessible from your living room or wherever you've set up your battle station.

- **Virtual Meetups (via Meetup.com)**: There's a buffet of data science groups on Meetup. It's like speed dating for networking – you can bounce from one group to another until you find your perfect match.

Remember, kid, networking isn't just about schmoozing and playing the "who's got the biggest...brain" game. It's about learning from others, sharing your own insights, and hopefully making a few pals who won't look at you funny when you start talking about Python – and I don't mean the snake.

So get out there – or stay in, your call – and start mingling. Just don't forget to have fun while you're at it. Life's too short to spend it all on data – said no data scientist ever.

Boolean Search

Looking inside of LinkedIn:
"Data Scientist" AND "Neural Networks" AND (Matlab OR Octave)

Using a site search to X-Ray LinkedIn:

site:linkedin.com/in "Data Scientist" (Tableau OR PowerBI OR SAS)

Using a site search to X-Ray Github:
site:github.com/ ("Data Science" OR "Data Scientist") ("Big Data" OR Hadoop OR Spark)*

Using a filetype command to uncover resumes:
filetype:pdf resume "Data Scientist" "Machine Learning" Python PHd (SQL OR NoSQL) "Data Visualization"

Infrastructure Engineer

An Infrastructure Engineer is a type of IT professional who is responsible for the foundational computing and networking systems that underpin all other IT systems in an organization. They design, install, maintain, and support computer systems and networks within an organization. These professionals typically work closely with a team of other IT professionals, such as software engineers, network engineers, and database administrators, to provide infrastructure solutions and manage performance and security.

Key duties of an Infrastructure Engineer may include:

- Designing and implementing new network solutions and/or improving the efficiency of current networks.

- Installing, configuring, and supporting network equipment including routers, proxy servers, switches, WAN accelerators, DNS, and DHCP.
- Procuring network equipment and managing subcontractors involved with network installation.
- Implementing and managing security tools, like firewalls and intrusion detection systems.
- Monitoring network performance and troubleshooting problems and outages.
- Securing network systems by defining and enforcing policies, and monitoring access.
- They need to have a broad knowledge of network architecture, server design, and the cloud, and strong problem-solving skills.

The term "infrastructure" in IT refers to the hardware, software, networks, and facilities upon which an organization's information technology services are built. This includes all of the IT resources that are used to deliver IT-enabled business processes, applications, and services - such as the network infrastructure, storage infrastructure, and computing infrastructure.

Applicable Technologies

We're going to dive into the nitty-gritty world of Infrastructure Engineering, and trust me, it's as scintillating as a new tech startup popping up in Silicon

Valley, even though it might not sound as glamorous. You know, the kind of world where servers, networks, and databases are as important as a perfectly brewed cup of coffee for a late-night coding session.

One: Networks. Infrastructure Engineers live, breathe, and maybe even dream networks. Now, you might think of networks as your WiFi going down at the worst possible moment. But for these tech maestros, it's about TCP/IP protocols, understanding things like DNS, VPN, Firewall configurations, and don't even get me started on subnetting and IP addressing. Imagine a highway system, but for data - that's your network.

Two: Servers. You can't talk about Infrastructure Engineering without getting into servers, the hardworking backbone of the internet. These folks deal with Windows, Linux, you name it. They're configuring, maintaining, and troubleshooting physical and virtual servers, which is as complex and critical as it sounds. It's the very core of what we know as the cloud. So the next time you watch Netflix or check your Dropbox, think about these engineers working their magic behind the scenes.

Three: Databases. Let's not forget about databases, the world's storehouses of digital information. SQL, MongoDB, Oracle - our Infrastructure Engineers need to be fluent in these languages. They design, implement, manage, and tune databases to ensure they're running like well-oiled machines.

Four: Virtualization. Tools like VMware and Hyper-V have become a staple in their repertoire. It's like inception but for computers. A computer within a computer? Yes, it's a thing, and it's incredibly efficient. Virtualization technology is about maximizing resources, and honey, let me tell you, it's the future.

And last, but certainly not least, is the cloud. Companies are shoving data into the cloud like there's no tomorrow. Services like Amazon Web Services (AWS), Google Cloud Platform (GCP), and Microsoft Azure have become the new kids on the block. Our Infrastructure Engineers have to be comfortable working with these platforms, setting up environments, and managing resources there.

So there you have it, a whirlwind tour of the technologies an Infrastructure Engineer uses on the daily. It's not for the faint-hearted, and it's the backbone of our digital world. Trust me, next time you tweet, share a meme, or stream your favorite show, you'll know there's a hardworking engineer ensuring your digital life stays on track.

Screening Questions

When conducting a phone screen for an Infrastructure Engineer role, recruiters often focus on assessing the candidate's technical knowledge, problem-solving abilities, and experience with infrastructure management. Here are 15 interview questions that a recruiter may ask:

- Can you provide an overview of your experience as an Infrastructure Engineer?
- What infrastructure components have you worked with in your previous roles?
- How familiar are you with cloud computing platforms (e.g., AWS, Azure, Google Cloud)?
- Can you discuss your experience with infrastructure provisioning and configuration management tools (e.g., Terraform, Ansible)?
- Have you worked on implementing high-availability and disaster recovery solutions for infrastructure?
- How do you ensure security and compliance within infrastructure environments?
- Can you explain your experience with containerization technologies like Docker and container orchestration platforms like Kubernetes?
- Have you worked on automating infrastructure deployment and management processes? If so, what tools have you used?
- Can you discuss your experience with monitoring and troubleshooting infrastructure issues?

- Have you worked on scaling infrastructure to meet changing demands? If yes, how did you handle it?
- Can you explain your experience with networking protocols and technologies (e.g., TCP/IP, VPN, load balancers)?
- How do you handle configuration management and version control of infrastructure resources?
- Have you worked on implementing infrastructure-as-code practices? If so, what tools and languages have you used?
- Can you discuss any experience you have with database management systems and data storage solutions?
- How do you stay updated with emerging technologies and industry trends in infrastructure engineering?

These questions help the recruiter evaluate the candidate's technical skills, experience with infrastructure components and tools, problem-solving abilities, familiarity with best practices, and their ability to adapt to new technologies and trends in infrastructure engineering.

Networking Groups

Alright my friend, let's dive into this.

Infrastructure Engineers have an array of networking events that are more intoxicating than a can of White Claw on a Saturday night. And yes, in the realm of tech, networking is as crucial as the mighty algorithms that are powering our life, because as we always say, it's not just about what you know, it's about who you know.

Firstly, in real life, they've got the heavy hitters like the **O'Reilly Velocity Conference**, where the greatest minds in tech gather and dive deep into cloud infrastructure and site reliability like it's the freakin' Mariana Trench. The speakers are the crème de la crème, the content is as rich as Jeff Bezos, and the networking opportunities are hotter than Miami in the middle of July.

Then there's the **Gartner IT Infrastructure, Operations & Cloud Strategies Conference**, which is like the Harvard of tech events. If you're an Infrastructure Engineer not rubbing shoulders at Gartner, you're as missing out as a vegan at a steakhouse.

Now, virtually, engineers have been flocking to events like the **SREcon (Site Reliability Engineering Convention)** - it's the Burning Man of the infrastructure world, minus the sand and eccentric costumes. From digital transformation to practical problem-solving, it's where you learn, connect, and get inspired without leaving your ergonomically designed chair.

CloudNativeCon and **KubeCon** are other gems in the virtual space where Infrastructure Engineers can tune in to grasp Kubernetes and other cloud-native tech. It's like Netflix, but instead of binge-watching Stranger Things, you're binge-learning about cutting-edge infrastructure tech.

And let's not forget the meetups on platforms like Meetup.com and LinkedIn events. They're the grassroots of networking, brimming with tech aficionados ready to share a pint of knowledge.

So whether you're going IRL or keeping it virtual, networking is the unsung hero of the tech world. It's the multi-vitamin to your career's health and the Red Bull to your professional growth. So go ahead, jump in, the networking water's fine.

Boolean Search

Looking inside of LinkedIn:
("Infrastructure Engineer" AND virtualization) AND (VMWare OR "Hyper-V")

Using a site search to X-Ray LinkedIn:
site:linkedin.com/in ("Infrastructure Engineer" OR "Network Engineer") (CCNA OR CCNP OR CCIE)

Using a site search to X-Ray Github:
site:github.com/* "Infrastructure Engineer" (monitoring OR Alerting) (Nagios OR Prometheus OR Datadog)

Using a filetype command to uncover resumes:
filetype:pdf resume ("Infrastructure Engineer" OR "Cloud Engineer") ("AWS Certified" OR "Azure Certified")

Site Reliability Engineer (SRE)

A Site Reliability Engineer (SRE) is a professional within the software engineering industry whose primary responsibility is to ensure that software systems and services are highly available, reliable, and performant. The role was first developed by Google, but the principles have been adopted by many tech companies.

The philosophy of SRE takes many of its cues from software engineering and applies them to infrastructure and operations problems. The main goals are to create scalable and highly reliable software systems. Some of the key responsibilities of an SRE include:

- **Incident Management and Post-Mortem Analysis**: SREs often take on-call responsibilities to handle incidents as they occur, and then work on root cause analysis and remediation to avoid recurrence in the future.

- **Designing and Implementing Reliability**: They work on designing and developing software and systems that add to the reliability and stability of the overall system.

- **Capacity Planning and Demand Forecasting**: SREs also help with anticipating future infrastructure needs by understanding trends in service usage.

- **Automation**: Automation is a key component of the SRE role. They develop software to automate manual tasks, thereby ensuring efficiency and reducing the chances of human error.

- **Performance Tuning**: SREs analyze system performance and suggest improvements. They might work with other developers to ensure best practices are followed for optimal performance.

- **System Design Consulting**: They may also consult with other teams during system design to ensure that the system is scalable, resilient, and manageable.

An SRE requires a mix of deep technical knowledge, including networking, systems engineering, and coding skills, as well as broader abilities like project management, communication, and the ability to balance the trade-offs between the perfect solution and the need to deliver business value.

Applicable Technologies

Alright, so let's dive into the world of Site Reliability Engineers, or SREs as they're typically called. You'd best believe they're some of the most important players in the tech scene, keeping things running smoothly while the rest of us tweet, binge-watch, and stream with reckless abandon. But what tools are they wielding behind the scenes to keep our beloved internet up and running? It's a powerful and complex mix of technologies.

Firstly, SREs have to know their way around cloud services like a tech-savvy Sherpa. We're talking about platforms like AWS, Google Cloud, Microsoft Azure, you know, the giants that essentially run the online world. These guys can set up, manage, and troubleshoot issues on these platforms faster than you can say "server downtime".

But there's more. These engineers have to understand Docker and Kubernetes like they're their native language. Docker is the go-to solution for creating and managing containers, which essentially package up the code and all its dependencies so the application runs quickly and reliably from one computing environment to another. And Kubernetes? It's like the traffic cop of the container world, making sure everything's orchestrated and runs smoothly.

On top of that, we've got infrastructure as code (IaC) tools like Terraform and Ansible. These aren't the new kids on the block anymore, but they're crucial. They let SREs automate a ton of manual work, allowing them to handle large scale, complex systems. And let's face it, in this day and age, who isn't dealing with large scale, complex systems?

Monitoring and logging tools such as Prometheus, Grafana, ELK Stack are also part of their arsenal. These are like the Fitbit for systems, tracking performance and making sure everything's in tip-top shape.

And, of course, our SREs need to be coding wizards. They need to be proficient in programming languages such as Python, Go, and Shell. It's not enough to just keep things running, they need to be able to build and optimize tools, and solve problems on the fly.

Last but definitely not least, these SREs have to be well versed with CI/CD pipelines using Jenkins, GitLab, or similar tools. Continuous Integration and Continuous Deployment is all about making small changes frequently, testing them, and getting them into production rapidly. It's like a rapid conveyor belt of improvements.

That's the 101 on SREs. It's a tough gig, but someone's got to do it. Without these tech wizards, our connected world would probably be spinning in chaos. So, the next time your streaming service doesn't buffer, maybe take a second to thank the invisible army of SREs keeping it all together.

Screening Questions

When conducting a phone screen for a Site Reliability Engineer (SRE) role, recruiters typically ask a combination of technical and behavioral questions to assess a candidate's qualifications and fit for the position. Here are 15 interview questions a recruiter may ask a candidate:

- Can you explain the role of a Site Reliability Engineer (SRE) and its importance in modern software development?
- What experience do you have with incident response and managing system outages or service disruptions?
- How do you approach monitoring and observability in a production environment?
- Can you discuss your experience with designing and implementing scalable and highly available infrastructure?
- What tools or frameworks have you used for configuration management and infrastructure automation?

- Can you describe a project where you collaborated with developers to improve application performance and reliability?
- How do you prioritize and address system-level bottlenecks or performance issues?
- Can you provide an example of a challenging incident you handled and how you resolved it?
- How do you approach capacity planning and resource allocation for a distributed system?
- What strategies do you employ to ensure disaster recovery and business continuity?
- Can you discuss your experience with cloud platforms like AWS, Azure, or GCP and the services you utilized?
- How do you stay updated with new technologies, tools, and best practices in the SRE field?
- Can you explain your experience with implementing and managing service-level objectives (SLOs) and service-level agreements (SLAs)?
- How do you approach incident postmortems and learning from failures to prevent future incidents?
- Can you discuss your experience with containerization technologies like Docker and orchestration tools like Kubernetes?

These questions help the recruiter gauge the candidate's technical knowledge, problem-solving abilities, experience with incident management, familiarity with infrastructure automation, and their ability to collaborate with development teams and prioritize tasks. It also provides insights into their familiarity with cloud platforms, continuous learning mindset, and understanding of SRE best practices.

Networking Groups

Well, strap in because we're about to dive into the exhilarating world of networking for Site Reliability Engineers, or SREs as they're known in the biz. This isn't your run-of-the-mill, nametag-wearing, chicken-or-fish conference scene. This is the tech industry's answer to Burning Man, minus the neon and desert dust.

First off, the reigning champion of IRL networking events: **Google's SREcon**. These guys literally wrote the book on SRE (no, really, they did), and SREcon is where the brightest minds gather to network, share ideas, and chow down on some truly mind-boggling amounts of free snacks. It's like the Met Gala for nerds, but instead of discussing haute couture, we're deep-diving into latency issues and system dependability. It's sexy, in its own way.

Next up, **DevOpsDays**. They're popping up in cities worldwide like overzealous tech-themed dandelions.

But, unlike dandelions, they're a welcome sight, offering local techies a chance to discuss all things DevOps and SRE, and probably some spirited debates about Star Trek vs. Star Wars.

Then there's the virtu-rama, the digital symphony, the Zoomtopia of virtual events: **The ONES: Open Networking & Edge Summit**. It's an orchestration of cloud natives and edge computing aficionados, showcasing the latest advancements and diving into the complexities of open source systems.

We've also got **Failover Conf,** a virtual conference where failure isn't just an option, it's celebrated. A fascinating space to hear tales of epic tech fails, and more importantly, how they recovered and what was learned.

And let's not forget the **Kubernetes Forums and Days** around the world. Kubernetes is like the mitochondria of the tech world, the powerhouse of the cell (remember 7th-grade biology?). If you're an SRE and you're not up to speed on Kubernetes, it's like being a chef who can't boil water.

Now, bear in mind, these are just the tip of the iceberg. The world of SRE is vast and the events are plentiful. Like your mother probably told you: get out there (or log in there) and meet some people! Share ideas, make connections, challenge conventions, and don't forget to enjoy those free snacks.

Boolean Search

Looking inside of LinkedIn:
("SRE" AND "Docker") OR ("Site Reliability Engineer" AND Containerization)

Using a site search to X-Ray LinkedIn:
site:linkedin.com/in ("Site Reliability Engineer" Automation) OR (SRE Scripting)

Using a site search to X-Ray Github:
site:github.com/* ("Site Reliability Engineer" OR SRE) Terraform

Using a filetype command to uncover resumes:
filetype:pdf resume ("Site Reliability Engineer" OR SRE) (Kubernetes OR k8s) (DevOps OR SysOps)

Chapter Eleven

Final Thoughts

In the vast expanse of professions out there, being a technical recruiter might not immediately pop out as the most glamorous one. You may not be stepping onto a rocket ship and flying off to Mars, but I'll tell you, you are doing something just as remarkable, if not more.

In a world that's rapidly bending towards digital, being a technical recruiter isn't just a job. It's a noble mission. You're not just shuffling resumes, you're shaping lives. That's right. Every time you connect a talented coder with a promising startup or place a seasoned engineer in a tech giant's team, you're steering the trajectory of their career, their life. And let's not forget, the families that are supported by these jobs.

Moreover, you are an architect of companies. You handpick the bricks and the mortar that build not just the physical but the very soul of organizations. This isn't about filling vacancies. It's about sculpting the character of an enterprise, piecing together the mosaic of personalities and talents that will birth products, services, ideas that change the world. The next intuitive solution that makes life simpler? You could be introducing the genius behind it to their dream team right now.

The satisfaction you get from this role?

It's immeasurable.

You get a front-row seat to the grand opera of life, where dreams intersect with opportunities, where hard work finds its reward. And you're not just a spectator. You're the conductor. You engage with talent on their terms, understand their ambitions, their strengths, and help them shine in the best light.

The algorithm of value is pretty straightforward here: You find talent, you open doors, and you help create something larger than the sum of its parts. And in that process, you drive the evolution of our world. You, the technical recruiter, are at the intersection of technology, talent, and opportunity. And let me tell you, that's a thrilling place to be.

And if that doesn't make you feel grand, well, I don't know what will.

Made in the USA
Columbia, SC
25 June 2023